My First Two Hundred Years

My First Two Hundred Years

From Budapest to Hollywood to Buchenwald and Beyond, a Beautiful Life

Pál Királyhegyi

(Paul King)

Translated, from the Hungarian, by Paul Olchváry

Anzix Publishing

Published in 2017 by Anzix Publishing

English translation by Paul Olchváry

First published, in Hungarian, in 1979 by Gondolat Könyvkiadó, Budapest.

Photo by Irén Ács (1924-2015). Courtesy of Hungarian National Museum, Historical Photo Department.

ISBN-13: 9780999158715
ISBN-10: 0999158716

First English-language edition

10 9 8 7 6 5 4 3 2 1

Introduction

He who has a sense of humor knows everything
He who doesn't is capable of anything.

—PÁL KIRÁLYHEGYI

It may be true that exceptional lives make for exceptional books. But when you have a writer who has lived so fully, one who has experienced the most soaring heights of success and history's ultimate example of human evil, then you have a book that stands in a very select category, a memoir written by one of the great talents of his age that could only be made believable by a writer of his caliber. Though most native speakers of English are not familiar with Hungarian-born Pál Királyhegyi, or Paul King, as he was known as a novelist and screenwriter in America, this book is set to change that.

Királyhegyi was always a restless soul and fearless wanderer. As a young man, he endured near starvation as he stowed away on a New York–bound cargo ship. In the New World he rose from the status of vagrant and busboy to journalist and banker before making his way to Hollywood, where he wrote films for Paramount Studios and mixed with the likes of Charlie Chaplin and *Casablanca* director Michael Curtiz. But, as he was known to say, "One always wants to leave the place one is at."

And so it happened: "My (next) trip was urgent, lest I miss the Auschwitz Express." Indeed, after tiring of Hollywood and discovering a new life and love in England, where he covered the spread of World War II from his office in London, the writer opted to return to his homeland so as not to abandon his family, many of whom were confined behind the walls of Budapest's Jewish ghetto. There, not even his quick wit could save him from deportation. His account of his time as a prisoner in Auschwitz, among other notorious concentration camps, is heartbreaking while remaining uplifting, and even funny. Királyhegyi maintained a touch of breezy, wry humor to all the horrors he encountered. Indeed, when he returned to Budapest broken and half-starved, upon collecting the small reparations made by his government for all the injustice he had been subjected to, he simply took a look at the thin stack of banknotes and remarked, "Next time I am going to charge more."

This volume stands alone in Holocaust literature due to Királyhegyi's voice, which, while unflinching, is that of a natural born humorist. It may take a few pages to pick up on his characteristic wordplay. Királyhegyi was ironic long before it was in vogue, something hinted at by the titles of his books and writings: *Face to Face with Myself*, *Up the Slope*, *Honesty is Not a Shame*, *Only You! And Them*, *How to Make Enemies?* Sometimes the reader can't help but wonder if he used a little imagination to aid him in writing down the facts of his life to liven up the story. But as a historical figure, with his name on films, novels, plays, and countless articles for newspapers, we know that Királyhegyi was the author of his life and not created by the collective unconscious of an era that desperately needed a belly laugh. Királyhegyi treats arriving broke in New York City with the same deadpan wit as striking gold in Hollywood's early years. Along the way he is the casual profiler of characters like Horthy (Hungary's head of state through the interwar era), Rothschild, and Mengele, but saves his most acerbic barbs for himself.

A good example is an episode from after the war that finds Királyhegyi being exiled from Budapest by Hungary's new communist government.

Once he had returned from a communal farm to the city, he was forced to live in a windowless basement room, with but a naked light bulb hanging from the ceiling. After wooing a dancer, he turned to her the next morning and said, "Tell me, do you love me?" "Of course," the girl answered. "And if I were poor, would you still love me?" was his rejoinder.

No doubt it is this kind of levity that made the diminutive Királyhegyi so popular as a conversation partner in postwar Budapest's most famous cafes. A member of both the intellectual elite and circles of artists, the author was prized company in a time when government authorities made much of silencing dissenters, particularly writers, as well as anybody else who dared to speak out against the absurdities of communism. But, of course, it would be Királyhegyi who in one Moscow-bound telegram stated, "J.V STALIN, MOSCOW, KREMLIN. THE SYSTEM HAS NOT WORKED OUT STOP PLEASE STOP IT STOP KIRALYHEGYI STOP"

When asked why he entitled his memoir *My First Two Hundred Years*, he replied, "If it's true that war years count twice, if I say I am two hundred, I am actually pretending to be younger than my age, since I had as bosses Franz Joseph I, Horthy, Szálasi, and even Hitler, because I worked in Auschwitz, as a simple deportee, and it is common knowledge that time there passed quite slowly, as long as one was still alive, anyway."

Királyhegyi published his memoir of the Holocaust *Not Everyone Has Died* in Hungarian in 1947. A huge hit in his home country, but unavailable in English, much of this essential historical document is incorporated into *My First Two Hundred Years,* which you are holding now, in the loving translation of Paul Olchváry. On the seventieth anniversary of Királyhegyi's first publication of his Holocaust work, we are proud to present *My First Two Hundred Years* to an English-speaking readership.

Királyhegyi was a worldly man with a singular voice, a conqueror and a prisoner by turns. But no matter what circumstances he found himself mired in, his humor remained irrepressible and his optimism undiminished. It is our hope that this volume, one of Királyhegyi's best, will be cherished for what it is: a human spirit forged in language, a translation of dread misery into humor, and the work of a writer whose life and words we are sure you will find irresistible.

Dr. Tamás Otrok, publisher, with Matt Henderson Ellis, editor

Contents

Introduction v

One I am born in a hurry and other inconveniences. 1
Two Chess is a fine sport, but sometimes life does the checkmating. 10
Three Suicide is a temporary solution. Death is preferable. 16
Four We always want to leave the place we happen to be. A straight path is best: lying is necessary. 20
Five Nothing amiss in our family, but Grandpa will take care of everything, and even America visits home. 23
Six Work is nothing to be ashamed of, but there is none. The Italians don't speak Hungarian, but that's their problem. 25
Seven Starving is no way to make a living, and besides, Venice is not just for honeymooners. 28
Eight Every ship has a bottom, but not even rats are rats to the bottom. 35
Nine Even in America there are only trees, houses, and people, and the girls, too, are like at home, except everything is completely different. 39
Ten Don't start with women—only if you must. 42
Eleven The sun shines, the banker cheats. Life isn't about simple declarative sentences. 47

Twelve	It's good everywhere, but worst in jail. The basic law of life is injustice.	52
Thirteen	The woe of the honorable burglar. Yelena writes her letter, which changes everything. The priest is strict, but sly as an ox.	60
Fourteen	You can be in prison even when you're free. Girls always spell trouble, but a minister isn't child's play, either. Even the straight path is crooked.	64
Fifteen	Every fine fur starts out as a rabbit. Sleeping in a bed is possible, you just need to be sly. "No Experience Necessary" is not a serious trade.	68
Sixteen	Freedom is lovely but it requires a flat. People are heartless, kudos to exceptions. One always leaves the place one is at.	76
Seventeen	At gambling you can lose, too. Homesickness is strong even without a home. No distance is too great, it's just a question of money.	84
Eighteen	You should water people only at Easter, lest you get fired. Bankers are human, too, if not quite. Escape.	89
Nineteen	Yelena wrote her letter. Geraniums grow big if allowed to. Life is good everywhere, but it's best somewhere else.	93
Twenty	Hollywood doesn't even exist, but what does is just enough. I don't know English, but Yelena takes care of it. Everyone is rich, except for the poor. The sun shines day and night, but it rains for six weeks.	98
Twenty-One	Destitution is no delight, but success is harder to endure. Aggression is not strength, but love conquers all. Homesickness can't be cured with a Mimosa.	106
Twenty-Two	In Hungary everyone speaks Hungarian. Two weeks is a lot of time if it lasts for years. Meetings with everyone who is alive. I make a new career at a Budapest newspaper.	118

Twenty-Three	There are English troubles, too. Writers write if they're allowed to. My meeting with the three Kordas.	127
Twenty-Four	Rothschild has no money. The Germans even lie. Scotland Yard is not a unit of measure. It's bad everywhere, but worst at home.	137
Twenty-Five	I arrive home more often than I depart. Budapest is no more. Dirty Fred, the Captain. Friends don't change. I died in London; the rest is just an encore.	146
Twenty-Six	Minor inconveniences, but that's quite enough. Are the Germans human beings, and are the Hungarian fascists Hungarian?	152
Twenty-Seven	Horthy lays down his arms. Szálasi picks them up again. Éva loves me, and so does Brother Surányi, but several people have already died of the latter.	163
Twenty-Eight	Life in cheerful Germany is sad. Everything is forbidden, even living.	190
Twenty-Nine	Eating snow is unhealthy if you get shot at meanwhile. Benedek is all dancing and decorum. You need to know how to salute.	205
Thirty	Even at death's door carrots are stolen. Everyone goes faster than they can. During work I unexpectedly stay alive.	224
Thirty-One	Even as you're beaten dead, you've got to be secretive. Pleasure, too, takes strength and nerves. Pineapple is food, too.	238
Thirty-Two	There is no time for regret. Ursula laughs, I don't know why. I walk on the train. The past haunts.	247
Thirty-Three	Life becomes ever more beautiful. We're afraid again, but exuberantly. Every cow in Adács looks the same. Epstein's chickens are immortal. You can haggle upward, too.	279
Thirty-Four	Judit, though a lab technician, is beautiful. This of course has its consequences. Not even	

destitution is free. Roth is the main tenant but insists on the rent. Vienna is close, but why? Our compatriots who've wound up abroad return in spring, like storks. Roulette strengthens the heart. 296

Thirty-Five Writing a play is easy, having a flop is hard. Language skills: power. My troupe and I travel the country. I came from America, but when? 322

Glossary 333
Publisher's Acknowledgments 339
About the Translator 345
About the Author 347

One

I am born in a hurry and other inconveniences.

I was born at the age of thirteen, because that is when I became the coeditor of the weekly *Student Humor.*

In fact, I am two months younger than my age, for I was born at seven months even though custom has it that this sort of thing lasts even nine months. Why I was in such a hurry, I don't know, because my memories of those days are hazy. It was others who told me that I started out very little and weak and that I passed two months in the company of heated mason jars pressed against the maternal breast to get the milk flowing, and perhaps that is why, even today, I feel homesick on seeing a jar of appetizing preserves.

We mimeographed *Student Humor* in Vilmos Kunstätter's stationery store, which still deals in stationery though old Kunstätter is missing.

My coeditor, Ferenc Kálnay, my classmate and best friend, was a genius, pure and simple. But he quit being a genius, just like he quit everything he began. No one had as much genius for quitting as did my friend Kálnay. Even in his very tender youth he wrote stunningly beautiful poems—indeed a collection of his was published—but then he suddenly quit writing poetry and took up something else.

Kálnay was a handsome, strapping, well-built young lad with an indefinable, elusive, wild allure, so everyone loved him.

After graduating high school, he enrolled in the naval academy at Fiume and became an officer, but he quit that, too, and once again changed course.

He ran off to America, and though I ran after him, I didn't catch up to him. But more on that later.

Despite its enormous success, *Student Humor* was banned by our school's faculty, in part because we had criticized the teachers, and in part because in a lead article I had called the country's attention to the detrimental institution of the monarchy, even though back then, in 1913, Franz Joseph still reigned, and there was no sign that he would ever quit. At the time I was attending the Realschule on Horánszky Street in Budapest, and I had lots of run-ins with the teachers. Arithmetic never was my strong suit, and I outright abhorred mathematics.

It was in the wake of this that, one fine day, Mr. Priváry asked me in class what I knew about univariate equations. "I don't like variables. As for how many there are, that's their business, and let it stay that way."

Miraculously, the teacher was unsatisfied with my answer, and indeed he fell into a terrible rage in which he called me all kinds of names and threatened to have me kicked out of every last high school in the country.

Also most relevant here is the fact that Maison Frida was, back then, the loveliest, priciest, and most distinguished brothel not only in Budapest, but in the whole country. The finest gentlemen patronized it; the entrance fee or, rather, the coatroom fee being five *pengős*, or, rather, crowns. These days the building, on Magyar Street, is a home for old actors, and it is still beautiful. Elegant plush armchairs and divans; a choice selection of lovely young damsels; and a refined community of gentlemen patronized this institution of the arts. Among others who came here were Sicu (Henrik) Major, the world-famous caricaturist and painter; and Marcell Vértes, who bequeathed the institution with a whole volume of drawings. The stunningly beautiful, if somewhat risqué set was titled *My Little Meat*, and if it still exists somewhere, it is worth a fortune.

It was with my close, all-around chum Karcsi Schatz that I first visited Maison Frida. Karcsi and I lived in the same building, at 40 Hársfa Street—he on the second floor, me on the third—so our friendship was undisturbed by the outside world. Karcsi was a very handsome, blue-eyed boy with coal-black hair, and he always had enough money on him, because his father, Gusztáv Schatz, had an art dealership on Váci Street.

Our arms and legs were trembling with excitement the moment we first crossed the institution's threshold. We were worried they wouldn't let us in, but the concierge just listlessly took our admission fees, and we went upstairs unhindered.

Music was already playing in the elegant salon, compliments of a blind pianist, as the girls danced gracefully with the gentlemen, though their attire was a tad too insubstantial, if, that is, the flimsy blouses they had on could be called attire.

We ordered a coffee, and after the first gulp I saw our teacher, Mr. Priváry, heading right toward me. When he saw me, he was thunderstruck.

"Mr. Királyhegyi—you, here?" he asked, gasping for air.

"I'm a single man, sir, with no one to account to. Besides, we're just having coffee."

Priváry, who was married and the proud father of two children, ran off, and that was that. He did not report me to the principal, for he would then have had to also explain how he'd ended up there. In fact, it seemed that after this encounter he was kinder to me, and at the end of the year he didn't fail me in mathematics, though I would have richly deserved it.

On but one subsequent occasion did he erupt with that bygone rage of his, when he asked me in front of the class to cough up the answers to my homework, which, however, I'd been unable to do. Why, I told him flat out, with that sincerity I'd been blessed with by the Creator, that it wasn't out of laziness that I hadn't done the assignment, but because I get a headache from counting.

He acknowledged my answer and wrote the following in the class register: "A self-professed imbecile."

And yet there was among the subjects one that I hated even more than arithmetic: freehand drawing, which back then counted as a very important subject in Realschule. Yes, but. I had even less talent for drawing than I did for math. I couldn't even manage to draw a straight line, and even as a child I sensed that I would never become Hungary's greatest painter.

Tatay, the art teacher, was a painter on the side, and art class invariably meant two whole hours of high-tension boredom. The teacher himself would retire to his room behind the classroom, and paint, while we were expected to complete the assigned drawing.

On one occasion Tatay put a rose on his desk. That's what we had to draw. I had a drawing board, a pencil, and paper. Only that I couldn't draw. Luckily I still had on me the little bottle I'd made the customary rounds with, sprinkling girls with rose water at Easter. Well, I now filled it with water, and then went about the classroom diligently watering my classmates' drawings, because even back then I knew just how important life-sustaining water is for plants.

It was the art teacher's custom to appoint a class monitor charged with writing on the blackboard, while the teacher was busy painting in the back room, the names of any unruly students.

Everyone dreaded the strict teacher, so only rarely did one of our names wind up on the board.

But my name, on account of the sprinkling I'd done, blossomed up there on the blackboard. Toward the end of hour two, Tatay came into the room to examine our drawings, and on seeing my name on the board, he called me up front:

"Slap or note?" he asked coldly.

By then I'd long been familiar with this custom. He always asked the victim which he wished, and if a slap, why then, that would include hair-pulling and ear-twisting before, finally, one gargantuan slap, which usually resulted in temporary deafness. If the unfortunate student chose a note to his parents, the teacher would fail him in art and behavior, which was considered a death blow. Thus it had been decades since a student had asked for a note. Everyone opted for the slap, which was painful, but faded away without a trace, and one's parents would never know about the matter.

"It's a bad question, sir. Ask me if I want a salami sandwich or a movie ticket. That, I can answer. But I would like neither a slap nor a note."

Tatay went pale. He then turned beet red. A vein was throbbing wildly on his temple. He was raving with fury. He stomped his feet. Never before had this happened to him since he'd become an institution. He'd slapped up several generations over the decades, but so far no one had dared speak out against his regimen.

Once he calmed down a bit, he hissed:

"I'll get you expelled from school. You won't graduate. Get lost!"

At home I told my father the whole thing, fessing up completely, and awaited his paternal slaps, which were hard but at least familiar. Not like a stranger's!

When disagreements arose, my father invariably began with two surprisingly powerful slaps before saying, "Just pay attention to see what big slaps you'll get." And I sure did pay attention: I took him for his word, for the two slaps he'd delivered without notice convinced me that his promise had gold reserves to back it up.

Except that, this time, the slaps didn't come.

"What you did was really clever. I'll figure something out. I don't want this sadist to have you expelled from school."

My father soon came up with a brilliant plan. He discovered that Tatay lived at 49 Ráday Street. That apartment building belonged to my uncle, József Himmler, a wholesale butcher and, incidentally, not just a millionaire but well-to-do on the side.

My father arranged to have the resident landlord, the next time he hosted an evening in his sumptuous, six-room apartment, invite Tatay, the poor art teacher and even poorer painter.

A dazzling and elegant army of guests had gathered: lovely young girls and boys who were in on it, and who were showering attention upon Tatay, who was basking in bliss. They offered him food, drink, and fawned over him.

When they introduced my father to him, he shuddered.

"Is something the matter?" my father inquired compassionately.

"No, no," said the art teacher, collecting himself, "it's just that I have a student with a similar name, a monster, who corrupts the others, too, and is utterly without talent."

"That's my son," said my father humbly. By then the others had gathered round, too, and with collective effort they managed to persuade Tatay not to have me expelled, but that instead by the end of the academic year my father would arrange to have me continue my studies in another school.

Tatay, in order to ingratiate himself with the landlord, gladly assented. Even under this scenario he would free himself of me, which was, for him, the whole point.

Thus I wound up in the Downtown Realschule.

Here too I had to study, but there were new acquaintances and friends, new teachers, and no Tatay. I was becoming almost happy, and didn't even suspect how near tragedy was.

The tragedy was called Éva Völgyi—Évike, as everyone called her. I think we were about the same age, except for her, who was one year younger. She wasn't the most beautiful girl I ever saw, but she had a sort of verve, something mystical, some sweet wonder that gave me the sense that she was the one and only. One look told me that this was no ordinary girl, but that something had happened here.

That day my father had not given me money for the movies, even though right on the corner, the Royal Grand Cinema was playing an incredibly exciting crime film—God only knows how many sequels there were—with the spine-tinglingly beautiful, honey-blonde Pearl White in the lead role. I was even fonder of this woman than of the *Fantômas* films. Perhaps because, though she was but a damsel, she was almost sawed in two. It's hard to find such a woman.

After pondering briefly, I decided to head out to the zoo. For that I didn't need capital, because from the age of thirteen on I'd had a pass.

A fateful gift it was!

This day distant pleasures were waving at me and pleasant thrills were showing themselves nearer still. Perhaps because I had on my new, blue sailor's suit or perhaps because I was ever anticipating excitement, I don't know. No doubt I was not an unpleasant sight, making my way along the street, in navy blue, deep in thought.

True, I was small, decidedly short in stature, and indeed during arguments in school my classmates sometimes even called me a midget, which was of course an exaggeration, but by then I'd resigned myself to the fact that never would I become a Hercules.

In the zoo I'd just been climbing down the crag from the foxes when I saw her. I knew at once that this little gal with dirty blond hair would mean the world to me. Quickening my pace just so, if only to get a better glimpse of her, I'd already forgotten the foxes completely, but then she stepped under the awning of a vendor's pavilion, greeting the middle-aged woman standing behind the counter—her mother, as would soon turn out. The girl then disappeared inside, only to reappear in no time wearing a little white apron and getting diligently down to work.

I noticed right away that her motions, as she stirred the raspberry syrup into the sparkling water and handed the result to customers, were gracious, graceful, delicate, and discreet. Nor did it escape my all-encompassing attention that my knees were trembling a bit as I paced nonchalantly to and fro in front of the little stand.

After a while the girl vanished, and that was when courage flared up inside me, because her mother remained alone behind the counter. I went over and asked for a raspberry soda, which I then slurped down slowly, praising it to no end.

"The syrup is homemade," said her mother, "but unfortunately folks don't appreciate that. Lots of folks just don't care if it's factory-made or homemade."

"We make it at home, too, which is why I know raspberries so well," I exaggerated. With that, I knew I had nothing more to say about this nonsense. A pause was ready to take hold when I noticed a little white box in the corner. It was full of tiny holes, and I knew at once that it could only be for breeding silkworms.

"Évike, my girl, collects them, silkworms," said the mother, sensing my interest in the box.

"There is nothing more beautiful and lovely than breeding silkworms," I declared without blinking an eye, though the truth is, I'd always hated grubs, be they silkworms or velvet worms, because they were soft and they squirmed. Their touch disgusted me, though with my eyes now fixed upon that box, I suddenly found myself believing that I was partial to these odious maggots.

"Évike loves them very much."

So she was called Évike! Even this?! The first woman was Eve, too. A veritable miracle.

"May I examine them?" I asked with an expert's superior air.

The mother handed me the box full of silkworms. I opened it, and observed those squirming larvae with faint horror.

Still I managed to force my hand to touch one of them. It wasn't as horrible as I'd imagined. If you don't consider their countless tiny feet but touch only their backs, which are soft, it is quite tolerable although not a great pleasure.

"Well-fed insects, they are," I stated reassuringly. Nothing else had come to mind. After all, I couldn't say that they were smart or clever when in fact they were simply revolting this way, at first sight.

"I myself don't much like these bugs, but my girl, Évike, adores them. Do you know her?" She asked this just a moment after Évike suddenly appeared on the horizon from who-knows-where.

My heart was beating every which way.

"I am Éva," I said in my embarrassment, God knows why, and I felt like dashing off toward all four corners of the earth at once. Sailor's suit or no, I sensed that at that moment I looked as romantic as a toothbrush.

It often happens that you're crazy about someone, and then you get to know them, and it turns out that you could have saved yourself the trouble, for the person is completely different than what you imagined.

But with Évike this was not the case. Our friendship deepened with each passing day, and that grand, good feeling grew within me, that strange, sweet sensation called love.

Amid such circumstances I naturally persuaded myself in no time that mid-morning snack was pointless, and, with the money I'd been given to buy it, I bought flowers for the girl, blissfully and daily.

True, Évike often gifted these bouquets to the winners of dumb track races. And yet life was so sweet and colorful, so worth living, that because of this, back then I didn't even think of suicide.

Two

Chess is a fine sport, but sometimes life does the checkmating.

As time raced along, I loved Évike more and more. She was my life, my sustenance, my dream, my everything.

Objects, people, and food had meaning only if I could somehow relate them to Évike.

Although for the time being she was not in love with me, she *liked* me, and I trusted that the time would come when she too would understand that we were meant for each other.

No one in my family was ever tired, but all the same, each and every summer I had to go off on holiday with them. I loathed these pointless vacations, which lasted two whole months.

One summer we went to Abbazia. That's where I saw the famous Adriatic Sea for the first time. But that big water, the hotel, the people—none of this interested me. It only morphed into a subject I could write to Évike about. These were never-ending letters, but interestingly enough, the girl replied to not a single one. Women! And yet I longed so much to get a few lines from her, though she probably didn't have time for correspondence. She had too much work at the zoo. I wrote my first poems here by the sea, comparing Évike to the endless sea, although no doubt she and the sea had nothing in common, for she was beautiful, while the sea was just wet and salty.

At last the holiday came to an end and I could return to Budapest. By then I'd nearly gone mad from homesickness, that's how much I wanted to see the zoo once more.

I had a friend called Berci, a handsome lad and immensely popular with the girls. He wanted to be an actor, which is in fact what he became.

Though I was only a year older than him, I was two grades ahead, since Berci was a bit lax when it came to Latin and Hungarian. Thus he always spoke to me with the respect due to elders, and sought out my advice about everything. He trusted me.

Even my best friends didn't know how madly in love with Évike I was, and so not even Berci suspected a thing.

"Hey," he said to me one day out of the blue, "know that gal at the zoo, that pretty little brunette whose mother sells raspberry soda and animal feed at the stand?"

My heart stopped beating. Then it swung back into action with terrible vigor, and I worried Berci would hear the racket. I didn't like to speak about HER with anyone. Even the word "stand" bothered me, for I thought of it as a pavilion. I asked him coolly:

"Why?"

"Because I heard that the little runt is really stand-offish with the boys. I made a bet with Géza that I'll hook her in two weeks. I gave myself two weeks. Out of caution."

"Oh, don't be silly!" I said blithely, though in fact my knees were trembling with anxiety.

"You know, I thought you know her better than I do. I saw you with her a lot at the zoo, and I thought you could fill me in on her. It's good to know the territory. What a gal likes, what she doesn't like, and stuff. Know what I mean? You give me some tips, make my job easier. I don't really care a whole lot about the chick, but as I've made the bet, I'd like to win her over."

I was dizzy, but I gathered my strength. I knew Évike didn't like wild boys, so I advised Berci to be rough with her. As with a rag.

Knowing that the girl loathed lowbrow pranks and practical jokes, I naturally mentioned that he should try the stock pranks that always worked: sneezing power, itching powder, the sooty bottle, and other novelties, because the chick lives and dies for that sort of stuff. Évike was different, she loathed sweets, especially licorice, which due to its size was the rage among us back then. I recalled that Évike had said of licorice with disgust, "Can you believe that some people like this stuff?!"

So I told Berci to go out and buy some licorice for the woman right away. I even gave him money, just to be sure. One less mid-morning snack didn't matter anymore.

A few days later Berci came running toward me on the street. He was gleaming.

"I'm so grateful. What you did for me was really nice. Without your help I wouldn't have succeeded so fast. You should have seen how happy she was to see the licorice! She was all smiles as she asked me how I knew she loves the stuff? I just smiled right back mysteriously. The chick is a bit dumb, don't you think? But now the whole thing is almost over, since I've achieved everything. She's softened up."

"Terrific," I stammered, choking back tears. "But what do you mean by saying you've 'achieved everything'?"

"Évi asked me to go out to the zoo, and then we'll climb up Little Rock and make out."

I shuddered.

"Listen to me. I've given you good advice so far, right? Don't go on the date, don't go with her to the rock, don't try kissing her. With that, you can be sure she'll love you even more."

Before he answered I could see that my attempt was useless. He didn't get it. Nor did I.

On the fateful day I went along with Berci to the zoo. He sure did look elegant, with even a walking stick flashing in his hand.

On reaching Évike's stand, I coolly greeted the woman and dragged myself listlessly onward.

But near the stand I sat down on a bench. With strained interest I stared upon the people walking by, and even turned a passing eye to Little Rock.

Évike stepped out of the stand and went with Berci toward the rock; the girl musingly, head bent down, like a sacrificial lamb; Berci shamelessly, haughtily. He even had time to give me a secret wink, signaling that everything was going exactly according to plan, thank God. *Goddamnit.* As I sat there on the bench, thinking of the lady of my dreams, whom I'd already lost forever, out of the corner of my eye I noticed a boy coming toward me. I looked up. A stranger. With a chess board under his arm.

"Excuse me, but I noticed that you're here alone, too. We could play some chess."

Alone, I thought. *Whoever this wretch is, he's right in this one thing. And at this very moment Évike is making out with Berci on Little Rock.*

Without even waiting for my answer, the chess player had already sat down beside me and began placing the pieces on the board. Utter chaos and darkness reigned in my mind. Shattered, I looked down upon the chess board, but instead of knights, rooks, pawns, and bishops, I saw only Berci and Éva, embracing and kissing wildly.

"Well, excuse me, but you can't move so far with the king!" my chess partner protested.

Poor kid! How was this wretch to know that what he saw as a king was in fact Berci, who did not love Éva as he should have. The whole thing had been only a bet, and yet, or precisely on account of this, he was now up on Little Rock hugging her tight. How could this hapless fellow know that Berci must be driven from the chessboard, Little Rock, the entire world?

"I say, that's a bit much! Have you gone mad? You can't jump that way with the rook! Why, you have no idea how to play chess!" So he shouted as he went about picking up the pieces and putting them furiously away.

So the match remained unfinished, and if it's up to me, never again in my life will I take a chess piece into my hand.

I remained there alone with my tears, and I lacked the strength even to feel pain, when I saw them approaching merrily, smiling, from Little Rock. All was lost, no doubt. What did it matter? I thought, knowing I'd never look again upon this fallen girl. She was like most women. I could have killed her now, as she stopped before me, smiling away, the last courtesan.

"Berci will walk me home," she declared, but Berci was firm and manly in his reply.

"Pali will come with us, and that's that."

I looked up in hope that perhaps they'd start a fight, but Éva liked this determination even though she could clearly have done without my presence.

I didn't want to go with them. I wanted to coldly, languidly remark that I was sorry, but it was my custom to only walk home respectable girls, not those who run off on rocks like mountain goats. But to do so when I was so happy to be near her, even if in a manner unbefitting my rank?! I said barely a word on the way home; I felt only pain, as if I were attending my own funeral. Berci was kind only to me—putting his arm around me, coddling me, and otherwise signaling to me in all sorts of ways just how grateful he was for all my paternal advice. Évike invited Berci in to their place, but I secretly gestured to him, and so he stayed with me. She meant nothing to Berci. That's why it worked for him. She knew I'd die for her. He'd been confident.

But starting tomorrow, I thought, *everything will be different. I will be as cold as an icicle. Or even colder. I'll never go with her on dates. I'll woo other women instead. Of course this coldness and indifference will really work only if it's genuine. Maybe if Évike were bald or pockmarked . But enough of this nonsense already! After all, it's not her hair and her pockmarks that I love.*

Fortunately, Éva quickly forgot the whole little adventure with Berci, and a few weeks later she herself told me everything. As for me, I admitted how much I'd suffered, knowing as I had about what was going on, and I even confessed that I'd sought to have Berci's courting go down in flames by doling out bad advice. By the time we'd talked over everything, and were happy and relieved, I couldn't resist risking the question:

"The one thing I don't get is how you were able to love that disgusting black and sticky licorice?"

"Oh come now, I just wanted to pull Berci's leg."

Life was sweet again, but at the bottom of my heart I knew that something still wasn't right with licorice.

Three

Suicide is a temporary solution.
Death is preferable.

I was past seventeen when I decided to take Évike as my wife.

I was to meet her at ten in the morning. That's when she and her mother opened their little refreshment stand at the zoo. The truth is, by that time of day I should long have been in school, but that's for another page, and besides, who insists on the exact truth? In short, then, I decided to play hooky, as I'd done so often already for my love.

At the usual time, a bit before eight, I left home, books in hand, and I could hardly wait until ten, when I could again see Évike. I stood there in front of their stand and waited. After two or three eternities the woman finally arrived, and business started with a frenzy. People were thirsty, and raspberry soda was in great demand. Naturally I helped serve customers.

"Hand me the syrup," said Éva.

"The half-full bottle or the new one?" I whispered to her, though I knew full well that they never opened a new bottle as long as there was anything left in the old one. But I liked to whisper to her, leaning near, as if we had a secret, because this somehow brought us closer to each other.

"You know very well," she said, with a kindly smile.

I did know, I did. Quickly, I leaned down to pick up the large bottle of raspberry syrup, and when I rose back up, my father was looking at me from among the customers. At first I thought I was hallucinating. I couldn't believe my eyes. But then my father's characteristically deep voice pealed like a bell as he turned to my mother, who stood beside him.

"I had to live to see this! Your son is a waiter—a waiter!"

My mother cried ladylike tears while my father yelled a manly bloody murder.

"Out of there! Get over here!"

Slowly I got moving. There I stood, trembling, in front of my father in the radiant morning light. He grabbed my arm; he was quite a strong man.

"Yo*uu*!" he growled. And he slapped me. Hard. Twice, lest I misunderstand. I just stared at my own father, who'd just slapped me and ground my pride into dust in front of my great love as if I were a beggar.

Twice. And I only stood there, helpless, devastated, slapped up. I wished vaguely that the earth might swallow me.

But that's just a generality, something anyone might say: I was well aware the earth is solid and seldom swallows anybody.

Évike was stunned. She had no idea what had happened, and why. Before she might have been roused to consciousness from the slaps that I, as she saw it, had received from this complete stranger, my father was tramping about before her like a lion, waving an enormous finger in the air like a flag.

"I'm the father of this wretch! Are you the one who keeps him away from school? If I see you with him one more time, it will cost you dearly, do you understand? I'll have you booted right out of this city! You little hussy! You are seducing my son and ruining his life!"

Évike didn't say a thing. She only stood there, pale, her lips quivering.

A few minutes later she said calmly:

"May I speak with your son for a minute? Now."

And not even waiting for a reply, she took my hand. I went.

"Look," she said, "I'm really sorry about this unexpected and horrible scene, but you're not responsible for what happened. But the man doing the slapping is your father, and I don't want to be witness to such a thing again. Promise me you won't come here even after school until you're your own man, as long as your parents support you."

I stood beside her weak and pale, still holding the bottle of raspberry syrup, which, in all the drama, I'd forgotten to put down.

I raised the bottle so Évike could see it, too, and with a slightly trembling voice but with conviction, I said:

"It's got dregs."

Évike looked at the bottle, and then, with misty eyes, at me.

"Dregs, but ..."

"I ... I ..."

But by then my father was standing beside me, tall and dark, ready to take me home. I handed the bottle to Éva and left. My mother was still crying. We went home in silence. Along the way I began to brood. I would have liked to die. I was practically eighteen and was a nobody. A slapped-up young gentleman. Even in the best-case scenario, years would pass before I'd be able to support myself. Not even serious professionals got jobs nowadays, in these troubled times. True, times are always troubled. Perhaps life without Éva was possible, but it wasn't worth it, and I had no hope of seeing her for even a minute. Twice, in front of her—my father! Horrible.

I saw at once that only one thing would help somewhat: killing myself. People make too much fuss about death. It's not such a big deal. Anyone who's alive has got to die, no matter how old the person is. The two are not in proportion. Let's say someone lives to be a hundred, which is a nice age, though not too common. But how long will he be dead? Take King Matthias. He lived forty-seven years. And since then he's been dead, and so it will be for who knows how long. *It would be best if I have a word with Karcsi. We live in the same building, anyway, and his father has an officer's revolver full of heavy, military bullets. I won't write any letters. Who can a dead man correspond with? Ridiculous.*

Although it wouldn't hurt to write Évike a nice, short, manly letter. Évike would cry. My father would shed tears, too, that stone-hearted man. Perhaps he'd then understand what a fateful error it was to slap a grown man. In front of Évike. Twice.

Even he would be terror-stricken on hearing the bang of the weapon from the other room. Or maybe it's best to leave home in such cases, to let strangers bring home my lifeless body on a simple stretcher, pale and stiff? There is no escape.

Suddenly I had an idea. The Aster Revolution had come and gone, and Béla Kun had taken power. On the way home that day I noticed a poster exhorting young men to join the Red Army. What a heavenly idea! To die for an ideology rather than of cowardly suicide. I was a huge fan of Hungary's great poets Petőfi and Ady, after all. I knew nearly every one of their poems by heart. That was it! World liberation! I'd fall in battle like Petőfi wrote and then did! What a very different, lovely death!

I enlisted. In a matter of moments I received my high school diploma and joined the army. After brief basic training I was assigned to the 28th Assault Company. I was happy. My life had purpose, after all. We'd head out to the front to fight for freedom. What a lovely thought.

My father cried when I told him that from the next day on, we'd be strictly on call at the base, that no one could go home, and that we were off to the front. My mother cried, too. It seems they loved me, after all, in their own way.

I bid farewell also to Évike. A soldier can't be slapped by his dad. Those days were over.

But before I could get to the battlefield, the Hungarian Soviet Republic was toppled, and Regent Miklós Horthy entered the country astride a white horse. Horrible times ensued. Father had me decommissioned. He confiscated my weapon (I had only a bayonet) and destroyed my uniform, so not even a trace would be left of my military days. Such was the terror that reigned in Hungary that killing myself didn't even cross my mind. All I thought was that amid such circumstances, even living was impossible.

Four

WE ALWAYS WANT TO LEAVE THE PLACE WE HAPPEN TO BE. A STRAIGHT PATH IS BEST: LYING IS NECESSARY.

Karcsi was a decent fellow. Though we were friends, I respected him. My best friend! Back then I didn't even have friends. Only best friends to whom I was tied by blood pacts.

One day Karcsi invited me for an important conversation to the New York Café, which later became the Hungária Café, since we got angry at New York.

Karcsi ordered me two rums. I couldn't drink even one, since I hated the smell, but it was a manly spectacle, me sitting there with the two shot glasses in front of me. Karcsi was giddy with excitement.

"I've got a great idea! We're going to America! A fantastic country! Freedom, happiness, wealth!"

"The Statue of Liberty … The Woolworth Building …" I said, recalling a couple of landmarks.

"Time is money! Rockefeller! Pearl White!"

"Cowboys … Corned beef … Edison …"

"California … Gold miners …"

"There are opportunities there. Every man is equal! There are no m'lords and right honorable gentlemen."

"And the money? We need money to set off."

Karcsi gave a dismissive wave of the hand. He was great at that.

"Don't you worry, I've thought of everything. We don't need much. Between the two of us we need about a hundred dollars. I'm already figuring in dollars. With that much money we'll get to Trieste no problem. There we'll hire on to some America-bound ship as sailors."

I shuddered. "What about passports?"

"That's nothing. I've got contacts. If you know people, anything is possible. Besides, we need passports only as far as Trieste."

"But where will we get money for the trip?"

"Leave it to me. And if there's a problem, we can always head out to the flea market on Teleki Square to sell some things."

We paid, and walked a little bit toward America. We parted on the Grand Boulevard.

"Bye," said Karcsi. "Gotta go to a little rendezvous. A really important and exciting one. A gorgeous gal."

What a nice guy Karcsi was! God. So he had a 'little rendezvous'. He always had important and complicated affairs. America! Terrific. Of course my father wouldn't like this, either, but come what may, I thought, I was going. This was my fate. According to my dad, everyone should die where they were born. If Columbus had listened to my dad … but he cut his own path. And he even had a wife, who tormented him to no end—why the hell a new route to India when the old route was still working? Instead of getting a real job on some ship as a sailor. We too—this nice guy Karcsi and I—would sail off, like Columbus did back then. Karcsi lied a lot, true, but his lies were always lovely lies, and he had great ideas.

Random memories of our long friendship now came to mind. There was the time he kicked around a one-krone coin like a soccer ball. He was seven at the time, we were attending the same school, and Karcsi happened to have a krone on him. A bona fide, spanking new, sparkling krone. In today's currency it would correspond to at least a twenty-forint coin. It was an incredible sum, for kids of our sort sometimes got a shiny kreuzer, but never a krone. A one-krone coin was grown-up money. We were headed home together, and I, concealing my wonder, asked him how he'd gotten his hands on such a treasure.

"Oh, we have lots of these at home. I don't even need it." And while my heartbeat came to a halt, he tossed the capital to the ground and kicked it absentmindedly all the way home.

We lived in the same building, near the school. By the front door I called out an anxious and hasty "bye," but then hid behind the door and spied to see what would happen. I wanted to get my hands on that krone. But Karcsi, too, glanced about cautiously, to be sure no one was looking, and then with a sudden motion he leaned down, picked up the money and pocketed it, like that, and ran up to the second floor.

Later there was the king's visit. I had to swear not to tell anyone.

"It's a deep, dark secret," he explained. "The king dropped in at our place last night."

"The king?" I asked in amazement.

"Yes. He came to borrow a sack of krones from my dad. We've got tons of money; we keep it in a secret hiding place in the basement. But no one can know about this. The guards who watch over the treasure are mute. That's how we bought them, with their tongues already cut out."

He was excited; his eyes were glittering. I shuddered. A visit from the king! A bag of money! What a dad!

Despite his tales, or perhaps precisely on account of them, I liked Karcsi a whole lot. And I respected him. For years after he told me, he was the boy whose dad had given the king a sack of money. Later, when I found out that this money never existed, my respect for him still held fast.

Dear, lying poet!

Five

Nothing amiss in our family, but Grandpa will take care of everything, and even America visits home.

"Get washed up and get dressed, we're going to Grandpa's!" said Mother after lunch.

"What? Another family council? I'm not going."

"Didn't you read about it in the paper? Márton has come home from America. You mustn't say no to Grandpa." With that, she ended the argument.

Márton had come home? He'd be there, too? Sure I would go. I was happy. Finally I'd get to meet Márton Himmler, who had been the black sheep of the family, because fifteen years earlier, when he was sixteen, he'd been expelled from school, whereupon he'd gone to America. For a while the news we received of him was fantastic, but then during the war, nothing for years. Now, however, huge newspaper articles were appearing about my American uncle. He was the president of some big American mining company. But he also owned a hotel, a newspaper, and a bank, according to the news. And so I knew it would be worth my while to go to this family gathering.

My Grandpa, who was then ninety years old, ruled over our family like the head of some ancient dynasty. With his long white beard, his youthful face, and his large, dark, intelligent eyes—he didn't wear glasses—he evoked the biblical Abraham. Whenever some important matter came up, he invariably summoned his multitudinous family. An upcoming divorce, marriage, birth, company bankruptcy, or dowry for a poor girl in the family—all this fell within the old man's scope of authority. He had six daughters and four sons. The girls all wed early, at the age of sixteen or seventeen. Their father had married them off mercilessly, ensuring himself a whole bunch of grandchildren and, indeed, great-grandchildren and great-great grandchildren.

He always had a gold coin for good students, and he was the one who reconciled married couples aiming to get divorced.

One young couple in the family was living separately. No one dared notify the old man of the awkward matter. The couple kept attending family gatherings diligently, as if nothing had happened. Before Grandpa they behaved as if they were living in the best marriage ever. My grandpa, who knew everything, just kept an eye on them and continued scheming until the illusion of peace became a bona fide reconciliation.

He'd now summoned the family together celebrate the return of the prodigal son, even though Márton had in fact returned from America as a wealthy and revered man. The family members were moved as they gathered round the enormous table in my grandpa's sumptuously furnished dining room.

On the right of the master of the house sat his oldest son, and Márton had the seat to his left. The relatives deluged him with questions:

"Is it true that every miner in America wears a silk shirt and has his own automobile? Is it true that Negro slaves work the plantations? Is it true that there are no houses, just skyscrapers?"

Márton tried amiably, smiling, to satisfy everyone's curiosity, but I didn't even pay attention, for I knew that soon I would personally witness all the wonders one can find only in America.

Six

Work is nothing to be ashamed of, but there is none. The Italians don't speak Hungarian, but that's their problem.

After fiery arguments (including two whole slaps from my father), Karcsi and I left for Vienna. This was my first time in Austria, but I didn't even look at Vienna, since it was but a stop along the way to America. Three days after we arrived, Karcsi got a bit of money from his relatives there, and we went on to Trieste.

Trieste: beautiful. The smell of Trieste. The smell of snails. The smell of fresh fish. The smell of the sea. All kinds of good smells were about, but we didn't have a dime, so we were by turns starving and fasting.

Of course we weren't just lolling about. We wanted to work, but on day one we learned that only members of the Sailors' Union could get work on a ship. Those days there were no more than thirty thousand unemployed people in the city. We were living hard times, as we always have since someone invented humanity.

"Well, kid," said Karcsi with a sigh, "let's go home."

I was stunned. "You're a spineless dog," I said in a huff. "You want to turn back when we've barely set off? At the first obstacle? You can go if you want, but I'm staying."

The next few days were suffused by melancholy. Usually Karcsi did the talking, but almost always about America. He berated that hapless country for all that is bad, but in vain, for in my eyes it remained an unattainable wonder.

Dear Karcsi was a charming boy, a born poet full of imagination, except he couldn't write, so he became the greatest liar of all time. He always had gripping tales at hand. Usually about himself, for he was lyrical. On one of our days in Trieste, the moment he stepped into our small, bleak, ramshackle furnished room, he began excitedly sputtering:

"Guess who I met today?! Polnay. In case you don't know, he's the managing director of one of the world's biggest ship companies. He knows my parents. We had a friendly chat, and he happened to mention a law the government has enacted. Under this law, no more ships can go to America. Understand? Not a single ship. So the situation is completely hopeless. We might as well go home. Even with monumental thrift our money will last two weeks at most. Then we'll starve to death."

"Which government brought this unusual law?" I inquired.

"The government. Which one? Does it matter? It's a law, a law."

"You didn't even meet Polnay."

"No, but we've got just enough money to get us home."

"Fine then. You go home. I'm staying."

"Don't be mule-headed. If you don't want to go home, let's go to Vienna. We do speak German, after all, and we'd be close to Budapest in case something unexpected happens. America is not for us. Strangers, and besides, we don't even know a mouthful of English. What the hell is a sensible person supposed to do there? I'm utterly fed up with America. In Vienna I've got relatives, too, if need be."

"And I have a relative in New York, Uncle Márton. I'm staying, come what may."

I walked with Karcsi to the station, and we agreed that for the time being he'd go to Vienna, but we'd write to each other.

With slow steps and a heavy heart, I headed alone back toward the city. I stopped in at an ugly little tavern for dinner. No sooner had I stepped into the smoky room than I stopped in my tracks. I heard a Hungarian folk song. Looking through the thick smoke in the dingy space, I saw a young man ardently, beautifully singing *Only a Girl for Me.* A fleeting thought of Évike passed through my mind, who knows why? For a while I just stood on the steps and watched, until finally I strode over to the fellow, put my arm around his shoulder, and sang along with him, in heartfelt Hungarian, to the tavern's Italian patrons. We sang for a while, and then the unfamiliar but agreeable young man went from one drunk guest to another, an upturned hat in his hand, and almost everyone threw a bit of change inside, mainly *centesimi*, which back then counted as money.

When he finished, he beckoned me and we stepped outside together.

There he scrupulously counted the money, divided it in two, and was already extending half toward me. I didn't understand what he wanted.

"We worked together, so half is yours."

"But I didn't do it for money. I just got carried away."

"No matter. These people give more to two than to one. Today I earned more than twice what I usually get on my own. Feel free to put it away."

"What's your name?" I asked while carefully pocketing the money.

"Karcsi Vidor's the name."

"Where do you live?"

"Nowhere. I've just been looking for a place. I'm an actor from Budapest and am preparing to go to America. I've been in Trieste for two months. It's a tough city."

"It so happens I'm looking for a roommate. My friend just left—he is also called Karcsi—and now I'm on my own. I have the feeling that we'll be roommates. I'm also headed for America."

From the moment we met I was fond of this affable, handsome, tall actor who was likewise headed to America. So it was that I found a new friend to replace Karcsi, whom I'd temporarily lost.

Seven

STARVING IS NO WAY TO MAKE A LIVING, AND BESIDES, VENICE IS NOT JUST FOR HONEYMOONERS.

Karcsi moved in with me, bringing both of his shirts. He had no other furniture. We kept singing with iron diligence, though I mostly confined myself to Ady poems, for, after all, it was all the same to the Italians. Business wasn't booming, though. Most Italians prefer to have dinner in silence, without listening to Hungarian poems. That's what they're used to. Or maybe the Italians are poor, and since they've got to budget their limited funds, nothing was left for us. Slowly my reserve capital dried up, too, and Karcsi had no significant assets to speak of either. There were days when we ate not even a bite, despite going to restaurants and little taverns to sing and recite.

Hunger itself was not so dangerous, it's just that our future seemed bleak. Mostly we just sat in our room, the rent past due, and racked our brains, but no bright ideas came to mind.

Our landlady was a patient, kind, older gal who had only one leg to seriously stand on, since the other one was made of wood.

She became suspicious that we didn't even go grocery shopping, but when she inquired, we explained that in Hungary customs are completely different than here. Hungarians do not have lunch and dinner at set times but on a whim, sometimes late at night, when it happens to cross their minds.

She must not have been too impressed with our national customs, for she often brought in a huge dish of boiled potatoes, just a bite, she said, so we could have a taste, and of course the two of us tasted every last bite in a matter of moments, no matter how large the helping was.

We learned Italian incredibly fast, since, as it turned out, it is a phonetic language that closely resembles Latin. We were already able to express our thanks for the bites, and it was in Italian that I appraised the landlady's beauty, which she acknowledged with a maternal smile, knowing full well that in fact we found the bites she brought us beautiful, not one of her legs.

It was easy to get old bread from good-hearted bakers, and sometimes we bought fresh bread, too, when we happened to earn a bit of money from singing, but somehow the Italians were generally in no mood to spend money on us.

Nor could we really be happy, in our heart of hearts, that our landlady confessed to us one day that she needed money, and that if we were unable to pay, she would have to rent the room to someone else. Due to a lack of funds, we had to move. We went out to the seacoast, at first aimlessly, but then it proved to have been a useful idea, for all sorts of ships were arriving from America and who knows where else, and everyone had luggage. We helped carry this luggage, and sometimes the owners were not ungrateful. Not that they spoiled us, no, for they could see that we were not professional porters but amateurs. And yet we earned enough for bread and cigarettes.

We slept in the park, since it was a lovely summer, and I even managed to sell my hat to some Italian optimist for a lira. That was enough for a day's worth of food for the two of us, but then it started to the rain, and only then did it become clear what a hat is good for. Karcsi still had a hat, though, so we took turns wearing it.

Meanwhile, Karcsi recited Hungarian poems just beautifully, and then night came, when we were able to head off to work in some dive.

We were singing away unsuspectingly when a little team of Hungarian ship's officers arrived and ordered supper. They were speaking in Hungarian with each other, though they sported Italian merchant marine uniforms.

We got to work. Enthusiastically. We sang only for them, happy to finally have a Hungarian audience. We were working like ladies of the night, and I'd just begun reciting Ady's poem "Sailing on New Waters"—*Fear not, my ship / tomorrow's hero is sailing upon you / Let them laugh at the drunk oarsman*—when one of the officers waved me over to their table and invited us to join them for supper. The four officers, it turned out, served on the formerly Hungarian, now Italian vessel *Szterényi*. Among them was a giant everyone called Peaches, who later played a decisive role in our lives. After the sumptuous supper, which comprised not only bread, we fell into a jolly good mood, laughing a whole lot, forgetting our lodging and financial concerns, and as happy as could be over our new, Hungarian acquaintances.

I'd just begun to tell a story when I suddenly stopped in my tracks on witnessing a strange, incomprehensible scene. At the table beside us was a young couple, the man with an arm around the woman, as appropriate, and meanwhile the woman, silently, by way of signals, agreed to a rendezvous with the sailor sitting across from her. I only watched and wondered. Peaches, too, looked upon the scene in confusion.

"Is that fellow stupid or blind? Why, doesn't he notice that the woman is cheating on him right before his eyes?"

I stood up and went right up to them for a good look. It turned out that the man embracing the woman was in fact blind.

"The guy is blind," I reported to Peaches, who was disheartened at the news.

"Jesus Christ!" he hissed. "That sailor deserves a beating for carrying on with that blind man's woman."

"God will punish him," I said to placate Peaches, but without much success.

"We won't wait around for that," said Peaches enthusiastically. "You'll pick a fight with him."

"If I'm a fool," I replied. "He'd beat me dead in a minute."

"I'll be there, too," said Peaches to put me at ease. "The reason you've got to start the fight is that I look strong. Folks usually don't want to mess with me."

I pondered for a bit. Meanwhile Peaches taught me a short sentence in Italian that triggers a punch if the individual is Italian.

I made up my mind. *Whatever will be, will be*, I thought, and meanwhile I'd learned that Peaches's ship would be leaving for America in a few weeks—only the government can't get wind of it! Moreover, I trusted that my Italian pronunciation was still far enough from being perfect that perhaps the sailor wouldn't even understand what I said, and so he wouldn't take offence. Maybe he'd hear "You're a jackass" as "Your jackets." Hence my words would lose their sting.

I went over to him. I stepped on the sailor's foot, gently, almost lovingly, but the sailor just screamed at me, not that I understood what, to which I responded with that magical Italian sentence which triggers a punch, and indeed he turned pale and was already raising his mighty fist to beat me dead, when from out of nowhere Peaches appeared, as if the angel of revenge, shoved me aside, and spoke thus to the sailor:

"Have you no shame? Picking a fight with a kid like this?" and no sooner had he said this than he'd already struck a blow in Hungarian, at which the Italian's head crackled in Italian, before he crumpled to the ground, likewise in Italian, and then we left him then and there. We weren't doctors, after all—what were we to do with him?

After that excellent fight the officers invited us onto their ship, where we spoke at length about this and that. It was a delightful evening.

When Peaches inquired as to our address, we gave an evasive reply.

"We're just in the process of moving," I said, whereupon we agreed that we would look him up on the ship.

Peaches was a good-hearted fighter, but a fighter he was, and he loved the sport. The next day, refreshed by sleeping in the woods, Karcsi and I happened to be sitting in a café, brimming with enthusiasm and youth, but Peaches was in a sour mood, listening on in silence.

"Shall I start a little fight?" I asked softly. The sailor's eyes came to life. He nodded. I stood up, looked about, set my sights on a strapping young Italian, and got the subversion underway. For a moment I felt sorry for the fellow as he sat there, unsuspecting and young, dreaming of home, but—duty calls!—a moment later I'd already pronounced that certain, untoward Italian sentence in which, alas, his mother figured, too, whereupon he gasped and was all set to throw a punch, but once again Peaches appeared in a flash and finished the fight I hadn't even begun.

Refreshed, we left the café. Peaches seemed distracted, posing random questions to himself that he didn't even answer.

"Impossible! Don't be foolish! You shouldn't even think this. Nonsense—you can't get to America this way."

"What way?" I inquired, teeth chattering from nerves, my brain tight as a fist and yet hopeful.

"No way. It's nonsense. I was just thinking aloud. Crazy. You'd die that way before the ship would reach port."

"Nothing is impossible when it comes to America. I'd even be willing to undertake the little trip tied to the ship, swimming. What did you have in mind?"

"I was thinking that maybe I could hide you away on the ship, but it's not really comfortable in the hold, in the bottom of the ship. I think it would be unbearable."

At length I explained that of all bottoms, my favorite was the bottom of a ship, that I'd always dreamt of just that.

"All right. I don't care. If you want to go to America so much, I'll give it a try. Our ship leaves in a few days. I'll hide you away, and then we'll see what the future brings."

I was giddy with joy.

"God, if it were true! I'll tell Karcsi Vidor straight away, let him be happy too."

"Who said a thing about Karcsi? I'll hide you, completely alone, and that's it."

Horrible. Hope had flashed before my eyes and then fluttered up and away like a butterfly.

Of course I couldn't even think of leaving Karcsi here while I swam comfortably to America. *No problem,* I thought. *Something else will come up. Peaches is not yet America.*

I had a whole hour to kill until meeting up with Karcsi. We always met at the Piazza Pozzo Del Mare and went from there to our usual headquarters.

In those days we were staying in the Boschetto, which was a pleasant mix of forest and park. There no one bothered us about paying rent, and we rose early, before the sleepyhead Italians. We washed up and shaved in strangers' yards, which is to say, by their wells. Sometimes the owners caught us in the act and sent us packing, but no problem, we continued our morning ritual in the yard next door. There are lots of yards like that in Trieste.

It was a lovely morning. We'd bathed in peace, Karcsi had gotten bread from a kind-hearted baker, and we set off on our daily walk, as fitting.

All of a sudden Karcsi leaned down, picked up something from the ground, and whispered excitedly: "We're heading back to the Boschetto for a consultation."

"What happened?"

"Good God, you didn't see it? I found a fifty-lira note on the street! This is a first!"

Fifty liras! Wealth, lodging, food, cigarettes, happiness.

In the Boschetto we relaxed on the grass and began to consult. An entire lunch didn't cost more than one lira. Indeed, if we wished to start off on our new life with thrift, we could have a fine lunch for even fifty centesimi. We'd have forty-nine liras left.

After a fruitless consultation we headed off toward downtown. Along the way, we bought a bottle of fine cologne for thirteen liras, two bars of brand new chocolate, rented a room for five liras a week, and Karcsi haughtily paid for two weeks in advance. We even had money left over, with which we were at a loss for what to do, since we had everything.

We bought cigarettes, too.

The next day, though it was bright and sunny, we didn't feel like going out. We just enjoyed lodging all day.

Then I went alone out to the street, not entirely without purpose. Karcsi stayed home, so our room would not be entirely unoccupied.

I stopped at Peaches's usual café, and spotted him from a distance.

"Our ship is leaving tomorrow. Do you want to come with us to America, alone, or stay in Trieste?"

"Without Karcsi I'm not budging an inch," I said firmly.

"You're in luck, since if you'd been willing to leave your friend behind, I wouldn't have taken either of you. But this way, you can both come along. I repeat, we're leaving tomorrow, and after supper we're meeting right back here."

I ran like a maniac home to tell Karcsi the sensational news. He gasped for breath.

Only that night did he calm down, once Peaches explained things in person.

"We're leaving at eight tomorrow morning. But you two will come this evening and spend the night on the ship. From here we'll go to Venice. In Venice you two will disappear, and I'll let you know when you need to return. The next stop after that will be America. As for what happens after that, we'll see."

That night we walked right onto the ship, and soon we found ourselves in Venice. There we thanked the captain for his generosity, bid him farewell, and headed off together with Peaches to look up our relatives in Venice, who didn't exist, but that wasn't our fault.

Eight

EVERY SHIP HAS A BOTTOM, BUT NOT EVEN RATS ARE RATS TO THE BOTTOM.

Venice. Honeymooners, gondolas, lagoons, and all sorts of things. It may be a lovely little town, but we were only interested in the ship that would take us to America.

We just happened to be standing about toward evening near the ship when an enormous figure approached. It was Peaches.

"Don't say a word!" he said under his breath. "Follow me!"

We boarded the ship, where Peaches again began to whisper.

"Go down here. I'll look after you. Take it slowly, because it's very dark."

He opened an iron hatch, and we descended a ladder into a dark void. Then it suddenly became even darker. Peaches had closed the hatch. In the dark we hung from that ladder between heaven and the hold. Slowly, carefully we climbed, further and further down. Finally we reached the bottom. We couldn't see a thing. In the darkness Karcsi looked for my head, which was in its usual place, and, leaning up quite close to my ear, whispered, "Don't breathe so loudly. No need to be huffing and puffing."

And so I hardly breathed, lest someone should hear it and throw us off the ship before we even set sail. Slowly our eyes became somewhat accustomed to the dark, and yet still we more sensed, than saw, that the *stiva*—the hold—was a colossal chamber full of cargo. It turned out that half of it comprised hard blocks of Magnesite; and the other half, calcium carbide, which was easy to recognize due to its smell. We had enough space between the two loads to stand, sit, or lie down by turns as we pleased. After a while it felt to us as if the ship had embarked. We were happy, which was not so easy, since it's hard being happy in the dark, holding back your breath. In the dark we got hungry twice as often as before, but we couldn't even think of eating. Somewhere I'd read that a person can last three weeks without food. True, the journey to America would take thirty-three days. We would starve to death. Silk-shirted miners would later find our skeletons among the pieces of calcium carbide, and would wonder angrily what was wrong with their carbide lamps.

Despite the worry and excitement, we somehow fell asleep. I awoke to the sensation of something soft grazing my face. Wet fur was tickling the skin under my eyes. And two tiny eyes were staring at me. Anxiously I flailed my arms about in the dark, managing to scare away the individual, who, I now realized, was a fat, grown-up rat. What a fine place we'd wound up in! I adore animals, but somehow I'd never had occasion to truly come to love rats. I recalled terrifying tales about rats that gobble up an entire person. In no time another rat approached. The same one? They do bear a striking resemblance to one another. With one exception. The most brazen of them all, the one that simply didn't want to leave. Karcsi named him Hugo B. Bimsenstein so we'd recognize it, but then Karcsi got so angry with him that in a blind rage he grabbed the creature by the neck and began to strangle it. Hugo felt increasingly uncomfortable in that strong hand, and when Karcsi flung him to the Magnesite with all his might, the rat passed away. That's how we figured out that we didn't have to fear these wild beasts, for if you squeeze their necks with two fingers, they stretch out, and that's when you've got to fling them at the mineral.

I too tried my hand at this excellent technique, but no matter how hard I threw them they just became dizzy and staggered back to their feet.

Therefore I granted Karcsi the authority to carry out executions on my behalf, for he was strong and merciless.

What a ship!

The exercise made us more and more hungry. Who could tell how long this ghost ship had been swimming on the great water?

After a while we heard some sort of noise above our heads. We were done for. They'd discovered us and would perhaps throw us into the ocean. A yellow streak of light shot down into the darkness, and I heard Peaches's voice.

"Quiet. It's me, Peaches."

He'd brought us dried fish and zwieback, which is hard and counted as bread in the merchant marine.

"How long have we been here?"

"Two days," he said, and handed us a remarkable iron rod to shoo away the rats.

Darkness, darkness, the roar of the ocean as the ship cut through it, and hunting with the iron rod. Our amusements were limited. Sometimes we couldn't even bring ourselves to talk with each other. We just sat in silence waiting for food.

Twenty-five days passed. We started to go slowly mad. We couldn't wash ourselves, our beards grew as if being watered, our eyelids stuck together, and I dreamed of being able to bathe one more time in life, truly, from the heart. I remembered our beautiful, sparkling bathroom at home, and the white, piled towel that I had never before managed to appreciate. Perhaps I'd be able to take a bath one more time, just once, if we arrived. If, that is, we'd last that long in the torturous bottom of this ship.

After an eternity or two, it came to pass that Peaches did not throw down food but, on opening up the hatch, called down.

"Come on up!"

The ship kept swimming on the ocean as it seemed set to do forever. We obeyed wearily. We didn't expect anything good to come of this. Maybe he'd report us to the captain? Peaches was on duty. We couldn't see anyone else on deck but him. He gave a wink.

"Tomorrow we'll be in New York. Tonight you can sleep in my cabin."

We got two hours to spend on the deck. We became dizzy and drunk with freedom. We ran around and bathed our faces in the balmy breeze. Karcsi noticed the mast and waved me over, and then the two of us climbed right up. The wind blew Karcsi's dark hair, and with his strong, rat-killer arms hanging on to the rope, he began to recite that Ady poem I'd spoken in the restaurant when we first met the ship's officers. At first he did so quietly, and then louder and louder, crying, singing, and blaring as he thus announced himself to the New World:

Fear not, my ship, tomorrow's hero is sailing upon you
Let them laugh at the drunk oarsman,
Fly, my ship,
Have no fear, my ship: tomorrow's hero is sailing upon you.

In the early morning Peaches led us from his cabin up to the deck: there, before us, was New York City.

Karcsi cried, who knows why. After all, we had arrived.

Nine

EVEN IN AMERICA THERE ARE ONLY TREES, HOUSES, AND PEOPLE, AND THE GIRLS, TOO, ARE LIKE AT HOME, EXCEPT EVERYTHING IS COMPLETELY DIFFERENT.

Peaches said we had to go into the city on our own, since he had work yet to tend to on the ship. He gave us five dollars; we could pay it back once we were millionaires.

"Now you can say about me whatever you want! I'm a rotten beast for having left you two to starve in the hold among rats. Go right ahead and chew me out."

"But Peaches, for God's sake, how can you talk like that? We'll be grateful to you forever. You're the nicest beast I've ever met, and that's the truth."

As we left the ship and headed toward the city, a tall, strong man blocked our path. He was just like we imagined American detectives to be. We were done for. Everything got found out and now we'd be deported, to our shame. The whole thing had been in vain. I struggled to stand up straight, to keep from collapsing on the spot. My knees were still working, but only so-so. The detective started to say something in English, and his words were like barks. We didn't understand, but we replied with the word Peaches had taught us on the ship.

"*Walking*," we said, as that is fair to say when you get off a ship.

This gentle word failed to have the desired effect, and he promptly gave us some hugs, even checking our pockets, and then said something in that impossible language before giving a nod.

"*No whiskey*," he said, waving us on.

This, we understood. He was searching us for liquor, for back then prohibition was still the law of the land in America. Well, he was sorely misguided. Slowly, very slowly—in case he might want to shoot—we went forward, and all of a sudden we found ourselves on the streets of New York. Interesting, even here the trams jingle like in Budapest as they rumble along the tracks. All those people swarming about! On the outside they seemed normal, but not one of them could talk.

I called out to the first seemingly trustworthy fellow, showed him my uncle's business card, and turned myself into a question mark. He said something, and I really paid attention, figuring perhaps I'd understand, but I couldn't. He even pointed toward something, and we took a couple of steps in that direction, whereupon I again waved that business card under someone's nose. I wanted to be enthusiastic, but I was weary and deflated. Karcsi felt a toothache coming on. In America, of all places.

Finally, after traipsing about for hours, we found the office of the newspaper Márton—Martin, in America—owned. We were just about ready to collapse from exhaustion and sleepiness when the cashier saw us and quickly closed the safe door. He thought we were burglars. Our ragged clothes were reasonably clean, though, and we did what we could to conceal our torn shoes. But we must have been a bit dirty.

I stepped over to the cashier and asked if he spoke Hungarian:

"*Beszél magyarul?*"

"Yes. *Mivel szolgálhatok?* – What can I help you with?" he asked coldly, as if he'd prefer not to help with a thing.

"I'd like to speak with the boss."

"I'm sorry. He's in Kentucky."

"How much is the fare?"

"A hundred dollars."

"When is he getting back?"

"Maybe in the winter," he said with a shrug. "I don't know." He'd already turned away and began calling out terse orders to a clerk. He had no desire to talk to us. He wasn't one for small talk.

Karcsi now assumed command.

"Please, here is a card. The publisher of this paper is my friend's uncle. He gave this business card to him back in Budapest and told him to look him up here in New York. My friend must get in touch with him by all means."

The little man's face changed as if by magic, and he immediately telegrammed Márton. He then took us to Márton's hotel.

There were two beds in the room—two white beds with white pillows and white sheets.

And a bathroom!

I issued a command to Karcsi use the bathroom before me; he had a toothache, after all. Then it was my turn. I just couldn't get enough of all the hot water and American soap. We fell asleep as soon as we lay down on our real beds. When I awoke the next morning, Karcsi was already standing there by my bed, dressed, and glowing.

"Come on, Paul. They're waiting for us at the office. Márton telegrammed. They're buying us shoes, suits, and everything."

An uncle!

Ten

DON'T START WITH WOMEN—ONLY IF YOU MUST.

We happened to be having breakfast in the "lunch room" across from the office when a young woman stepped in. The lunch room was full of people; only our table had a spare seat, so that's where she strayed over. Her hands were lovely; one of her fingers bore a silver ring with a large black stone.

"She has beautiful hands," I whispered to Karcsi, "but I don't dare look up. I'm afraid that she is ugly."

"You can look up," he said nonchalantly. "She is not ugly."

"Is she beautiful?"

"No."

I looked up. She looked interesting and intriguing, with sleek hair and big, black eyes veiling distant woes within. I now spoke to her, but did so in Hungarian, while facing Karcsi, for I knew that these hapless natives did not understand our beautiful and useful language.

"Hey, girl, you stranger with those fantastic hands, I'd like to talk to you in that odd foreign language of yours, which I don't understand a word of. Why were you born American, you poor, woeful girl with those heart-rending eyes? I'd tell you a lot, things you will never learn or understand in this wild, foreign language. Too bad you were born American and cannot know that there are stunningly beautiful Hungarian poems that have been dedicated to your melancholy eyes."

Slowly she rose from her chair, just as I was quietly reciting this:

My queen, the flames are lighting up,
Our golden carriage, lo, arises,
Today we mingle among the people,
You, the queen, and me, the king.

That's as far as I got. That's when she looked upon me, with her sad smile, and slowly, with feeling, finished the poem:

The time-worn cab bumps along.
And we, pale, shiver.

She paid for her breakfast, and left. We stayed there, stunned, wonder-struck, just staring at each other. Karcsi anxiously shook his hands the way he used to on the ship when shooing away rats, but a moment later we sprang up and dashed out to the street. The girl was gone. She'd vanished, like an apparition. Perhaps she wasn't real at all? Perhaps I'd only conjured up this girl for myself? For a while we went on looking for her, but then we had to call it quits, because it was time to go to the newsroom.

There, still distracted, I started to work when the typist told me that the paper's editor had returned from a two-week vacation and wanted to speak to me.

I stepped into her office. Some sort of woman was sitting behind the desk, smoking a cigarette. She turned toward me with a polite if guarded smile that froze the instant she saw me. I turned dizzy on recognizing the woman who'd completed the poem.

"Of course you could not know that many Hungarians live in New York. It's not advisable here to make comments aloud in Hungarian about people you don't know."

"Are you angry?"

"Of course not. I like that poem, and you recited it well. I might have figured that you are the nephew whom—as per the boss's orders—I'm to treat sternly. I just returned from two weeks with your uncle, and he appointed me as your guardian." She laughed. "Márton does not wish to make his nephew's life any easier. He told me to work you hard. Behave properly. I've got to go to the printing press now, and in the meantime you can read through the paper's older issues to get an idea of what it is actually about. Naturally I do not yet expect you to know the situation of Hungarian American miners and what they would wish to read about in their paper, but soon you can try your hand at writing an article. At first it will be hard, of course. Good-bye."

She left. I didn't see her all day long, because when she returned from the printing press she wrote, dictated, and had meetings with advertising agents; in short, she was busy. A couple of minutes before closing she came by to see me.

"Come to my place for dinner. I have a Hungarian cook. It's tough at first getting a handle on American food."

She didn't even wait for a reply. Off we went.

The pleasant, cozy apartment was crammed with books—including poetry, plays, novels, and short story collections by my favorites, Endre Ady, Dezső Kosztolányi, Lajos Bíró, Zoltán Somlyó, and Ferenc Molnár. We ate Hungarian food and spoke Hungarian. It was a pleasant evening, and I could hardly wait to get home and fill in Karcsi.

"I have bad news," he began when I got there. "I couldn't find her. I scoured the whole neighborhood, in vain."

"She's my boss—the editor of Márton's paper. Her name is Yelena, and she has lots of Hungarian books. She gave advice all night. It doesn't matter how much you make, you've got to set something of it aside so you'll have capital for a rainy day. In America you've got to work hard, but it's worth it. So then, she spoke such words of gold, but otherwise she's a pleasant gal. I'm not obliged to hate my boss."

The next day Yelena took me to a bank, where I opened a savings account with five dollars. Now the capital would grow as if being watered. All I had to do was save. After all, we were in a foreign country.

Every week I went to the bank, like a bandit, and deposited five dollars.

Yelena found Karcsi a job, too. He became a choir member in a beautiful theater, and sang enthusiastically with the others.

Ivan, Yelena's older brother, had started out as a strong man in a circus, and then became a painter and sculptor, but he could sing and play the violin as well. He was like some hero out of a great nineteenth-century romantic novel. A man for all seasons. Only that he earned very little, since he started out on this new life only around then, but later the whole country knew him as a famous and wealthy painter.

Ivan held a soirée, to which Yelena invited Karcsi and me.

We milled about, meeting the guests. There was Delly, a tall, black-haired painter with a lumbering gait; Jack, a Swedish sculptor with colossal hands and a gigantic frame; and Jack's lover, Fatime, a beautiful Turkish girl who looked up at him with devotion. We were introduced to some actress; a German baroness who wrote poems in English; a wealthy, gorgeous American gal who was hopelessly in love with Ivan; a talented Hungarian writer who worked in a factory by day, wrote by night, and happened to be in love with Yelena; Rita, an American dancer; and a Russian princess who painted.

Ivan called my attention to Rita, who, he said, was an exceptional dancer.

I took in Rita with fresh spring eyes, but she didn't really strike my fancy. Neither pretty nor ugly, she was sprawled out lazily on the settee. Ivan got the evening underway by singing and quietly playing the violin. A little man sat behind the piano, whereupon the others began to dance.

Karcsi danced with Yelena, too. Everyone danced with everyone, and only two of us, Rita and I, remained off to the sides.

Around midnight Ivan announced that Rita would dance.

And Rita began to dance.

Flickering lissomely, jauntily about. Then she vanished, and returned shrouded in a thin veil. The piano music began, and after a few steps Rita cast aside the veil and continued to dance, completely naked, with her beautiful, supple, youthful body, with every last bit of herself.

And a miracle happened. This girl who just before had seemed insignificant now became significant. Talent rendered her beautiful, conjuring her into loveliness to behold. And there she danced before us, afire with passion, electrified as she swayed and turned with dizzying verve, like some sort of sprite.

Dawn was breaking by the time the party ended.

I was happy the next day, and even the day after that.

This happiness lasted for a few months. Every week I put the five dollars into the bank enthusiastically, and I already saw myself as a budding millionaire when lightning suddenly, unexpectedly struck. It turned out that the paper, whose zealous employee I was, was relocating to Kentucky.

Márton, my charming uncle, invited me to join him there, and Yelena, too, should have moved there. But Yelena didn't. I decided that I wouldn't move, either, that I wouldn't leave New York. If Yelena wasn't concerned about losing her job, well, I wouldn't be, either. I was no girl who shrank from difficulties.

I thanked Márton for his generosity, and that was that.

A few days later Yelena got a job at a New York daily paper. I didn't. I spent my days looking for work, and now I understood what a smart thing it is to save. Those dollars I'd buried each week at the bank were lifesavers.

Naturally it would have been ideal, had I been able to work at the same paper as Yelena, but there they rejected me with the excuse that I didn't know English, and the news comes in on the *ticker* in English, and if I don't understand what it's about, I can't write about it, either. There was a grain of truth to this, but, alas, that grain counted against me.

Time passed, and as it did, my savings account kept dwindling, too, until—as was foreseeable—it finally disappeared. Although I sometimes got ambiguous dollars from Karcsi, destitution was already baring its teeth on the street corner.

Then, out of the blue, Yelena notified me of a kindly printer in New Brunswick who owned a paper called *Magyar Hírnök* (Hungarian Herald). Speaking English wasn't as important there, because it was mainly about Hungarian matters. Yelena had already talked with the printer, and I had a job.

I was happy again. New Brunswick was but one dollar away from New York, and so I would continue being a New Yorker, just a bit farther off.

Eleven

THE SUN SHINES, THE BANKER CHEATS. LIFE ISN'T ABOUT SIMPLE DECLARATIVE SENTENCES.

The train clunked its way toward New Brunswick. It clunked a whole lot for that one dollar, and I began to experience qualms. What kind of man might my boss be? How much would my pay be? Would I be able to do the job? Pure fear and doubt.

New Brunswick was a typically boring small American city, with not so much as a trace of the verve of New York.

My boss, Mr. Lengyel, the printer, was a short, strapping man of about forty-one, a Hungarian with a plump, pleasant wife who was ever on the verge of giving birth. In the end she gave birth, too—sometimes a boy, sometimes a girl. They had four children so far. The printer had been a soldier back in Hungary who'd served long enough to become a platoon leader, and he liked to regale me with tales of his military years. He raised his numerous children with military discipline, too, and spoke to them rarely. He limited himself mostly to short, hard, snappy commands: "Put it down!" "Get out!" "The door!" "The window!" "Off to bed!" This is how he dallied with with the kids, whom he loved but beat with enthusiasm. He explained concisely what I was to do, and that my pay would be fifteen dollars a week. I got a flat, too, at the Lengyels, who were hospitable folks whose home was frequented by guests. I tried to befriend these strangers, but it was hard to pay attention, since my mind was in New York with Yelena and Karcsi.

There was a whole lot of work, for I was not only the editor but also the business manager, and moreover, I also solicited advertisements, mainly from Hungarian businesses, and that's not all: I had the privilege also of sticking the subscribers' names to the papers using a primitive little machine; fortunately, there were few subscribers, and their names stuck pretty well.

Laci also belonged to the family, working at the press in the rank of brother-in-law, but without pay, in view of the bonds of kinship. The bulk of my own pay went to the printer, too, for he charged ten dollars a week for room and board, leaving me with five; or, rather, with nothing, since it was easy to see five dollars disappear on cigarettes and all manner of nonsense. Saving was pretty much impossible.

My name wasn't yet in the paper, which meant simply that I was still in my probationary period. But then one day, a few weeks later, Mr. Lengyel turned to me with these words:

"You're getting twenty dollars. Your name in the paper. That's all."

Twenty dollars was at least a thousand more than fifteen. With twenty dollars an editor had enough dollars to afford everything. As far as I can recall, there were few important people who, at the age of twenty, edited the *Hungarian Herald* for Mr. Lengyel.

One surprisingly warm day, as I was sauntering along French Street, in the Hungarian district, I wandered into a confectionery. Standing behind the counter was a pretty young gal.

"I'd like a raspberry soda," I said, blushing. Moments later, as I stirred the ice-cold drink with expertise I conjured up out of age-old memories, I remarked, "This is the finest raspberry soda in town."

"I know who you are," said the girl, scrunching out the Hungarian words with a bit of an American accent. "Because my daddy is a subscriber and you're the editor. It must be easy work."

"What's your name?"

"I'm Alice," she replied.

The next time I went into the confectionery I could hardly speak to the girl, since it was Saturday and she was managing the place on her own, with amazing speed. Various liquids were flowing in slender, toothsome flutes, but Alice navigated it all with remarkable finesse. Here, it was unnecessary to lug around heavy, wide-bellied bottles. Interesting. This was America.

Suddenly a young man popped in the shop and asked for cigarettes, but Alice happened to be serving another customer, by which time the customer seeking cigarettes was about to go back out the door. I happened to be standing next to the cigarette rack, and so I lifted out a pack of Lucky Strikes and handed it to him. The next customer turned right to me and asked for Camels. I served him too. Alice looked at me gratefully with her blue, beautiful eyes. Her hair was blond. How strange. . . .

I worked there diligently until midnight, like a day laborer.

When we finally closed shop, I offered Alice to accompany her home.

"I live here above the shop," she said, adding cleverly, to help ease my embarrassment, "but we could walk around the house a bit. Did you work in a confectionery back in the old country, too?"

"No. But I had an acquaintance I used to help sometimes." My father's monumental slaps came to mind as a distant memory.

The next morning, being Sunday, I hurried right over to the confectionery and again worked there all day long. There were lots of customers. There was not even a minute for conversation. After closing, once again I accompanied Alice for a bit around the house.

"We're putting on a performance to benefit the paper," I said, "and I thought you should be in it, too."

"I'm crazy about theater. I'd love to perform, because lots of people have said how much I resemble Mary Pickford."

"I noticed right away!" I said, exaggerating, whereupon we went back into the closed shop to discuss the performance. Only one faint light was on all night to discourage burglars, and Alice's father had long been asleep above us.

"There is a really interesting scene in the piece," I explained, "when the boy comes home from vacation. He has a little sister whom, of course, he adores. He worships this sweet, blond girl, since she is a good sister. They are orphans, their parents having died long before, and they have no one except each other. Anyway, this orphan boy comes home from somewhere, and when he sees his little sister, he puts his arms around her and gives her a passionate kiss, saying, 'Darling, I'm so happy to see you again.' And he is happy. Anyway, we can rehearse this exciting scene right now so I can figure out if you'll be right for the role. So then, I'm the boy, and you're the girl."

I kissed her.

And then I had to do so again, since I forgot the rest of the scene, and she kissed me back and stayed there in my arms, happy sister, as customary. It took quite a few tries until I was convinced that this girl would be good in the role of this little sister who worships her big brother. Naturally the two of them kiss a whole lot. We kept embracing there, in the shop, for a good while, entirely forgetting this strange play that was so bereft of complication and tension.

Dawn was already breaking when I got home, weary from the rehearsal, but I couldn't sleep. I just kept seeing Alice in front of me and reliving those passionate kisses, feeling her slender, supple body, her firm little breasts as they pressed tight against the thin fabric of her dress, and that very night I decided that to begin with, I'd make her my wife. Then we'd see.

Alice's father had been a blacksmith before he bought the confectionery, and he had an irritating resemblance to his daughter. This pained me. But he was a kind-hearted confectioner, like every decent blacksmith, and he sent various sums back home to his poor relatives in Hungary.

"I just got a letter from Mihály, whom I sent a hundred dollars to with Birkás, the banker. Birkás sent him fifty thousand Hungarian crowns for those dollars, which is a fortune back in the old country."

I turned pale. This was suspicious. I looked into it, and it turned out that under the exchange rate back then, Mihály should have gotten at least seventy-five thousand crowns. When I reported my discovery to Alice's dad, he was furious.

"I'm going to kill that thief!" he shouted.

In the course of my further investigation I determined that Birkás was constantly cheating and plundering poor Hungarian workers who knew nothing about exchange rates.

My first order of business was to publish the crown-dollar exchange rate not only for that day but also going back several weeks.

As later turned out, this was a fateful error, for no sooner had the paper appeared than Mr. Birkás showed up, in person, in the newsroom.

"Stop publishing the exchange rate at once, otherwise I'll stop advertising with you."

"Go ahead," I said confidently. Mr. Lengyel, the boss, was away in New York for a few days.

"If I'm a friend, I'm a good one, but if you make an enemy out of me, you'll be sorry for the rest of your life," said Birkás menacingly.

The next issue had the first article with my name on it, accompanied by the dollar-crown exchange rate, cautioning readers that Birkás cheats them terribly when wiring their money to Hungary.

As I published more and more information every week about Birkás's swindling, I became a national hero among the Hungarians, and Alice's dad was swelling with pride about this.

"We'll show the dirty crook!" he said over and over again.

The banker sent his lawyer to pay me a visit, and the man demanded that I publicly apologize to Birkás and stop publishing articles exposing him, or else he'd have me locked up. The poor guy. How could he have even thought to have me locked up—me, who'd saved the Hungarians?! The thief! The cheat!

Twelve

It's good everywhere, but worst in jail.
The basic law of life is injustice.

One fine day a short, mean-faced man stopped by the newsroom looking for me, summons in hand. Soon I appeared before a distinguished old judge, who explained that they had received a complaint against me for criminal libel, but for three thousand dollars bail I could remain a free man until the trial.

I didn't have that much money with me at the moment, so pending further proceedings they placed me in a police station holding cell.

I saw it all as an interesting experience, sure as I was that within an hour, Alice's father or the printer would arrive with the bail.

I tried looking at the situation with a brave face, with a supercilious, cheerful air, though I couldn't see much in the poorly lit, narrow, dirty little cell. I tried imagining myself as a hero, a martyr being crucified for the truth. But I was locked up in a cell, like a common prisoner. A pretty lowly rank for an editor-in-chief.

Three hours later I began getting antsy. Perhaps they'd completely forgotten about me? Who knew what a formidable enemy was capable of in this foreign land? Fear crept in. I waited, settling into my newfound role as prisoner, when suddenly the cell door opened, and a policeman who looked to be six-and-a-half feet tall carried in a giant with a bleeding head. The new prisoner, who must have been a strong man, was wrestling and tussling with the huge policeman. He spat, too, wanting to free himself by any means, which was perfectly understandable in this situation. He shouted and he swore, cursing the policeman's relatives, including even his mom. I watched as the billy club rose up into the air and came striking down. The giant stopped cursing at once, whereupon I heard a body crashing down, and then, silence. The policeman stepped back out and nonchalantly locked the door.

Well, I'd sure wound up in a fine place. I became ever more nervous, and pounded a fist against the bars. I shouted, too, for them to let me out, and also that I was innocent, but it seemed that nobody cared.

Silence. The wind of death struck me. No doubt I'd meet my end right here. Had all the suffering been worth it to get to America? No one knew what had happened to me and no one cared. Injustice was the basic law of life, and there was nothing to be done about it. The situation is the same among wild animals, for what sin has the gentle, plant-eating antelope committed to then be torn apart by the lion, which even growls into the bargain? The lion even feels annoyed. My legs buckled at the thought and I flopped down on the bunk, as a bed is nicknamed in jail. All at once I sprang up in terror. The darkness seemed to start moving around me. As I now tried hopelessly to penetrate the thick dimness all around me with burning eyes, I saw a teeming mass of strange, American bugs climbing all over the walls and the floor. I tried frightening them away by stamping my feet. But, alas, these were brave bugs, accustomed to robbers and murderers, not about to be scared of me. I then resolved to kill them, but they were big and fat. To think that in Japan or wherever, they eat bugs! But I didn't envy even swallows. *Whatever will be, will be,* I thought, and stepped on one of them, which so crackled under my foot that I nearly fainted in horror. I gave up the futile struggle. There were lots of them, and they crackled. *If I were Japanese or a swallow....*

I tried avoiding them. I stood on one leg, like a stork, so fewer bugs would get on me, and I don't know how much time passed this way before the cell door suddenly opened up and a policeman stepped in, inadvertently crushing three bugs in quick succession, but he didn't even wince. This was his workplace.

Well, I thought, *the hour of freedom has struck.* But, then, the policeman said to the broad-shouldered detective standing beside him, "Transfer him to the county jail."

I'd already learned that "jail" means prison. The detective nodded, and took out a pair of handcuffs. He deftly clicked one of the rings to my wrist, the other to his own. Strange custom. So it was, pathetically, that we headed off somewhere. We boarded a bus where everyone was staring at me and the cuffs. *My poor, dear father,* I thought, if he were to see this now, no doubt he wouldn't be able to stand the sight of his son, in handcuffs, being dragged across America like some thieving murderer.

Collapsed into myself, I hardly noticed when we arrived.

In the new jail I had to hand over my money, my watch, my everything. Then it came time for a bath. Afterward they had me put on a pair of rough pajamas, and I entered the cell. The heavy iron door slammed shut behind me.

But somehow here, in the jail, it wasn't quite as bad. I even felt a twinge of delight as the detective undid the handcuffs.

My fellow prisoners gave me a warm welcome. No matter how small I was, my presence did break the monotony of imprisonment a bit. I'd been placed in a large cell comprising ten small, cagelike stalls. Each prisoner got one compartment. I could hardly stand up straight from nervousness. I looked around carefully before lying down to sleep, but I saw no bugs. They'd all stayed behind in the police holding cell. I only wanted to sleep, but something always happened that roused me awake.

Languishing in one of the cages was a poor young Italian guy who'd been crying and shouting all night, wanting to see his mother, sometimes voicing his thoughts in English, sometimes in Italian. The others were talking or, rather, shouting at each other. No one was concerned the least bit about the hapless Italian's mother. In the cell beside mine an old man was molding away. With his snow-white hair and beard in the dimly lit cell, the handsome gentleman looked like some biblical prophet. What was this graybeard doing here among these prisoners here awaiting trial?

For lack of an audience, the prophet talked to himself continuously. Sometimes he paused his one-sided conversation, took some straw from his mattress, and chewed on that for a while. Straw must taste good in American prisons.

"Maggie, my little white angel," he murmured, "don't run away, don't be afraid of me, I won't hurt you. I love you, don't you hear? Maggie, I'll strangle you if you don't pay me attention. Why are you looking so terrified? It's just me here, after all. Don't be afraid, I'm telling you. Give me your hand, that sweet little kid's hand, and ..."

Here he got stuck, perhaps because of some trouble with the little girl, or perhaps he was just seeking more straw. In times of trouble a person will eat every last straw, I thought. After a bit of silence he began to recite a poem—so he was a poet!—in a soft, soothing voice, intelligently indeed, and with feeling:

I love you for your velvety youth
I will serve you day and night
I will serve you always, ever
I will be your loving knight
All I want is to be loved
By your velvety youth my dear
Put your hands on my forehead
So in my dreams I'll be with . . .

It was easy to remember the poem, because he repeated it over and over again. From it I gathered that he sought to be the loving knight of some young gal, and all he asked in return is that the girl in question love him, too—him, this pleasant-faced whitebeard—and that she put her hands on his forehead, to ensure him sweet dreams. He was partial indeed to the word "velvety," which he used more than once. And in comparing the girl's youth to velvet, it must be said that this is not a bad idea for a contemporary poet.

When not reciting, he was calling out, amid gasping sobs, the name of this certain Maggie, this unfaithful girl who of course did not come with her velvety youth, whereupon the old man tore apart the mattress in his rage until finally collapsing to the ground and falling silent.

Women.

I had a bad night, mainly on account of Maggie. I could hardly sleep, though I was tired. At seven in the morning the cage doors opened and breakfast appeared—which wasn't rich. Only later did it turn out that the strange purple liquid was coffee, and perhaps the slice of bread had once been white, but the iron teeth of time showed. It was grey, dirty, sticky, hard. Even the water tasted like mold. Maybe here this was the law.

I began to get to know the other inmates, since during the day we could meet up in the big cell.

The Italian kid, it turned out, was sixteen years old—a tall, lovely boy—whose crime was that he'd broken into a candy store and stolen a few bars of chocolate and cigarettes, which is strictly prohibited. He'd been caught while committing this criminal act, and though he would have been released for fifty dollars' bail, no one in his family had that much money. And so he'd been locked up for now. He was a first-time criminal, deathly afraid of the execution that awaited him, and cried constantly day and night. Without pause. I couldn't believe how so much crying could fit inside one Italian. Even when he did drift off to sleep for a few minutes from sheer exhaustion, he awoke screaming, for he'd dreamed of the electric chair.

Languishing in another cell was a Hungarian peasant named Lajos Nagy. A fifty-year-old, short, brawny Hungarian sporting a big moustache. He gave the impression of being a respectable fellow.

"How did you wind up in here?" I asked.

"I've thought a lot about this, too, but I don't know. All my life I was an honorable, church-going sort, and back home in Hungary even the gendarmes shook hands with me, since I had a little plot of land, and still these people brought me here. Just why, only the good Lord could say, not me. It had to be a mistake."

It turned out, meanwhile, that my neighbor the graybeard was indeed a poet. And a bogeyman of little girls. Which is why he'd recited so enthusiastically about velvety youth. That very day he was taken to the observation room, but he was crazy, so they observed him in vain. For when even I alone had observed him, all that chewing of the straw and all those proclamations addressed to Maggie had already struck me as suspicious.

Also with us was Fuhrman, a young German who'd been arrested for running a brothel and smuggling liquor, even if he did claim to be a respectable fellow who'd never wronged anyone:

"A fellow has to get by somehow," he kept saying.

Before long I had befriended every resident of this big cell. From a Hungarian perspective, in America the meals are pretty bad even in the outside world, and in jail they are a bit worse, and so I got sick soon enough. My fellow inmates liked me, since I spoke little and I listened to what they had to say and did my best to cheer them up. The residents of such cells just walk back and forth all day like wild beasts, telling their sad stories a thousand times but never paying each other attention. Everyone just spouts his own words.

From day one I missed cigarettes, though smoking was allowed in the cells. Those who had cigarettes could smoke to their heart's content. Most of my new colleagues smoked, but I was afraid to ask how they'd gone about acquiring their stash. Instead I suffered. I'd have liked to write letters, too, but I had neither paper nor pen. When I turned with my request to the guard in charge, his face turned stern:

"What do you think this is, anyway, a hotel? And paper, too?"

"Sorry," I said.

The next day a new, young prisoner arrived. He was nicknamed Handsome Joe, rightfully so: he was a tall, handsome, strapping man. He possessed some sort of wild charm, some sort of allure, some sort of verve, and as if it were the most natural thing in the world, in no time he became the leader of this coterie of loonies. A chemical engineer in civilian life, he was, as later turned out, facing the most serious crime of us all: he'd held up a bank, and while escaping he'd killed two policemen who'd been chasing him. The trouble was that five more followed.

Since being in prison I had not been feeling well, but then I became seriously ill. One morning I could not get up onto my feet from the straw sack. Every day a different one of us was responsible for mopping the floor of the big cage. That morning, as I was trying to persuade myself not to be picked, I felt a gentle hand on my chest.

Handsome Joe was sitting on the edge of my bed.

"Can I help?"

"I don't suppose it's possible to get a pillow around here?" I asked, wearily. "Though at the moment this would be my one and only request."

We began talking about theater, film, and books, and the honorable bank robber was surprised to learn that I hadn't read a single novel by Theodore Dreiser, his favorite writer. I didn't understand everything he said, because he spoke English well indeed, but his pleasant, gentle voice lulled me to sleep, and when I awoke, a pillow was under my head.

I was sick for a few days, and this good-natured murderer nursed me like a father. By the time I recovered, we were friends.

"I'm twenty-eight years old and a chemical engineer," he said. "My parents are rich, and my father is one of the richest men in the city. He buys things for ten bucks and sells them for fifty. He cheats within the law. They call him a respected businessman, and I'm a crook. The dregs of society."

"But you are smart and talented. You could easily make a living as a chemical engineer."

"Ah, nonsense! If I need money, I go to the bank and take it."

"I heard you killed two cops. Aren't you afraid?"

"No. At most they'll send me to the chair, but even then I've won. Two for one. Once you're out of here, which will happen soon, I'll give you a few addresses where they sell opium at a relatively cheap price. That's the best, though I like heroin too. Don't believe the fools who are against it. Life is short but sweet. We ought to make that short time pleasant. What's a long life worth without giving it some substance? I didn't live long, but it was worth it. Some folks live a long time. They're born and they die, and nothing happens in between. My life was colorful, exciting, and interesting. Delicious tastes have been in my mouth, amazing giddiness in my head. I'm not afraid of death. Death isn't an enemy.

"I was twenty-one, strong, healthy, and happy. I wanted to see everything with clear eyes. Back then I still lived with my folks, and I was in love with a girl. Beatrice was eighteen, and I was meant for her. We were made for each other. But my folks didn't see it that way. The girl was poor. They talked her dad into taking her on a tour around the world. He got lots of money. And Beatrice disappeared. I wanted to kill myself. That's when I found opium. I smoked a pipe; it was bitter. But by then I knew that every very good thing is bad at first, so I kept at it. I was right. Because the opium put me to sleep, and I had the most beautiful dreams in the world. What dreams! In a regular dream everything is foggy, indefinite, and most often you forget the whole thing by the time you awake. But with opium, dreaming is different. First of all, the good feeling is with you all around, the happiness is perfect! Your body is as light as a feather, and you feel as if you could fly, though it's not urgent. Once the dream gets underway, everything really happens. It's much more poignant, true, and colorful than real, gray existence. Just as if a veil were suddenly lifted from your brain or, more precisely, you see everything more clearly. The meaning of things becomes clear. It's just otherworldly.

"And with opium, even woe is as good as if you're meeting a lover you haven't seen for a long time and kiss her on the lips. Such is woe. Every night I lived a lifetime. Now they'll kill me. On account of two stupid cops. Why did they chase me? They started the shooting, I was only defending myself. I didn't want to hurt anyone. The bank isn't a person. But that's not important. It's not even what I wanted to talk about, but about Beatrice. Interesting, how another person has a bigger influence on you than anything else. Ever since they took her from me, I've seen her only in dreams. Since then she has become my lover in place of Beatrice. Opium. She is faithful. You needn't be afraid of opium, because it's beautiful and good, and that's why I told you these things, so you get to know it."

Thirteen

The woe of the honorable burglar. Yelena writes her letter, which changes everything. The priest is strict, but sly as an ox.

Fuhrman, the German, was very sad. No one wanted to listen to him, and so he complained to me:

"My lawyer has deserted me," he began. "My wife is pregnant and expecting the baby any minute, and there's not a cent in the house. My lawyer wanted a hundred dollars before the trial. I'm going to kill myself; there's no other choice. I don't know why God is beating me down like this, for I've never done anyone harm."

"Is this your first time in jail?"

"No. But that wasn't my fault, either. I didn't do anything. Imagine, we got a tip that Lefkovich, the grocer, had thirty thousand dollars in cash in his safe. Thirty thousand! Well, my man, would I not hold up even my father for that much money? I told my friend the good news, and that very night we pulled the job. We got in the store easily, but the safe was hard to blow up. It was a helluva heavy, thick-armored safe, the devil would have imagined it of Lefkovich, that fat little Jew. So anyway, I just kept saying to myself, *thirty thousand*, to ratchet up my strength. I worked hard, until the crack of dawn. And finally it worked. That's when we heard a noise. A man never has a moment of rest. Right away we hid in some barrels and waited there a long time, not moving. Until we could hear nothing suspicious. We then ran over to the open safe to get the dough, but found nothing. There wasn't a red cent in there, just meaningless papers. I was so mad! So this is what I'd worked my tail off for? Even a day laborer makes some money with one night's work! I was so mad that I started to wreck the place, and my friend even broke the big glass windows, since he too was furious. Then we left. No one saw us. The next day they caught us, and to this day I don't know who ratted on us to the coppers. Well, and now I'm here! And this is what people call law and justice!"

I complained to Handsome Joe that I'd like to write but had no paper, to which he explained that I had to give the guard half a dollar, and I'd have everything I needed.

I gave it a try, and a miracle happened. The guard brought cigarettes, paper, and everything, and he even smiled. For another half dollar I made friends with the guard, and I asked him why this kindly, good-natured Hungarian named Nagy was in here.

"He nearly killed his wife, and he was threatening to wipe out his whole family too."

As for the details, I preferred to get those from Nagy himself, so I turned straight to him.

"I heard you had some sort of disagreement with the wife, and that's why you're here."

"Just a family matter, sir," he explained, "because sometimes the wife and I didn't see eye to eye. I like to drink a bit, and the wife, she doesn't like me to. One time I was getting home late, and the wife locked me out of the house. I'm a good man, young fellow, everyone can tell you that, but enough is enough. The bitch locked me out of my own house. 'Hey,' I say, 'you scum, you're locking out your wedded husband so he goes and drops dead? I'll teach you a lesson, I will.' With that, I picked up the hatchet that was there nearby so I could break in the door, since I wanted to have a word with her. Then I went in, and then said to her nicely, you can't go locking your wedded husband out of the house, right? But she just keeps saying, 'You've been drinking again, you drunk pig. I don't even want to see you!' She was the one who was offended! But, I say, because

I'm the man of my house, because by then all the ire was really bothering me, sir, so we got to arguing, because she was just lashing her tongue, and then I stepped on her neck so she'd shut up. I told her this is either my house or I'll squeeze your ugly soul right out of you and fling your kids out the window too. Everyone could tell you I'm a good man, that I don't bother anyone, but at a time like that you've got to show who's the boss in the house. I'm a pretty strong fellow, sir, so the wife, she was squealing like a pig being slaughtered. She then called the police, the American police, on her wedded husband, sir. This is the seventh time they brought me here for a family matter. If they let me out of here, I'll whack that bitch upside the head, you'll see, mister."

One day I received a letter from Yelena:

My darling little criminal, how can I explain to you that there is no such thing as a prison cell? For aren't you free to think whatever you want? No one can imprison your imagination, your enthusiasm, your dreams. I know you're young and that you're inexperienced in the ways of the world. You won't be there for long, but meanwhile I'm sending you this volume of Ady poems all the same, though I know that only prayer books are allowed to be sent to jail, but they probably don't know Ady, besides, this is a prayer book. I'm sending cigarettes, too. Maybe I don't need to tell you it was foolish to write articles attacking the banker. But I love you for it. Newspaper writing is not your line of work. It has too many tricks and twists. You've got to be shrewd and know that the people don't want protection. It seems they have a need to be fooled. We'll talk about that later, once you're out. And that will happen soon, so don't feel as if you're the same as them, no, you're no criminal, and be careful not to let those poor crazy inmates' crackpot philosophies poison you.

The next day the guard notified me that a gentleman wanted to talk to me, and he led me out to the visiting room, where there were no iron bars. Waiting for me was a tall, elegant, stern old gentleman.

"I'm Reverend Wheeler, and I received a letter from a dear friend of mine asking me to help you out and see what you are doing here. I'm a wise old man and know your case. If you listen to me, you'll be freed; if not, you'll stay here. You must weigh every step carefully. This is a serious matter. Under the law you could even get ten years for slander in the media. But trust me and Yelena. I'll get you out of here. We'll meet again soon." He nodded, and left.

I was led back to my cell, where I could barely catch my breath, that's how terrified I was. *Ten years in prison.* I hadn't known. *But good prospects. May this minister be right. I never want to see another banker again.*

On that day I received my father's letter, which had been forward to me in jail:

> *... and I'm proud of you, my boy, for having become editor of a newspaper in America in such a short time. I know it's hard to give advice from so far away, but I'd like it if you don't write articles against the banker. You could get into trouble for that.*

My eyes welled up. I couldn't read any more. My dear, sweet, smart father! How he knew things in advance! But, by now, it was too late for the good advice, which I wouldn't have taken anyway.

The next morning the minister came to see me again.

"Soon you will be released," he began, "and then you'll be under my supervision. If they let you out, you can't write articles anywhere. And if you do, they'll take you back to prison the next day. I live at 15 Franklin Street. Once you're out, phone me. I'll then tell you what's next. Good-bye."

Fourteen

You can be in prison even when you're free. Girls always spell trouble, but a minister isn't child's play, either. Even the straight path is crooked.

I was released from prison in the early afternoon. It was cold and the street was covered with snow, so everyone was in a hurry. I inhaled the fresh, frigid air deep into my lungs. I could hardly wait to see this kind, stern minister, whom I had everything to thank for, and I resolved to thank him, too, even if I had to wrestle him to the floor for him to listen to me.

I rang the bell. A lovely young woman opened the door and politely told me to step right in. The jail, this clean girl, this house, and, well, everything made me dizzy, and I could hardly get my name out. But the girl—her name was Ruth—was already chattering away:

"I've heard a lot about you already from my father and in the paper too.... You're looking for my father, right? I'm really sorry, but I don't think he'll be home before dinner. It would be best if you waited for him. I'll make a little coffee, and we have delicious pastries as well."

Without waiting for an answer, she ran right out to the kitchen with quick, determined motions and got to business. She looked like her father, but was much prettier. And her shape was different, too.

She poured the coffee and served the pastries.

"I know your case well," she chattered. "I really liked the way you fought that swindling banker. Dad told me the details."

"I did my duty," I said simply, though by that time, after my sojourn in prison, I didn't have the fanatical conviction, the unbreakable faith, that is so characteristic of martyrs. "You can't imagine how grateful I am for everything. You can't even understand how much joy it brings me that you are here and that you are clean. I came from prison, from among thieves and sick murderers. I've arrived here from filth, from a swamp, straight into this clean, girl's room, to a fairy maiden."

Ruth took my hand and led me to a sofa.

"You see, most of the time I'm home alone in the house. Completely alone. I think we'll be good friends."

I then noticed her picture on the wall.

"Would you let me have it?"

"Of course," she said, and with her dear little maiden's hands she took it from the wall and wrote on the back:

To my old friend, with love, Ruth.

I thanked her and kissed her hand, which was "as soft as velvet," as the mad poet might have said, and then I kissed her mouth, but she didn't resist. In fact, she kissed right back, which I was very happy about. But not for long, for precisely at the worst moment imaginable, my valiant savior, Reverend Wheeler, stepped in. Choking with rage, he said, in a not at all sanctified tone:

"I told you to phone when you are released. You disobeyed me. Now get out of here, and don't you dare set foot in my house again."

He seemed not even to notice the girl, his own daughter. As if she weren't even standing there right in front of him, red with shame and confused.

I got out of there.

Outside the fresh, cold air sobered me up. I now had an opinion about ministers too. I went straight to the press, but Lengyel, the boss, was not very pleased to see me.

"You stirred things up around here terribly, you know. I warned you it's not a good idea to pick a fight with Birkás. But it's not too late. Birkás is willing to give you money if you get out of town. He'll even drop the charges, because he doesn't want a scandal. I suggest you accept these conditions."

"Out of the question. I can't be bought. Everyone knows he's the fraud and I was right."

The printer looked downcast.

"You're talking nonsense. You're still young and completely wet behind the ears. It's suicide to keep on fighting Birkás. Birkás would gladly sacrifice a couple hundred dollars for you to keep quiet. It's worth it to him. And you can use that money, since you don't have a cent. Listen to your elder. Life has stepped all over me many a time. If you want to be headstrong, that's OK with me, but you can't count on me. The minister who got you out of prison told me, too, that you are not allowed to write articles until the trial. And I meanwhile need someone at the paper."

He went back to work, but called back.

"Well then, God bless you. Good luck."

I went to see Alice. Her father was standing behind the counter looking like a belligerent, nasty blacksmith. But I didn't bother with him—instead I turned to his daughter.

"May I help you?"

It was the blacksmith, whom I hadn't even asked, who replied:

"Yeah, young man, you won't get help here," he began in poor Hungarian. "I don't like it when jailbirds hover around my girl. This is a decent house. What are your intentions, anyway? Who are you? You're a nobody, fresh from jail. Do you have some trade to support a family with? No! I don't want you coming here! We don't want customers like you."

It seemed I was not destined to have much luck in the ice-cream and raspberry soda business. Back in Budapest, my father had said my dalliance with Éva was beneath me, while here, in the home of freedom and equality and of Birkás and his sort, Alice was above me. God, what a fool I'd been! Like some turkey that's grown nice and plump for the chopping block. Yes, let's be honest, I'd started this whole Birkás affair on account of Alice's father. And now he called me a jailbird. There wasn't an ounce of decency in blacksmiths, either. All they do is shoe horses.

Birkás's money would have come in handy, true, but I could not accept a penny from that thief. Then what would the difference be between us? *Let destitution come,* I thought, *and then something will turn up.*

Fifteen

Every fine fur starts out as a rabbit. Sleeping in a bed is possible, you just need to be sly. "No Experience Necessary" is not a serious trade.

I still had a few cents left, enough to pass the night in a cheap hotel. Tomorrow I'd begin a new life. I wasn't allowed to leave New Brunswick as long as this awkward Birkás case lasted. I had to find work right here.

Take it easy, I told myself. *All you need is a little pep, and then everything will go as smoothly as a roll with butter.* I lay down feeling good, with a lawful pillow under my head, as a free man, in a free bed, and I entertained the thought of getting dressed and going out for a walk if I felt like it, but I was weary and broken, and so I fell asleep.

In the morning I bought coffee and a roll with my last pennies, and it was now in a composed, clear frame of mind that I tried to take stock of the situation, which seemed bleak and dreary.

But luck didn't abandon me even then. I met up with a huge young plumber I knew from my days as an editor. He was very sad, because he was just taking his babies to their burial. His wife had given birth to twins, but they had died as infants, and every time he began to talk about them, this big strong man wept, and yet he kept mentioning them again and again. Such is a father's heart. I accompanied him home to console him and his wife, who was likewise crying. While consoling them I asked if they had a room to rent.

"We have an empty room, but without any furniture, so it's not fit to sleep in," said the grief-stricken plumber.

"That is just the sort I'm looking for, since I just got out of jail, I don't have much money, and life is expensive for a man without a penny."

"Alright, then," said the plumber and mourning father, whereupon we settled on terms. Most furniture is superfluous anyway.

And when it came time for bed, I found out not only that there was no furniture in the room, but there was no blanket, either. Except for the tiny diapers which those darling, innocent little ones had used when still alive.

For the time being I lay down on the floor. The room was chilly, and it was only then that I realized how tiny the twins were. *Poor things,* I thought, *no wonder they died. Their diapers were not even enough to cover half of my body even though I am small even when I stretch out.* All night long I kept busy moving those wee diapers from my upper body to my legs and vice-versa. Despite my tireless efforts, I only shivered and shuddered with cold in the kind-hearted plumber's simple, unfurnished room, under the diapers of those poor dead twins.

I imagined an open fireplace, warmth, and Emperor Nero, who'd been so cold that he burned down all of Rome. It did no good.

I got up in the morning tired and worn out, like a frozen lumberjack.

I headed off in search of work immediately, but at first no one needed me. I was living from day to day by getting a few cents from people I used to know, when all at once my lucky star unexpectedly arose, after all.

One evening I went unsuspectingly to the cheapest lunchroom to have breakfast for dinner, and there I was dipping my roll in my coffee when suddenly there was a stink so bad that all I could do was swallow what was in my mouth, but not any more. The smell was unusually strong and odious, so thick and stationary in the air that I could have leaned up against it, and it did not want to go away.

Across from me a genial young man was slurping his own cup of staggeringly bad coffee. I said to him: "Pardon me, sir, but don't you smell something unusually strong? I can't figure out what it is."

"It's me who stinks so much. My clothes. I work in the rabbit factory. You see, it works like this: when rabbits die, they're brought to our factory, where all sorts of furs are made from the skins."

"Interesting. Do you need any experience to get a job in that factory?"

"You want to work there?"

"I sure would," I exaggerated.

"It's a terrific place, I'll say. A good factory, an open shop, white people. I'll take care of you. My word counts there. Be here tomorrow at seven, and leave the rest to me."

The next morning, we met in the lunchroom, and by ambling along after the smell, we quickly arrived at the factory. My new friend introduced me to the foreman, who received me warmly.

"Here an eight-hour workday is not in fashion. You can work as many hours as you choose, because we pay by the hour. Of course, thirty cents is not a lot at first, but if you're good at it you can get it up to thirty-five. Of course you've got to work."

He put me right to work.

The job was simple but aggravating. I worked in a small hall with twenty other men who'd arrived from all parts of the world. Sitting on a tall chair in front of us was a young American man who did nothing. He was the foreman. He was also the one who showed me what to do. A great big pile of rabbit skins was heaped up on a table. My job was to take one of those staggeringly smelly skins and rub it with some sort of sticky, revolting liquid. God knows why. I looked on in terror as my colleagues worked at lightning speed. Lightning was a slow motion film compared to them. No sooner had one hand picked up a skin than the other hand was already in the pot containing the liquid, and in a tenth of the next second they'd already rubbed the stuff all over the skin, which they then set aside as they picked up a new one.

I grabbed the first skin I saw and began rubbing it with the revolting liquid, because I'd resolved to keep this job even if it killed me as surely as death is apt to visit twins. I started to work ferociously. I lay the skin down flat, dipped a hand into the muck, and was raising that hand, preparing to rub, when a terrible thing happened.

My hand holding the sticky fluid paused in the air. A full-grown, surprisingly ugly-faced bug crawled out of the skin. I began to itch, and broke out in a cold sweat.

Glancing about hopelessly, I noticed, crawling out of my neighbor's rabbit skin, a bug of similar appearance that was enthusiastically wiggling its little head about, as if it had goals in life. I looked at the person at the receiving end of this particular bug. He was a tall, young, brawny Russian, and not a single muscle twitched on his smooth face. He wasn't a man of emotions. Following his eyes, I saw that he too had noticed the bug on the skin. Like some living stone statue, the Russian lifted his strong, bony hand, and, without the slightest indication of fear or revulsion, dropped that hand down, whereupon the bug vanished into the skin. It must have died from the blow.

Well. If the Russian could do it, I would try also. I was, after all, stronger than that bug. Some people collect the things. Horrible. Eyes shut, nauseated, I slammed down my fist. The individual had disappeared into liquid. Stealthily looking about, I saw that no one had noticed my hesitation with the insect.

From then on I worked with mind-boggling speed. Fortunately, after a while I didn't even feel my hands—as if I wasn't even picking up, laying flat, and rubbing the skins with that loathsome fluid. I knew that rabbits were prolific, but that they were so prolific, I would not have believed had I not seen ever more gooey sacks arriving, packed full of rabbit skins.

By the time evening came, I was dead tired and disgusted. I could have gone home, but I was only at three dollars, and I decided not to stop work until I reached five dollars. I wanted to pay my rent to the kind-hearted plumber. There were more and more dead bugs, but I didn't care; I didn't care about anything. All I wanted was for the kind-hearted plumber to see that he wasn't wasting that empty room on someone who didn't deserve it, not to mention the dead twins' diapers.

In the course of the night they gave us a lunch break, but fortunately I had no money, besides, my appetite had vanished amid those ill-tempered skins.

Finally morning came. I immediately got five dollars.

The rabbit factory wasn't far from the house of the kind-hearted plumber, but by this time I was quite tired, and it was a hard job to walk. Though I used my hands to help along my legs, by the time I dragged myself home, the kind-hearted plumber was asleep. I set the alarm so I'd awake in three hours, as I had to return to the factory, and the minute I reached the floor I was asleep.

I dreamed of the North Pole, where the icy wind brought bad smells. I woke up sleepy and cold. By then the kind-hearted plumber and his wife were up, too. I tried handing him the money but he didn't accept it, insisting I could pay them when I had more.

For a full week I worked in the rabbit factory without being sent packing. I then asked the foreman to assign me to some other department, thinking that perhaps it would be better there.

They transferred me to the "mill."

There was an enormous mill, full of wet rabbit skins. The skins had been soaking there in brine for who knew how long, and as the millwheel swung round and round, the brine splashed into my eyes with amazing accuracy no matter which way I turned my head. This posed me a bit of a challenge in watching with clear eyes, which was a problem, as the whole point of my job was to watch—or, rather, to notice when the wheel brought this or that skin to the surface, and to then fish out those skins with my hands and put them on a rack. Now, the fishing would not have been easy even if my eyes had not been stinging from the salty water, since the millwheel kept turning at a constant speed. Were I to have snatched out a skin but a moment late, the machine would have run away with my hand. And you can't go fishing for skins without hands. The foreman even said to me:

"The fellow who worked here before you is in the hospital, because the mill cut off his hand. This work is no place for a drunkard. Here you need a clear head, as you can see."

I didn't see. I didn't see a thing, since the brine stung my eyes. Even my legs were soaked, but the foreman promised I'd get boots once they hired me permanently, because the work would then be more pleasant.

I kept at it, but it was slow going, for I was afraid of nestling up too close to the mill with my blinded eyes.

At lunchtime I asked my colleagues what better places there were in the factory.

Well, there was one where sharp knives were used to flay the skin off the rabbits. There, the workers were always covered with wounds, because the skin is greasy and slimy, and it's hard to handle a slippery knife. It was piecework. There was another place where the skin was smoothened with a nifty little device, but there everyone loses their nails. You never know when you might need your nails.

Why had I come to America? To be among rabbits in stinking factories? To be a jailbird? Why? But, then again, this was not obligatory. I quit, and that was it. No more rabbit factory.

On the way home I bought a bottle of cologne, and on getting back I began taking a bath. Unfortunately, water was leaking from the tub, whereas the point would have been for it to stay inside; but there was a problem with the plug. Even the hot water flowed only half-heartedly. The pipe must have been clogged.

I got dressed, went back outside, and boarded the train to New York. The ticket was just a dollar, but perhaps Birkás's detectives were already waiting for me at the station. But they weren't.

I rushed right over to Yelena. She was home, reading. I had taken a few steps toward her when my knees buckled. Collapsing, I buried my face in her lap and felt her strong, smooth, smart caressing hand on my head.

"Hey, what's the matter, sweetheart?"

I told her everything—the jail, the minister, and the kind-hearted plumber—and then we wept together happily.

Yelena stood up and called New Brunswick. She spoke with the minister, explaining the situation and getting him to promise that he would not take retaliatory measures for my having left the city.

That night we had dinner together with my New York friends. Ferkó was there and so was Pista, and when that night in Pista's room I found myself in a bed on my own, a real, grown-up bed with veritable, warm blankets, I felt as if those unpleasant things had happened long ago, a thousand years, perhaps, in some half-forgotten past life of mine.

In the morning Pista gave me some money to go rent myself a room. I needed work, above all. I bought the evening paper and quickly began reading the "Jobs for Men" column. All the positions were for skilled laborers, but then all at once my eyes brightened up as I read these magic words: "No Experience Necessary." Finally. This was me. This, too, was a profession.

I ran to the addresses provided, but they were factories and they gave the time of day only to huge, strong men. I wasn't needed.

The next day, as I was rambling aimlessly along the street, a sign in the front window of a lunchroom caught my eye: "Busboy Wanted." I was inside but a moment later. The boss was an implausibly fat man who could barely drag his body along, and as he lurched glumly before me, I noticed immediately that missing from him was the encouragement, reassurance, and affability that can make looking for a job a pleasant experience for the job seeker. A sign above the cash register read, "KEEP SMILING," but he himself had surely never read it, for he was as grim as freezing rain.

"Do you have experience?" he asked belligerently, when he realized what I was looking for.

"Not just yet, but I'd like to learn this trade."

"I can't use you," he said, and waddled back to the kitchen.

I fell to pondering human stupidity. A person is born naked, with not a clue as to what a busboy needs to know. Later he fumbles about before finally learning how to clear tables of dirty dishes. But if every restaurateur behaves this way, what will become of the busboy trade?

At the next place I behaved more wisely, and when posed the question "Do you have any experience?" I gave this cavalier reply:

"Experience? All my life, especially in Europe's larger cities, for many years I was a busboy."

"All right. You can start right away, at fifteen dollars a week. Naturally you'll get fed too. Have you had breakfast yet?"

I got coffee and bread, and a dirty white cap and a smock. I didn't dare light a cigarette. I got right down to work. *Why is experience needed for this?* I wondered. I had to clear the dirty dishes off the tables and take them into the kitchen, and when there were no dishes then with a grimy gray wet rag I had to wipe off the tables. Big deal!

After a little while the boss waved me over.

"Here's fifty cents. Don't come anymore. You're too slow."

I left the lunchroom in relief, with money in my pocket and breakfast in my belly. For that day I stopped searching for a job.

The next morning, I found another busboy job, but again I was sent packing, because the boss said I had no talent, even though I insisted I'd already covered the world as a busboy. He wasn't buying it.

Sixteen

Freedom is lovely but it requires a flat.
People are heartless, kudos to exceptions.
One always leaves the place one is at.

Sure, I could have stayed on a bit at Yelena's had I not ruined everything with the ink. Often I stayed there until 3 AM, and this evening of all days, when I didn't have a flat to go to, I hurried off earlier. Oh well.

It was quarter after eleven. Now, in Hungarian this sounded closer to twelve—*negyed tizenkettő* (quarter of twelve)—but to be honest, it was barely a few minutes past eleven.

Well, I'll somehow manage to get through this night, I thought, *and in the morning I will start a new life. By six I can begin looking at the lunchroom windows, and by seven I can be working. No doubt there will be work. Up to now I haven't looked enthusiastically enough. That's the truth.*

Naturally I shouldn't have dropped that tray. It's all so simple, after all. You've only got to hold it from below with your whole palm, though it's good if the other hand is at the ready too. Then there's no problem.

I could have asked for my money back for the ink. It was a big bottle, ten cents, and I bought a pen too, so fifteen cents in all. That would be enough for a coffee and a sandwich.

No, I won't be going back now. She'd misunderstand. Though Yelena is one smart lady with lots of brains, maybe it's not out of the question after all.

Here, standing just inside the building entrance, I can calmly think the whole thing over. What's the hurry?

I'll run upstairs, gasping for breath as if I've left something important behind, and by the by I'll mention the fifteen cents. Ah, nonsense! Starting tomorrow I'll be working every day, after all, and I'll have lots of money. Fifteen cents! Ridiculous.

If I had two more cents, I could take the streetcar to the worker's hostel. They have good coffee there, and maybe I'd find someone to talk away the hours with until morning. Let work come.

I could go on foot, but the rain is unpleasant. True, if you're good at pulling in your neck it's outright pleasant, not flowing in as much. My shoes are in tatters; it's all the same to them, after all. That's their business. If only it would be mud, without rain, but this is a rich country with enough for everything, though in New York there are no farm fields, so rain is completely pointless.

Let's forget about that lousy fifteen cents! No way will I ask for it back. I'll walk down toward the worker's hostel, and we'll see.

Egad, they've locked their door so early? It's only 1 am. So I still have five whole hours left, and then I can look at the lunchroom windows. Of course what is eating away at me is hunger. No longer even hunger, but some strange pain that is curable. For the time being it's a moot point. We're men, guys, let's not forget that. In fact, I don't desire any food at all. OK, that's an exaggeration, because a coffee and two giant rolls in a nice warm place would not be bad. Only I mustn't talk myself into believing I'm sick or anything like that.

If I recite poems to myself like this, at a whisper, the time will pass more quickly:

If there were miracles on earth
If darkness glistened ...
A queen would step in my door,
Coming toward me and smiling....

A queen! She'd step in my door. She'd have long, blond, beautiful hair, and she'd be young and gorgeous, in a dainty little outfit, holding a silver tray in her hands, a tray with a heap of food. Awful. This is how I've got to hurry when I have nowhere to hurry to. This New York is an ugly little nest. A world capital! Why, not a soul is on the streets, and if I slow my pace, a cop will come over in no time and ask questions. If only I had money, five dollars, say, I'd give him a piece of my mind! We're free men, after all, so who can prohibit me from walking on the street at night, in this nasty rain, if my gentlemanly whim so dictates?

2 am. This night will never be over. Scholars will write about this as the world's longest night ever.

So then, in the morning I'll go to work, and by evening they'll fire me, yes, I'm tired even now, and I haven't even begun. No problem. I'll get three dollars all the same. That's enough for a deposit on a room, and a man can get to dwelling, or, rather, sleeping, at once. Later on I'll buy shoes, too. Out of fifteen dollars a man can comfortably put five in the bank. I've only got to get through this one night. At Pennsylvania Station you can wash up in the morning. Lucky my comb and toothbrush are still in my pocket. It's good to plan ahead. Just cough, my boy, just cough. The last thing you need is to get sick. OK, this isn't illness just yet, only hunger. Hence the dizziness. My eyes are stinging from sleepiness. True, this rain isn't helping, either, but I can get through it until morning, no problem, and then a new life begins.

I'll buy six shirts, too. I can't take it any longer.

It won't be a problem, after all, if I sit myself down in this doorway here nice and easy. If a cop comes by, I'll make as if I'm adjusting my shoes so he can see I'm no burglar. Of course you can't lie down, my boy, no, someone would misunderstand that. Just a couple of shabby hours is all, and then the lunchrooms will open and all my problems will go away.

In fact this doesn't yet count as lying down. It would be an exaggeration and ill will to call it that. Lying down is one thing, and it's quite another thing to lean on your elbow under a doorway just a tad like lying own. The view from here is interesting. The raindrops are falling to the ground so colorfully, beautifully, and bouncing back up like ballerinas.

I stretch out comfortably, no need to be concerned about getting a cold, no, I'm as warm as in a steam bath. That's young blood for you. If I want to, or if a cop comes, I can get up at any minute, but he'd do so in vain, for I'll say to the poor devil, the lunchrooms open only at six, what do you want from me?

I could still get up. I'm only pretending to be weak. Ah, it's not worth it. Dawn is breaking. The street is coming to life. Laborers are headed to work. A young American woman with make-up is coming straight toward me. Her boyfriend is looking at me too. I turn down my eyes. What are you staring at, you fools?

The boy gives me a kick.

"How shameful, how shocking! So young, and wallowing drunk on the street."

Others come, too, and stare at me. I now let myself go, though I have the feeling I could easily get up if I wanted to.

I see a big, shining disc above my head, and it's as if a storm were raging inside my skull. I can clearly hear the roaring of the wind. The rain has stopped.

A big, beautiful hall. Remarkable cleanness and silence. Someone is coughing. Everyone is whispering. This is irritating. I should tell them to please end the silence. A blackboard above my head. Numbers, written in chalk, and one word: PNEUMONIA.

A pretty young nurse leans over me.

"Do you speak English?"

I tell her I have no relatives and there's no one I know. Meanwhile I shudder at the thought of someone learning where I've wound up. Later, when everything is fine again, I'll tell the whole story amidst some good laughter.

My head is completely clear. I feel wonderful. So what's wrong?

"How are you, dear?" comes a wholly unfamiliar woman's voice from above me.

"Thank you."

"The nurse said you have no one, that you're completely on your own in New York. Is that so? The doctor said you'll recover soon."

"And who are you, if I may ask?"

"I'm a dancer in a cabaret, and I came to visit this old man, the one in the bed beside yours. He isn't too well, poor thing. We worked in the same place."

We talked a bit longer, and she reassured me that I'd be out in two days, maybe a week, but of course there was no way of knowing in advance. From then on she came by every day. She was the life of the quiet room. She always came over to my bed, too, reassuring me, caressing me. On a clean hospital day the old man beside me died, but the little dancing girl kept visiting even after that, now only me. She always brought something or other—preserves, flowers—as if I were a girl, and indeed one day she brought some Russian book thinking it was Hungarian. I didn't tell her she was mistaken, not at all. I praised the book, which might even have been good, who knows? Why, I even told her what it was about, so she could enjoy it as well. That's when it turned out that she was called Madge.

There were ten of us in the ward, which, sparkling though it was, reminded me of the jail all the same. Because here too, as in the jail, everyone spoke only of his own ailment.

So the days passed. I came to be very fond of the little dancing girl, who visited me diligently. Madge pampered me and loved me like a mother. Life was good here, and I was already dreading the day when I'd have to go back out into the world and keep an eye out for the "Busboy Wanted" signs in the windows.

Day by day my condition improved alarmingly.

One fine day Madge sat down with a smile beside my bed.

"I just spoke with the doctor. They're letting you out of here, but you mustn't work. So I thought I'd bring you to my place until you regain your strength. It will be better there than here."

"That's out of the question. We hardly even know each other, after all."

"I thought we were friends."

"Well of course we're … But I can't expect …"

"Don't be childish. I like you, so why wouldn't you be able to come to my place? We're only talking about a couple of days, after all. It would be good to nurse someone, to take care of someone. I too am alone."

When it came down to it, I didn't even have a place to stay. Who was I supposed to turn to suddenly? Where to go, now that I'd recovered so much?

"All right, then, I thank you. We can go."

She lived in a small flat afflicted with the usual, cheap American furnishings. But in vain they sought to tarnish Madge's life. Her presence triumphantly beat back the assault of the factory-made products. She had forty-two little stone monkeys, each one staring into the world with a different expression. Fresh flowers here and there, games, fortune-telling cards, photos pinned to the wall, newspaper clippings, small flags, long cigarette-holders, funny cigarette-trays (some with racy illustrations), buttons in myriad colors, pencils, knives: a veritable flea market. The smell of perfume and incense. Madge was fond of colorful bric-a-brac to ornament her dancing life a bit.

For days I only lolled about on the couch, waiting for the girl. And she always came, happily, singing, like a bird. Her hat flew off her head in a high arch as she flung it into the corner, and in an instant she was beside me with little packages she then began to unwrap.

It was bitterly cold that winter, as it is every winter in New York, and I passed the hours looking out the frozen window onto the icy streets of the city, so many strangers hustling and bustling about, busying themselves. Everyone had some aim—except me. Her face red from the cold, Madge merrily threw her hat in the usual corner and, laughing, gave me a kiss.

"So, how is my sick little boy? Things are starting to look up. I think I'll get a better job soon."

She made tea and sandwiches, and we smoked cigarettes.

"Madge," I told her, "you've been so kind and good to me. I don't even know how to thank you, but I now feel strong and healthy. Tomorrow I am going away."

"No you are not," she said, and kissed me on the mouth. My head moved down to her breasts. I didn't go away. Thus the days passed in idleness that was almost happiness. But I became increasingly impatient. Who was to say how many things she had to tend to? As for myself, I had to see not only Yelena but also Karcsi, and I had to do something.

I bid farewell to Madge, telling her we'd see each other sometime. I went down to the street, and as I put my hands in my pockets against the cold, I heard the rustling of paper. A five-dollar bill. I stopped in my tracks. *Oh dear, I can't accept it! I must give it back. But I can't. It's a life-saver. I'll give it back when I have money. It's a loan.*

With spirited determination I set out looking for a job. I bought a paper, from which I learned that an apartment building on Riverside Drive was seeking an elevator operator. When I got there, lots of others were already waiting in line, but the boss chose me, since the uniform he had happened to fit me to a tee. Barely had my luck begun to sink in when they had me get on my new outfit. I learned the trade in no time at all. I had to transport maids and laborers, because God had granted the bona fide residents a separate elevator.

Work began at 6 AM. I took up the milk and the ice, and brought down the garbage from the apartments. On account of the steep rent, this building was occupied only by the exceedingly rich. Even the garbage was friendlier than among the poor. Food was not a problem, since the maids provided me with that. They even gave coffee, if that low-grade liquid they served in colossal mugs could have been properly called that. The mugs were good.

The building was a wondrous palace enveloped by the air of wealth. Luxury laughed from the enormous marble walls. The wealthy swished in and out of the apartments; cleanliness and good smells were everywhere. Sometimes I saw the residents for a moment or two when the door opened to let their maids in, or when they accidentally strayed toward my elevator. But I had no business with them. I had to transport only maids and washerwomen.

The first week passed, and I still had a job. I got the pay I was due, fifteen dollars. They told me to come to work the next day, too, as if nothing had happened.

Evidently they were satisfied with me.

At 6 PM, when I finished my shift, I went to see Madge to return the five dollars. She wasn't home. No problem. I rushed to the cabaret she worked at. That`s where I learned that she was on the road. I was sorry.

I never saw her again.

For another few weeks I worked with the elevator, with flagging enthusiasm. Of course I'd been glad to get the job, but in no time I recognized its pointlessness. It's hard to make something of the elevator trade. What can a poor elevator boy do? Branch off on his own, with his own elevator, employing elevator boys, without a building? It's a hopeless trade.

I met up with Karcsi, who, fortunately, had just lost his job.

"My dear Pali, let's leave New York behind and head to Detroit, where I supposedly have some relative. It's a wealthy city, home of the Ford plant. Tons of automobiles. Well, what do you say?"

"Brilliant idea. I'll quit the elevator job today. We have money for the trip, and Detroit is more America than New York is."

And Karcsi, actor through and through, now enthusiastically reshaped a couple lines of an Endre Ady poem to the situation at hand:

Oh World, how lovely your
Every vista that we do not attain.

Seventeen

At gambling you can lose, too. Homesickness is strong even without a home. No distance is too great, it's just a question of money.

Though Detroit was foreign to us, we each found work all the same, on the day of our arrival no less. Not that Karcsi actually had a relative there—or, rather, there used to be one but he had moved to Cincinnati, which is the American city with the loveliest name, not as though that did us much good at the moment.

Once again I became a busboy, now with real experience, while Karcsi got a job as a host at a classy restaurant, where he used two fingers to point guests to the tables they should sit at. In English the term for this position was in fact "captain," though they do not belong to the army. Karcsi was tall, handsome, and elegant, and indeed the boss even commented that he'd been born for the job. We didn't dispute it. Between the two of us we earned forty dollars a week, which was a pretty penny back then. Naturally food was on the house.

I tried hard to keep my job, while Karcsi kept his with no effort at all. But neither one of us cared about the joy of work. We didn't care about anything. By then a terrible affliction had planted its seed and taken root in us, unnoticed—an affliction called homesickness. Not exactly for a home, since the home, under Hungary's head of state at the time, Miklós Horthy, was not the sort it was possible to yearn for. It even occurred to me that perhaps I would be arrested were I to go home, because back in New Brunswick I'd undertaken sharp attacks against Horthy and his regime, and I knew that every issue of that paper was available in Budapest, at the National Széchényi Library. But I couldn't even care about this any more.

We wanted to be in Budapest again, no matter what it took. Maybe it's not even homesickness, this feeling that besets you. It ambushed us after we'd read a Budapest newspaper. We wanted to see Rákóczi Boulevard and other places once again: Hársfa Street, where I'd been born, and the bench I'd carved into back in school. Maybe it's not even homesickness, but that you merely want to meet and shake hands with your bygone self. We were suffering. We wanted to get home! To kiss my father's hand for just two weeks, to be humbly obedient to him, which I'd never managed to do in my real childhood. This sort of thing needs to be made up for. I felt I must see those who'd stayed behind—the trees, the buildings, the people.

It seems I can't bear this America, I thought. *It is a country for people stronger, smarter, more talented than me.*

Karcsi and I talked about this nonstop after work, and sometimes we went out to the train station, aimlessly so, only to look at the departing trains.

We needed a thousand dollars. That would be enough for both of us to go home and live well on, and return. It wasn't an unattainable sum. In three or four years we could scrape it together. With iron will. With iron nerves.

Around 3 AM, when Karcsi would come home, I was usually long asleep. This particular morning Karcsi woke me up.

"How much money do you have?"

"Three dollars."

"I have seven."

I sat up in bed. Karcsi looked nervous and deathly pale.

"What's wrong, my dear Karcsi?"

"Nothing. Those damn waiters are driving me crazy."

"All day long they tell stories about that gambling den they go to religiously after work. It's open day and night. Some of them win, some of them lose. Last night, Jack, one of the waiters, won two thousand dollars. That's what everyone was talking about. He did it in a half-hour. He began with thirty dollars. At the moment we have ten dollars between us, and it doesn't matter at all if we hang onto it or squander it. Let's go. We can be there in a couple of minutes, and if we're in luck we can go home to Budapest."

I dressed in a matter of moments, and off we went without a word. I don't know why they call such places 'dens'. We went in. We had to go through lots of little doors until finally we reached a room where a man of around forty, with a rough exterior, stood in front of a footstool. He had us stand up on this footstool and then deftly rifled through our pockets in the blink of an eye. He even lifted our hats, looking for weapons. We had none. Next we clambered up a decaying staircase. Dim lights filtered through the walls as unseen individuals followed our every move from behind tiny peepholes. Finally, as if by an incantation, a little iron door opened before us. The door closed by itself, and we were inside the gaming room.

It was an enormous space with lots of tables that looked rather like billiard tables, covered as they were by green baize, except that they were much larger than needed for billiards and there was no sign of any cues. Someone was throwing dice at every table, each one of which was surrounded by a thick crowd. There was no sitting down.

Four men sitting on tall ladders were watching over the games.

A great deal of money was lying about on the tables, along with stacks of silver dollars. There were no chips. The players were talking in specialized jargon that might as well have been Chinese. We didn't understand a word. "We've got seven and eleven." "Hard four." "Come home to daddy." We heard magic words such as these.

I went over to one of the tables and observed the others.

The tables bore numbers and squares, and it was on them that the money was placed. I put our ten dollars on a number near us. *If we blow it, may it happen fast.* The dealer asked me something I didn't understand, so I just gave an airy nod. A bit of time passed, but no one raked money toward us. *Well, it seems we've lost our ten dollars. No problem.*

The other players around me were much more interesting than the game itself. Instead of winning I was watching them.

Elegant, silver-haired gentlemen looked on, trembling, as their last five-dollar bills swam away. Stalwart, ragged, pale men in tattered shoes lost without batting an eyelid only to pull thousands more from their pockets. Faces were red, hands were trembling, and the air was thick from cigarette smoke and sweat. There wasn't much talking. Everyone stared fixedly at the rolling of the dice, as if gone mad. Only the croupier, with his rake, was bored of it all. The whole scene reminded me of the jail.

Wait, what was going on? It was as if Karcsi had gasped behind me. I turned, and saw his face twist up, his eyes bulge, and sweat pour down in streams from under his hat, only without him noticing. He just kept staring at the table, then groaned, hoarsely:

"Take it out."

Following Karcsi's gaze, I saw a vast amount of money on the table. I understood what he was getting at. Slowly, conspicuously, so everyone would see if I were making a mistake, I reached toward the money. I was prepared for the croupier to strike my hand, but he didn't even bat an eye. By now I had the money. It sank in that our money had multiplied so smartly and nicely because I'd let it sit. I didn't dare count the winnings, but simply looking at it was enough to tell me it must be a nice tidy sum, since a good number of twenties and tens were crawling among all those greenbacks.

I immediately put more money on the winning number. I lost it. Now I put twice as much down. I won. Then I lost. What was this? Again I won. Now I threw down a hundred-dollar bill there, were it was supposed to go, because I'd won. And then, after a good many more rounds, I heard Karcsi's voice from behind me:

"Have you gone mad? Stop it right now!"

"Yes, I've gone mad," I said, and immediately threw two hundred dollars somewhere.

I won. Karcsi then dragged me away from the table, and we left. The magic door closed behind us. In the cold air out on the street I began coming to my senses. We counted our cash. Nine-hundred and ninety-seven dollars and zero cents. Now this was Europe. Budapest. Hársfa Street. Rákóczi Boulevard and whatever we wished. Akácfa Street too.

No, I wouldn't send a telegram. I wouldn't even write. My mother would open the door and would collapse into my arms. "Why, you've come back, my son?"

Life is so beautiful!

We danced on the street, in the Detroit cold, hugging each other and hollering with joy. We waved the cash, we smelled it. So it was true, after all: money doesn't have a smell. What an invention! And the police don't let you gamble. Nonsense.

Close to the building we lived in we saw two men coming toward us. Karcsi was aglow.

"Hey, maybe we know them. I'll die if I can't tell someone what happened to us."

The two men came closer. They stopped in front of us. All at once the barrel of a revolver was pointed between my eyes, and I heard the quick command: "Stick 'em up, boys."

I raised my hands. Slowly. *Let him shoot if he wants.* In a well-practiced movement one of the robbers reached into my pocket, precisely the one containing Budapest, and shoveled it out in one fell swoop. All of it.

We went home—without the money. Karcsi flung himself on his bed and wept. For me, it had yet to sink in. *We've been robbed,* I kept saying to myself so I'd understand.

Dawn was breaking. It was time to rise and get to work. There was no reason to cry; we weren't wild animals. A police complaint? Hopeless. They'd never find them, anyway. I didn't even know what the robbers looked like. I didn't remember their faces. Only that the ears behind the revolver were surprisingly large. Not that it matters. After all, if I think about it, we really lost only ten dollars.

Eighteen

You should water people only at Easter, lest you get fired. Bankers are human, too, if not quite. Escape.

I held fast to my job, which was, after all, my sole realistic way of making money. And you need money if you really want to go home so much. Homesickness grew like a debt.

One unsuspicious, completely normal day, a middle-aged, elegant, amiable-looking guest walked in the restaurant. No sooner had he sat down at a table, than I was racing toward him with a glass of water in hand, as appropriate. I did my utmost to avoid getting fired. My hand was still wobbling in the air, water and all, when I noticed that the guest had pulled out a cigarette and was looking for matches. Enthusiasm got the better of me. I wanted to give the poor man his water while also lighting his cigarette, the upshot of which was that while the cigarette did not light up, I did manage to spill water all over the gentleman's well-pressed trousers. Barely were there a few drops left for his coat. True, it was cold water, since we always put ice in the glasses.

The guest appeared to be vexed. His face turned red and his eyes sparkled like a meteor shower. The poor man completely lost control of himself. Springing up in fright when the icy flood hit him, he raised a clenched fist to give me a blow, but at the last moment he drew in his breath and with portentous calm he called my boss. Amid obsequious bows, the head waiter listened to his account of the tragedy, sometimes nodding sympathetically. The guest was a wealthy and desirable sort, while I wasn't yet exactly a genius of a busboy. He won. I didn't even defend myself. After all, the water was still visible on his trousers. Perhaps it had warmed up a little.

I was fired on the spot.

I was paid what I was due. I removed my white uniform, and I whooshed silently out of the life of the restaurant and of its head waiter. The soaked guest was likewise on his way. He must have lost his appetite from the icy water. We were even headed the same way on the street. I don't know why, but I invariably felt pure delight on losing such a job.

We looked at each other. From his rueful eyes I could see that he was no longer angry over the little bit of water. He seemed like a kind fellow with those water-splotched trousers of his, and I felt sorry for him.

"Please excuse me, sir. Believe me, it was an unintentional mishap. I'm really sorry, especially because of the ice. The truth is, I'm not an especially well-trained busboy."

"I am sorry too. I've got a bad temper, I lose it fast and when that happens, I'm capable of murder. Then I regret it. When you're not a busboy, what is your trade?"

"Nothing. I haven't got one."

"I can hear from your accent that you're a foreigner, but you speak wonderful English. How long have you been in America?"

"A few years. But I went to night school and also got my high school diploma in English."

"All right, then. Now I've got to hurry. Here's my business card. Look me up in my office. Maybe I can help you out."

Numerals, checks, pencils, more numbers, little deposit books by the hundreds.

Before I knew it, I was working in a bank. It had turned out that the kind stranger was a director of this bank. When I called on him, he told me he could use a Hungarian, since one of the bank's branches happened to be in the Hungarian quarter. My pay was 150 dollars a month.

They liked me at the bank. The boss declared that I had a big future ahead of me in banking. Perhaps someday I could even be manager of the branch. Later I might become an even more important person. I wasn't even tormented as much by homesickness anymore, because it occurred to me that maybe the hand of fate had decided that I was to get home for a visit with honestly earned money. Perhaps it had been the hand of fate, too, that had let me water those trousers? Who could say?

Another odd stroke of fate was that Karcsi—that Karcsi with whom I'd set forth on this journey from Hungary, was back in Budapest where, yes, he had married Éva, whereas the whole idea of America had been his to begin with. Éva wrote that they were happy. The letter didn't hit me in the heart as one would have expected. No, for in actuality I'd lost Éva a long time ago. So then, Karcsi had found a wife, and Éva had found a husband. *May they be happy*, I thought.

I was very careful about this bank job, which seemed solid, since the depositors were delighted to be able to talk over their business in Hungarian with a specialist who was a banker.

Among the bank's customers was the director of a Detroit theater. I spoke to him for quite a while about Karcsi—which is to say, that Karcsi I'd met in Trieste and who was now with me here in town. I told him what a remarkable actor Karcsi was, how honest and reliable and sensible he was, not a boozer like the bulk of American actors. He told me to have Karcsi go see him. Karcsi did so, and they hired him on the spot, with terrific pay. The director predicted a big future for him. Interesting, how everyone has a future, that it's just their present they have problems with.

Life was as exciting as a frozen lake. Like a wee little tiny frozen lake. I always had enough money. Karcsi was content, too. We still shared a place, and we shared dreams of great success. Of course we'd have to work for it. Nothing was for free. We only had to work, calmly and clearheadedly, every day. Finally, this crazy life of mine had veered onto the right track, and I was starting to make my way.

The weeks passed slowly and free of worry. I worked without fear. They wouldn't fire me. I was needed. I had a regular, serious occupation, and if anyone asked who I was, I could offhandedly reply: "A banker. And who are you?"

It was as if I'd awoken from an agonizing nightmare. Yes, I had had to suffer and go hungry so often only so I could appreciate the good life. No more aimless walks in tattered shoes, in the cold rain. Troubles harden steel, meaning me. Woe is the foundation of happiness.

Every single week I could put money in the bank. And every few months I could count on a raise.

And sooner or later I would no doubt marry some banker's daughter. A respected citizen of Detroit. *Most honorable gentlemen! Gentlemen and ladies! Most honorable mourners! Such is life. A man makes something of himself. Not to be some roadside weed but a pillar of support, a cornerstone. No,* I thought, *no longer can anything ruin this pleasant life, a life that will sweep me toward a banker's daughter, who might even be beautiful, for there is no reason a rich girl shouldn't be good-looking. Sooner or later a man gets married.*

Nineteen

Yelena wrote her letter. Geraniums grow big if allowed to. Life is good everywhere, but it's best somewhere else.

After a long pause, one day I received a letter from Yelena. We hadn't written to each other in about four months. I looked at the postmark with surprise. What had happened? Hollywood? Yes, Yelena was writing from Hollywood, as if she were some actress. Karcsi was burning with excitement as I read the letter:

. . . Yes, sweetheart, I am here in Hollywood. In this darling, dazzling, sunny place full of palm trees and flowers. I can hardly tell you what happened and how. In New York I was sad and sometimes even cried. The work bored and pained me. All at once it went up in flames, the whole barrenness, my aimless life. To be writing from morning to night about strangers' murders, about scandals, about loves that were not my own, and sometimes even about politics. And to do all this for years, for certain pay each month, among people so much the same, among white sheets of paper in the newsroom. I couldn't do it any longer. I went to the editor's office and resigned. And then I cried from happiness like a little girl, for I saw the new life that had opened up before me, I knew I didn't need to be afraid. This exciting life, this

hard life, this precious life, this uncertain life, this one and only life. I packed up quickly and here I am, a happy and zealous resident of Hollywood, and the sun is shining.

I have to thank you for this, sweetheart. Because you caused this whole imbroglio. You caused this fever, this pleasure, and all this beauty even if you don't know about it. Because as I thought of the past few years, I saw how much more exciting and colorful was your life than my cobwebby vegetation, tied to one place. Suddenly I was overcome by an irresistible yearning to stretch my hands out toward the unattainable. To experience bygone and forgotten flavors, to stroke a flower, to lean down, to pay attention, to be caught up in fervor, to be afraid, to exult, and to do so while young, fighting with both hands, in wonder, happily, and making plans—even if nothing will ever come of the dream. I hated New York, I hated circling the same streets forever. To go home to the same place, same comfort, same boredom: you can go mad from such monotony.

Just what I am going to do here, I don't know. But that's the beauty of it. "I don't know," "I don't know," I say, repeating these magic words a hundred times as if I've found the secret of life and happiness. Will my home be a furnished room or a Spanish bungalow? I don't know. Will I write screenplays or be an actress? I don't know. Or a starving Hollywood dreamer? I don't know. I don't know a thing. Why this is so good, I don't know. Geraniums are lush here, taller than me. The garages are covered with roses. Flowers grow all along the sidewalks, and these flowers, which are no one's, are beautiful. Red and blue window frames, people with make-up, men and women in funny costumes but no one minding one bit. Sweet freedom everywhere you step. Try to understand that I envied your uncertain days, which gave value to your every tomorrow. They enchanted the weekdays, promoting them to Sundays. I wanted to taste them, too. I wanted to get drunk on them at least once in life. I didn't care how much it would cost. We die anyway. Perhaps. I'm indebted already to Hollywood for the wondrous sensation of these first days.

I'm pleased that you are finally settled. I think you struggled a bit much. Now you doubly deserve the comfort and security you have. Don't feel sorry for yourself for the suffering you endured, for it has made you a more valuable, better person. And when you become a well-to-do banker with public respect, a chauffer, and a car, will you give the time of day, sweetheart, to a wandering nobody, to the tattered, black-haired girl I am?

At the moment I am still giddy with joy. I can't write a more sensible letter now, but in a couple of days I will write again. Give Karcsi a hug for me. I send you my greetings from here, the region of good sun, with love and, above all, with gratitude, for having shown me the road that can only go upward. Yelena.

After reading the letter we fell into a deep silence. Only around midnight did Karcsi speak:

"I think it was foolish of Yelena to leave behind her secure life and plunge head-first into uncertainty."

"Fatally foolish!" I exaggerated.

I didn't sleep much that night. I kept thinking of Yelena. Poor, foolish girl. Who knew what awaited her? In an unfamiliar city, completely alone. This sort of thing would not happen to me. I was settled for life. A banker. I had more than two hundred and fifty dollars in the bank and my account was growing.

I didn't even want to think of leaving Detroit. It was a nice city. But there was no reason why I shouldn't go out to the railway station occasionally. Karcsi also liked to do so. After all, that's where trains departed to and arrived from various places. Yelena was in Hollywood. A famous city. Its climate in particular was advantageous. A lovely, flowery city. Everyone knew about it.

I was earning well even above my regular pay. I wrote letters for Hungarians, seeing to their troublesome affairs, and all this brought money to my table. I had four good suits, more shirts than I could count, and three pairs of shoes, each of them flawless.

The cage in which you pass your days at a job is like a jail. Of course here you are not a real convict. It's voluntary. You needn't remain a prisoner, only if you want to. After work you're free but tired and go to bed early so in the morning you can jump out of bed fresh from a good night's sleep, because you need a clear head for work. Bankers are usually dry, boring maggots. They go stale from work. No wonder.

I like trains.

Money: success. The most important thing in a person's life. Money: everything. One thing alone is more important: life itself.

And health? True, I had no symptoms that would have concerned the average doctor. But I had a bad taste in my mouth, a sort of bitterness that worried me. That's not even to speak of the brutal winters in Detroit. Lots of folks, who knows how many, die there every year of pneumonia. Some die merely from the unbearable cold, like wolves.

Perhaps I was in need of a change of climate.

The climate in Hollywood is, by contrast, heavenly. The healthiest climate of all is, hands down, in California. Yes. The best climate in all the world. This thing about the climate is common knowledge. Hollywood is a nice city. The center of the world. Full of the most interesting people: actors, actresses, writers, painters, musicians. Directors. Everyone who counts at all is there. There, you can do big things. For Karcsi in particular, life there would be ideal. An actor. Talented. There he would have opportunity.

One night, as we tossed and turned in our beds, I said to Karcsi in a sulky, withering voice:

"This Detroit is a boring place. As an industrial park, it's not bad, I guess. It's irritating and mind-numbing. No variety. We ought to do something about this."

"Say, have you ever seen geraniums that grew as tall as Yelena?"

"I haven't. But how did that plant come to mind?"

"I don't know. It just did."

The next day Karcsi and I went for a walk.

"I just read in the paper that in California you can't starve to death," I said. "There's so much fruit on the trees. Oranges."

"Really? Nothing is lovelier than orange blossoms."

We spoke no more. In no time we'd telegrammed Yelena, notifying her that we were leaving for Hollywood the next day.

"Who wants to be a banker, anyway?" I said. "I'm always getting a headache from the numbers. I don't want to spend my life in a cage."

Karcsi nodded knowingly.

"Of course not. You're not a thief. It's ridiculous."

That it was. We laughed blissfully as we packed our bags. Indeed, we were even laughing the next day as the train raced toward Hollywood with us aboard. The other passengers were appalled at how loud we were.

The train kept huffing and puffing as it sped along, and finally the chugging simmered down to a serene sort of music, and suddenly, as if a curtain had been raised in my brain, I understood that despite trains, despite doing all you can to race toward other cities and foreign lands, you carry your fate, your life, with you wherever you go.

Hollywood, Budapest, Vienna. It doesn't matter.

It's best not to take it all too seriously—women, kisses, trains, cities, people, this whole wonderful everything called life.

Paying attention is a must, for this lavish play is colorful and interesting. What matters never changes. It's all an adventure, one without a beginning and without an end. There are only stations. We race along, huffing and puffing, chasing after happiness, but we can never reach it.

I was reminded of these two lines from a poem:

A person writhes and wriggles along
And then, like a leaf: twirls down, so long.

Yes. It's all that simple.

The train rumbled through the night with dizzying speed, the telephone poles fleeing backward in fright. Karcsi gave a sigh:

"Hey, Pali, I think I'm now as happy as can be."

Twenty

Hollywood doesn't even exist, but what does is just enough. I don't know English, but Yelena takes care of it. Everyone is rich, except for the poor. The sun shines day and night, but it rains for six weeks.

We arrived in that famous city, Hollywood, and took a cab straight to Yelena's, at 15 Gordon Street. Happiness, passionate pecks on the cheek, hugs, a few tears of joy, and then Yelena saying this:

"No resting, you two, no time for that now. I rented you a fabulous bungalow, right here beside me, and it's even mostly furnished, but first I want to show you the city."

We were awestruck. Surely we had arrived in one of the world's most beautiful places. Hillsides flooded with flowers, ocean and lake, mimosa trees sprawled nonchalantly over the streets, not even to speak of the palm trees, and this was where oranges grew, though I was surprised to see a little stove near every orange tree so they wouldn't freeze at night in the cold. But the scent of orange blossoms compensated for everything. It would have merited a serial novel with a happy end. An incomparable, divine smell struck our noses, and we just kept smelling, wordlessly.

And the houses! Here was a Spanish castle, there was a Chinese pagoda, and there, a hat. Then it turned out that the hat was a restaurant, a very elegant and pricey one at that. It was called the Brown Derby, and we just stood there gaping, as if we'd arrived in a new world with nothing to remind us of the America we'd come to know in New York.

Yelena had rented and furnished a gorgeous little bungalow likewise at 15 Gordon Street, behind Warner Brothers Studio.

We soon realized that Hollywood doesn't even exist. It is but a district of the sprawling city called Los Angeles.

Moreover, only a portion of the big film studios were in Hollywood. Most, like Universal, were in Universal City, and then Metro-Goldwyn-Mayer in Culver City, but there was a little Warner Brothers studio in Hollywood, along with Columbia, which was the first studio in the film-making city.

There was a surprising number of lunatics. Young men and women came here from all over the globe who wanted nothing more than lots and lots of money and world fame. I met a waifish little Hungarian gal who told me she bore a striking resemblance to Pola Negri. Well, she didn't resemble her, and I couldn't explain to her that even if I looked as much like Rockefeller as I don't, I still wouldn't be a billionaire.

One guy made himself up to look like Adolph Menjoun, though it didn't get him far, even though he had a genuine mustache.

In the restaurant Henry's, which doubled as an eatery and a bar, I met a Hungarian, an amusing eccentric who had been a lieutenant under his majesty Franz Joseph I, Apostolic King of Hungary, who began our conversation:

"Only a bit of luck, and world fame is mine. I am an actor. I'm the complete master of my facial muscles. Go ahead and name any feeling, thought, or action—my facial muscles can express anything."

"Sudden joy," I said, whereupon he assumed a motionless, somber expression, signaling that he was suddenly rejoicing about something, only that he couldn't show it. "A mother's death," I said, whereupon he shook his head and stared at me with the same, motionless expression. Then I said "lamppost" and "young female postal clerk," but the expression didn't change. He believed that he only had to stare into nothingness with a motionless expression, and world fame would be at his feet.

By then lots of Hungarians lived around the dream factories.

Sándor Korda and Mihály Kertész were already well-heeled directors. There was the actor Mihály Várkonyi; Béla Lugosi, who became world famous as the personification of Dracula and earned three thousand dollars a week; and many others on lower rungs of the ladder.

At first it bothered me a bit that I needed to learn Hollywoodese, because words had meanings entirely different than in other American cities. It turned out that "Shooting starts tomorrow" does not mean revolution, only filming; that an "extra" was no one extra special; that a "reader" was in fact someone who evaluated screenplays, and that "dough" was not for making the sort of bread you can eat, but was cash.

Our Hollywood life began in no time.

It was always possible to find work as an extra with Korda and Kertész if they were filming. Indeed, in the first film I had a part in, directed by Joseph C. Boyle, I was immediately named the Hungarian specialist, because the film, *The Whip Woman,* was set in Hungary.

My blood froze when I began reading the screenplay, from which it turned out that the count—count?!—of the small town of Siófok, who was played by Antonio Moreno, was bent on having the goose-herding peasant girl, played by Estelle Taylor (who in her private life was the wife of the world heavyweight boxing champion Jack Dempsey) join his harem. Harem?!

I offered my expert advice to no avail. In vain I explained to the director that in Hungary the harem was an unknown institution and that in a poor little Hungarian village it is not in a Ford that the young Hungarian couple would go to church for their wedding. He only laughed at me. Nor did he believe that rice and shoes are not thrown on the newlywed couple's car. But he only really became upset when I raised an objection to the Hungarian tavern scene in which young men decked out in Hungarian outfits took up proper boxing positions and got down to fighting as if inside a ring.

"Back in Hungary they do fight in taverns, but with pocketknives," I said.

Being too lazy to laugh on his own at such nonsense, the director called over his first, second, and third assistant directors, and then I had to repeat what I'd said about the pocketknives. They shrieked with laughter.

"Why, you can die if you get stabbed in the belly!" one of them exclaimed.

"Such incidents have led to deaths," I said, but I had no credibility, and now they were even doubting whether I'd ever been Hungarian.

Being an extra didn't pay well, except when they filmed Victor Hugo's masterpiece *The Man Who Laughs*, with Conrad Veidt in the lead role.

This project took six months, by the end of which I was no longer an extra but, rather, a bit man, who is a midway between being bit player and an actor. I played a beggar, for twenty-five dollars a day.

Over the six months a veritable community took shape from the many with small roles in the film. The dress men, who wore tuxes, earned fifteen dollars a day, but their elegant outfits went to their heads, because they looked down on the beggars and the midgets, strongmen, and others members of the film's traveling carnival.

Alice, one of the midgets, was a surprisingly pretty little gal, as tiny as an average-size doll. She was a good-natured, smart, and kind little being, and we talked a lot. One fine day she announced that she was in love with me, and that I should marry her. Presumably she saw me as her midget knight-in-shining-armor, though I looked like a giant beside her and could practically have pocketed the whole girl.

Nothing came of the idea, though Alice even showed me her deposit book to signal that I wouldn't do so badly, financially, from the marriage.

But it was here, too, that I got to know Goldie, a staggeringly beautiful extra who, for her part, was just my size and who in civilian life was a painter.

We met often after work in her charming little bungalow.

"Actually I'm from Detroit," she said, "but I hurried down here, to this amazing city, to try my luck. Everything is possible in Hollywood. I came only for two weeks, a year ago, but I haven't had the will to return. I love the warmth, and in Detroit the winters can be terribly cold."

"I came from Detroit, too, Goldie," I replied, concluding unexpectedly, "so do be my wife."

"Quite happily," she said, "though for now my parents can't find out I married a foreigner, because they're conservative, and they think anyone who is not American is not even a human being."

"My dear, your parents are no big concern of mine, and it wouldn't bother me even if we never met."

We got married straightaway, only that the officiating judge couldn't pronounce my name, although it was his duty to congratulate us on our marriage, which cost two dollars.

Goldie and I moved into my and Karcsi's Gordon Street bungalow, whereupon Karcsi moved out and rented another little bungalow next door. Rejoicing over the marriage, we even bought ourselves a rug, the lack of which hadn't come up earlier.

Hollywood's climate was incomparable, no doubt, though at night the air cooled down so much that women wore fur coats and there wasn't any heating to speak of, because the authorities insisted that the climate we lived in was tropical and that therefore it was warm.

I like birds in general, but mockingbirds, which truly deserved their name, got me down all the same, for they were in the habit of flying right at me, pecking at my face with their sharp beaks, and flying on. What pleasure the bird derived from this, I do not know, but I was scared of them, since I myself could not fly.

One night around 3 AM I awoke to see the iron, which was normally in the kitchen, coming slowly toward me. With fright I looked upon this iron that had come alive, without a clue as to how to behave in such circumstances. I awoke my wife, who opened an eye just enough to get a glimpse of the iron for herself, and then said only this much, "Earthquake," before falling back to sleep.

Such minor earthquakes are frequent in California, and the experts don't even pay any attention, sleeping right through them. I took the iron back to the kitchen, and it obediently stayed there.

I saw little future in a career as an extra, wanting instead to be a screenwriter, but soon it became clear that this was hopeless. I'd set my sights on

Paramount, on Marathon Street, in part because it was close to Gordon Street, and in part because I'd heard a lot about B. P. Schulberg, the associate producer, who was said to be a smart and kind man.

But it turned out that you couldn't even set foot near the studio without a recommendation letter, and such letters were accepted only from kings, princes, and presidents. Back then, unfortunately, I didn't know any kings—or, rather, I did have one, but that was none other than me, for I'd long before changed my name to Paul King (the first part of my family name, Király, meaning "king" in Hungarian), for Americans didn't even dare come near my real name, Pál Királyhegyi, much less pronounce it. So then, I wrote myself a recommendation letter:

Dear Mr. Schulberg:

The person handing you this letter, Paul King, is supposedly some sort of writer, but I think he is a talentless cur, and I beg you to send him packing. Forgive me, stranger that I am, for troubling you.

Respectfully yours,
B. M. Smith

Having sealed and addressed the envelope, I set off for Paramount Studio. With the letter in hand, I had an easier time of it, but even so, I had to fight my way through eleven secretaries, every single one of whom wanted to confiscate the letter, which I refused to let leave my hand. Finally, I found myself in front of the secretary who was right outside Mr. Schulberg's office.

"I will give the letter to Mr. Schulberg," she chirped.

"Unfortunately I can't allow that. The individual who wrote it ordered me to deliver it in person only."

In lieu of an answer, the secretary stepped into Schulberg's office, and through the crack in the door I could see her explaining that some little man was here with some big letter, and that he wanted to go in. The boss waved me in.

"You are Mr. Schulberg?" I said hesitantly, though I knew his face well even if I'd never spoken to him before, besides which, his name was written on his desk in letters as big as me.

Schulberg read the letter. I waited. I could see that he was choking back his laughter. He had Henry Herzbrun, Paramount's legal counsel, called in. After showing him the letter, Schulberg said:

"I think this cannot be resisted," he said.

Herzbrun nodded.

"Yes. I understand."

They hired me as a scenario writer, which is to say, as a screenwriter, for this is how Schulberg wanted to get back at the nonexistent B. M. Smith for being so obnoxious to a hapless writer.

It was a five-year contract, with a raise every six months.

Happiness had me seeing stars by the light of day. My starting pay was only a net three hundred and thirty-three dollars a week, while my weekly expenses didn't exceed thirty dollars.

True, I knew Schulberg couldn't lose money on the deal, because every contract has a clause saying that if a writer or actor does not devote his all to the company, he can be fired immediately.

So too, if a writer or actor makes disparaging remarks about his bosses in front of others, that too is punishable by immediate dismissal. To be fair, I should note that the bosses at Paramount did not exercise this right of theirs.

I was delighted on learning that Paramount had signed a contract with the Hungarian novelist and playwright Lajos Zilahy, for though I didn't know him personally, I was sure he'd tell me stories about my favorite Hungarian writer, Frigyes Karinthy.

By then the Hungarian actor Pál Lukács was also working for the studio—under the name Paul Lucas—for three thousand dollars a week.

When Zilahy arrived in Hollywood, I could hardly wait for us to meet, and my first question was what he knew about Karinthy, who by then was a successful and well known writer back in Hungary.

Zilahy broke into a smile.

"Frici called me a couple weeks ago. 'Thanks for the invitation,' he said, 'I'll be there tomorrow for lunch. Precisely at one, I know.' I hadn't invited him, but I agreed to the visit. I have a little villa in the Buda hills, with a garden and fruit trees. Karinthy arrived. I showed him around inside and the yard, and he took in everything thoroughly, in awe, and said: 'You know what, Lajos? I'm going to be a writer, too.'"

Zilahy's first job was writing a film treatment based on a short story by the American writer Ida (I. A. R.) Wylie.

One day he came into my office in despair.

"These people have gone mad. I read the story, 'Widow's Evening.' The lead role is supposed to go to Pál Lukács."

"And what's the problem?"

"According to the story, Emperor Franz Joseph's best friend is a gigolo who dances with old women for money, and when necessary, jumps into bed with them, too, if they pay him well. Pure madness. I can't do it."

I tried persuading Zilahy to do it. What did it matter what the American audience thought of the old emperor, who was dead by now, anyway? But Zilahy stood by his principles and turned down the project. As the studio's number two Hungarian and as an emperor-expert, I got the job.

I wrote the screenplay, and the film was screened in Hungary, too, under the title *Evenings for Sale*, starring Pál Lukács—Paul Lucas, that is. In any case, I don't think Spanish etiquette, of which the old ruler was such a manic devotee, would have prevented his majesty from having a gigolo as a friend. By then, I'd already been broken in by the story of the Count of Siófok.

Twenty-One

DESTITUTION IS NO DELIGHT, BUT SUCCESS IS HARDER TO ENDURE. AGGRESSION IS NOT STRENGTH, BUT LOVE CONQUERS ALL. HOMESICKNESS CAN'T BE CURED WITH A MIMOSA.

I made an interesting discovery. Lots of jolly paupers were milling about Hollywood, trusting that they too would one day be struck by world fame, but it turned out that success is the hardest to endure.

James Murray was a firefly in the cinema. He was the one who, with his tiny flashlight, showed people where to sit as they arrived in the dark. But to his disadvantage, King Vidor, one of the most famous directors, saw Murray in the light and signed a contract with him for the film he was then planning to make, *The Crowd*. The film was about an average American, and the director did not want to have the lead played by a star but by a real average man. Murray's pay at the cinema had been fifteen dollars a week, but King Vidor paid him one thousand five-hundred. A week. The film was made—it was one of the most exciting films of my life—and Murray was made, too. The high pay drove him nuts, and he began drinking. Then he drank more on top of that. Naturally he had a car, so he drove. He hit someone who died, and the company did everything it could to ensure that he got a light sentence, since they had lots of money invested in the former usher.

The trial date was set. Murray showed up stone drunk. He got five years for manslaughter.

When he got out, he had neither a contract nor money. He didn't drink, for he had no money. Every day he called on Datig, the casting director, who signed on people for bit parts. Murray stood up straight and smiled, but always got the same reply:

"We have nothing for you today."

Murray thanked him, and left. Datig watched him for a while, and then turned to me:

"Poor thing. He died a long time ago, only he hasn't noticed it."

And then there was Paul Fejős. One glorious sunny day he collapsed on the streets of Hollywood because he hadn't eaten for days. He was found by a little gal, an extra, who felt sorry for him, took him home, and gave him milk and bread. Three days later he was signed on at Universal Studios as a director. One thousand five-hundred dollars a week.

Fejős got his first film, but all the money soon drove him mad.

His script girl, just to say something, spoke thusly, "I love stories."

"Yes?" said Fejős, turning to his secretary. "Call Brentano's"—this was one of the world's largest bookstore chains—"and have them send this girl every story that can be had."

Naturally, when such an order arrives at Brentano's, it is the company that decides what's a story and what isn't. And at such time there are no ifs, ands, or buts, which is to say, there are stories aplenty, for Dostoyevsky is a story, as is Dumas, Victor Hugo, the Brothers Grimm, and Hans Christian Anderson too.

When the gaffer did a good job of lighting the set, Fejős had a box of cigars sent up to him. There were a hundred in a box, at a dollar apiece.

And that wouldn't have been a problem. But it turned out that he couldn't direct, and when he left Universal Studios he didn't have a cent, not counting his debt.

Not even he could take success.

Also working at the studio was an actor named Wallace, one of the great character actors of all time. At first he'd worked as an elephant washer, and when Cecil B. De Mille went to the circus for elephant viewing, because he needed these agreeable animals for one of his films, he suddenly saw the elephant washer.

"I'd like to speak with that man," said the great director.

"He's not an elephant, he just washes them," the circus manager replied with a laugh, but called him over to the director. Wallace took a break from the elephants, and with a gesture that would later become world famous, ran a hand all along his scruffy face.

"What do you people want from me?" he inquired.

"I'd like to sign you on as a movie actor," the director began.

"You gotta be kidding me. I'm not an actor. I have a good job here, one I'm quite content with."

"How much is your pay?" the director pried.

"Twenty-five dollars a week," the washer proudly proclaimed.

"With me you'll make a thousand a week," the director said, exhorting him.

So he began his acting career, this genius who was always cast to play villains and who was billed as "the man you love to hate."

Wallace, who had completed two years of elementary school in four years, wasn't particularly educated. He remained boorish scoundrel even as an actor.

Soon he became a star, with his own, separate, mobile dressing car. Once, while filming, after demure knocking at the door, in stepped Estella, a ravishingly beautiful, sixteen-year-old Mexican extra, and asked Wallace for an autograph.

The sun was shining brilliantly, as usual, and the girl had on hardly even a little dress. The actor watched her wordlessly for a while, and, liking more and more what he saw, in one fell swoop tore off her clothes.

The girl floundered helplessly in the man's iron arms, and when she finally came to, amid cursing and cussing, tried gathering up her torn-up dress, issuing threats as she marched out.

"You'll pay for this, you beast!" she shrieked. "You'll rot away in prison! I'll have you locked up!"

It was a monumental scandal. The bosses were there in no time and tried calming down the fuming girl, offering her money; for by then lots of money was riding on Wallace, and they knew full well that in America, even in the best-case scenario this sort of thing meant at least fifteen years in prison.

Estella was intractable.

"I don't care about the money! I want justice! Amends!"

After protracted imploring and persuading the bosses managed this much: the girl agreed not to file a complaint, on one condition:

"If Wallace comes up to my place, gets on his knees, and begs forgiveness, I'll show mercy on him," she said, and stormed off.

The bosses were happy. They would have been willing to pay the girl even a large sum, and this way they got off for free. They explained to the actor that they saved him from fifteen years in the penitentiary, and what this girl wanted in exchange was less than nothing. An apology. That was the least of what she was due.

Wallace nodded acquiescently.

But the higher ups did not trust that he could manage the thing on his own, and so the great director himself took charge of Wallace, and as if it were for the shooting of some real film, coached him for the scene.

"You knock quietly. The door opens. Estella is sitting there. You kneel down and say, 'Dear young lady! Forgive me. Your beauty robbed me of my mind. I am willing to undertake any amends.' Cut! And that's it."

They practiced the scene for some time, until finally the director expressed his satisfaction.

"Just be careful, Wallace, not to stand up meanwhile. You've got to recite the whole scene on your knees. It's not a long script."

On the designated day, Wallace dressed elegantly and went to the girl's flat, running through the script again in his mind all along the way to be sure he wouldn't get stuck.

He knocked, the girl opened the door. Wallace stepped in, the door closed. Wallace looked at the girl, who seemed to him more beautiful than the first time. Again he couldn't restrain himself. He fell upon her, embracing her and kissing her.

And then a miracle happened.

The beautiful Mexican girl was no longer angry. She forgave him on seeing that the actor did seriously like her, for he was risking fifteen years in prison over her. After that they lived together for years in sin, for the actor had a lawful wife, but when the girl had a child, Wallace accepted fatherhood and adopted the newborn.

Women's paths are unfathomable.

Karcsi Vidor married, too. He had gotten to know Frances, a fashion designer of Italian stock, and married her. The girl was sweet, young, adored Karcsi, and considered him a genius. The couple could live grandly on her pay alone, which meant that Karcsi no longer had to accept any role, only those which struck his fancy.

Soon he became first assistant with Alexander Korda, who was fond of him and said he had a bright future.

The Hungarian colony kept growing and growing, and after work we'd gather at each other's apartments—Sándor Korda, Lajos Bíró, Ernő (aka Ernest) Vajda, Oszkár (aka Oscar) Beregi, Mihály Várkonyi (aka Victor Varconi), Pál (aka Pál) Lukács, and Lajos Zilahy, whom everyone loved, since he could cook like no one else.

"Only a man can be a really great chef," said Lajos Bíró after one or the other of Zilahy's outstanding suppers. Even Pufi Huszár (aka Charles Puffy), who was not just the fattest actor in Hollywood, but also its greatest gourmet, recognized Zilahy's culinary art.

We met often with Ernst Lubitsch, too, who was among the most exceptional directors, and whom Korda named an honorary Hungarian.

Lubitsch's main collaborator and screenwriter was Hans Kraly, a warm-hearted, gentle giant. Together they made ever more successful Lubitsch films.

Kraly not only worked for the director but was also his best friend.

Lubitsch's wife, Gretchen, whom the director had brought earlier from Austria, was a beautiful woman and loved her husband, though she had one fault: fate had blessed her with a nymphomaniacal nature. Men feared her very presence and tried getting away from her, and they felt sorry for Lubitsch, who hadn't a clue about his wife's peculiar nature.

One day, Kraly happened to be working at the director's apartment on a screenplay, when the woman stepped in and began flirting with the screenwriter, who tried politely fending off her advances. He loved not the woman but her husband, whom he had to thank for his fortune, his career, his everything.

When Gretchen saw that speaking to Kraly was useless, that she was conjuring up her every charm to no avail, that her sex appeal was bouncing right off him, she began slowly undressing.

"Listen here, sir! If you keep resisting, I will complain about you to my husband and lie that you tried to have your way with me. Ernst loves me and will believe me, your denials will go unheard. Then your friendship will be over and never again will you work together. On the other hand, if you're kind to me now, at once, then Ernst will never find out a thing. Your choice."

Kraly was the type of man who knew how to lose. He saw there was no other way out, that he had to yield to the woman's desires.

The great director came home at the most awkward moment, unexpectedly, catching them in the act.

Never again did he give Kraly the time of day, and he filed for divorce, too. One evening, six months later, Lubitsch and I went for a night out at a place called the Silver Slipper, and the moment we stepped in, Lubitsch saw Kraly, who was dancing with a woman on the parquet.

Lubitsch was a short, scrawny little man, but, suddenly out of his mind, ran over to Kraly and clipped him over the ears. He could barely even rear up high enough to reach the writer's face, but that was unavoidable on account of the slaps.

The giant didn't even stir during the beating. He could have snuffed the life out of the little great director with one smack of his fist, but he didn't move, only his tears flowed.

A great and exciting experience of mine in Hollywood: my first two encounters with Charlie Chaplin.

There is in Hollywood a restaurant/eatery/coffee-bar called Henry's, whose owner is familiar to those who have seen old Chaplin films. That enormous, pot-bellied man with bushy eyebrows, who chases Chaplin in his old roles—that's Henry, the great actor's old friend, who was also a silent partner in the business. All his life he was afraid of poverty and starving to death, which is perhaps why he got a stake in the restaurant.

This is where actors, writers, and extras went when they happened to have money, though the prices were fairly steep.

One day it was drizzling, when by chance I arrived by the entrance at the same time as Chaplin, who didn't at all resemble his on-screen self.

Wearing a threadbare overcoat, he reached out his hand to check for rain. It was raining, but languidly, and I took in the sight of this brilliant actor, who seemed to be in a bad and dejected mood.

In America men easily make each other's acquaintance, but you mustn't accost a woman on the street, for that might land you in prison.

"Feeling blue?" I asked, initiating the conversation.

He was beaming with delight at not having been recognized, I could tell, and he nodded sadly.

"Very. Why do you ask?"

"I just thought that if you like, I could invite you for a coffee and a sandwich, which is as much as I can afford, but not in this lousy Henry's, which is very expensive, but instead there's this inexpensive little eatery of sorts here on the corner."

"Thank you very much," said Chaplin. "I'd really appreciate that."

I ordered coffee and a dismal, tasteless ham sandwich, and in the fifth minute of our acquaintanceship Chaplin took the risk:

"Say, don't you think I look like Chapin?"

"I don't think so. But in this crazy village everyone wants to look like someone. And if you did? Where would that get you? Chaplin is a genius. And what are you?"

Chaplin waved his hand.

"Nothing. But I have a friend at Chaplin Studios. A propman. He said he could get me on as an assistant propman. That's the only reason I asked."

"Don't believe him," I said. "Hollywood is the land of promises. Here they promise the world, but they don't keep a bit of their word. Assistant propman? Why not look for some proper occupation?"

"Why? What are you?" he inquired, biting into the wilted sandwich.

"I work as an extra, but not with much success. They just kicked me out of one studio where they were looking for party guests. They said I'm too small to be a guest. I said there are small guests, too, and that I myself have been a guest lots of times. They didn't believe me. With us a guest is tall and elegant, they said."

"No problem. If I end up getting that assistant propman job, I'll try getting you into Chaplin Studios as an extra."

I turned sad.

"It's clear you haven't got a clue about life. Why, don't you know that Chaplin Studios doesn't have extras? Normal studios pay extras seven dollars and fifty cents a day. At Chaplin, a day's pay is seventy-five dollars. But there, there are no extras. He is the editor-in-chief, the director, the owner, and everything. He himself works with every actor."

"No matter. Give me your name and address, maybe it will work out, after all."

I did so. Needless to say, in three weeks the invitation came. On arriving I made as if only then and there did I recognize in that little tramp the great actor, and I stammered out excuses. Chaplin, as happy as high heaven, slapped his knees while laughing away and told everyone how exquisitely he'd pulled one over on me. I was even happier, for filming lasted for six months for seventy-five dollars a day, which back then was a fortune worthy of Croesus himself.

Chaplin was fond of Hungarians, and one evening he invited me to his home along with Alexander Korda and Lajos Bíró. But that happened later. These parties, as they called such evenings, were important, for that is where loves, marriages, and careers were decided. Chaplin was a charming host. After doing impersonations of the guests one night, he broke out into song.

When he finished, Korda said, awestruck, "I didn't know you had such a wonderful voice and could sing so remarkably."

Chaplin waved a hand.

"Ah, it's nothing, I was just impersonating Caruso."

He himself wrote the music for his films, and everyone in his family was a music lover.

On that night it happened that one of his many children, who back then was perhaps eight years old, ran over to Chaplin, pulled at his coat, and said, as excited as could be, "Dad, imagine, there is Jascha Heifetz, the violinist! Such a famous person in our house!"

Interesting, how little a person knows himself and how little he knows how he would behave in certain situations.

One day, having a bit of free time, I went over to Metro-Goldwyn-Mayer Studios, were Karcsi was working as an assistant director. At the door I was received by cowboys who looked like cowboys, and when I asked them where I could find Mr. Charles Vidor, they gestured for me to accompany them. I obligingly followed along when all of a sudden they closed a door behind me, and there I stood face-to-face with a giant lion that, eyes half closed, was lying on the floor.

At first I couldn't believe my eyes. I figured it was some sort of film trick, but the lion stank like no one else and gave the impression of being very real indeed. I am calm in difficult situations, but now I was terribly scared; my heart began beating wildly and I didn't move.

I recalled that lions always leap on their prey, that they never attack while walking, and that they gauge the distance with their whiskers. If you ruffle up its whiskers, it can't leap. That much I vaguely recalled, and also that it only attacks when hungry.

But I was in no mood to edge up close enough to him for ruffling.

I waited. I figured that if I don't attack, maybe he wouldn't be angry with me, either.

After two minutes that seemed like an eternity, they let me out of the room, and one of the waggish cowboys observed, "You were pretty boring, kid. But let's just see the next one—and a minute later they shoved into the cage the next victim, who wailed in terror and anticipated the attack in a boxing pose.

He, too, was let out soon enough, and then they threw in the third victim, who, on seeing the lion, fainted and fell onto the wild beast, which, however, didn't even stir. Laughing, the cowboys dragged him out before shoving in another, who began praying and crying:

"I've been a depraved, wicked person, Lord. I know you don't want to help me. My sins are terrible, but so is my punishment! May your will be done!"

The whole thing was beyond me. Later it turned out that the lion was real; it was the trademark of the famous Metro-Goldwyn Mayer company. It had grown old and some wanted to put it to sleep, but Mayer wouldn't let this happen: "I'm old, too," he said, "and I still wouldn't want to be exterminated."

But the lion was in the final throes of old age. It couldn't even stir. It was fed meatloaf, for it hadn't a tooth left, and its famous claws had fallen away. Barely a thing was left of the once fearsome beast. The only thing he was good for anymore was to entertain the waggish cowboys.

At Paramount my circumstances were exceptional. The famous American rat-race seemed not to apply here. I was assigned a project, did it in two days, and then waited for two months to submit it, because I knew that Mike Levy, the boss, did not care for slapdash work. In a short time, it's just a thrown-together something, but if you've worked on it for months, it must be good. In the meantime, I worked a great deal and wrote, in English, my first novel, *Greenhorn*.

Homesickness tormented me more and more, meanwhile, and it also bothered me that my wife began to grow and was already much taller than me. And yet when I took her as my wife, I thought that a married woman stops growing. But she didn't know that, and kept getting taller. After four years of marriage we divorced, too, without anger, for she too understood that such a little man can't live with a woman as tall as she had become.

I'd always put off going home, thinking I'd get one more week of pay, and then another, that I'd wait a little longer, and then *Greenhorn* was published by the Macaulay Co. I received a thousand-dollar advance, the book even looked beautiful, and I was almost happy.

Karcsi meanwhile had directed his first, half-hour film, which was a serious success in the industry and saw him quickly signed on as a bona fide director. He too had divorced, but he married again. His wife was an in-demand American actress, and they seemed to be happy together, though I knew that he, like me, didn't like to speak in English before breakfast.

Meanwhile, Mihály Kertész—Michael Curtiz, as he was known in America—was directing a new film. I went out to visit him in the Yuma Desert, where they were filming.

I happened to be taking my two-week vacation, and Curtiz hired me right away as one of the cowboys. I told him I couldn't ride a horse, but he just gave a wave of his hand and said, "I won't even let you near a horse, but we'll pay a lot, since out here there's a danger bonus on account of the hazardous stunts."

Everyone got a real Colt revolver, since in the desert life was not without its dangers. Coyotes, which a long time ago must have been borne of wolves and foxes, were common, and there were poisonous snakes aplenty.

I tried boiling an egg, since I remembered from my studies a long time ago that you can do so in desert sand. It worked, but the egg was rather on the soft-boiled side. Regular cooking is better, after all.

I happened to be loafing about some distance from the wild horsemen when I suddenly found myself face to face with an enormous snake that stood up on its tail and, sticking out its tongue, hissed at me. In terror I flung out my Colt and shot it to shreds. That's when our desert expert arrived on the scene, looked at the dead snake, gave me a pitying stare, and said, reproachfully, "That was stupid. You killed a completely harmless snake."

"Forgive me, but there are enough left around here. I don't know much about snakes, and I couldn't give the poor little thing enough time for its innocence to be revealed. The next time I'll ask you if the individual is poisonous or not."

One day I was talking unsuspectingly with Michael Curtiz, when all at once the ground before us opened up, and a gaping chasm who knows how many yards deep opened up right under our feet.

By then I'd long been a native, and nothing could surprise me while a film was being shot, and yet this did irritate me, and so I said indignantly,

"You could have told me that you were doing such special effects. I nearly fell in."

I looked up at Curtiz. His face as pale as death, his lips trembling, he barely managed to falter out:

"Earthquake. A real one."

We began running away from the chasm, and when I got home, I'd already decided: I almost died in a foreign country, in a foreign earthquake, so I was now not waiting any longer. I would go home. To Budapest.

I spoke to Levy, the boss.

"I'm homesick. I want to go home."

"Why?"

"My mother, my father, and my siblings are over there. I want to see them. I haven't seen them in twelve years."

"Well, if that's all that this is about, you needn't go home. They should come here. For a visit. We'll send them tickets for the ship and everything. Let me handle it."

"But it's not just about that. I yearn for Rákóczi Boulevard, and I'd like to see Hársfa Street, where I was born."

"I don't understand. No problem. We won't bring the buildings here. But I'll give you two weeks' paid vacation. Go look at your buildings and come back."

Twenty-Two

In Hungary everyone speaks Hungarian. Two weeks is a lot of time if it lasts for years. Meetings with everyone who is alive. I make a new career at a Budapest newspaper.

The journey by ship toward Budapest or, rather, Paris, was beautiful, pleasant, and exciting, but I could hardly wait to get to port. This trip was different than arriving in America in the bottom of a ship. I was a traveler, and I was elegant, as befit a screenwriter with a bright future ahead of him. The excitement was much greater than what I felt when traveling to America with Peaches and Karcsi, for now I knew what and whom this would be about.

Inexplicably, as soon as I arrived in Paris, most of my homesickness ceased, and I grew calm. It seemed that it was Europe that I'd missed in that distant country. I couldn't get enough of Paris; days passed, and I was still at the Café de La Paix and the Champs-Élysées and the Boulevard Saint Michel.

That is where I became acquainted with Lajos Tihanyi, who, it later turned out, was a world-famous painter, but back then he was just painting this and that. We became fast friends, and though the poor man was deaf, he could read lips, and it was easy to understand his speech, articulated though it was in the singular manner of the deaf.

In the Dôme we drank exceptional coffee, which is completely unheard of in America.

But he soon died of deafness. There was a terrible storm in Paris, a hurricane and the works, and the poor fellow didn't hear as a gale uprooted an enormous tree, which crushed him to death.

When the train pulled in to the Keleti Station in Budapest with me on it, my whole family was waiting there. My mother; my father; my little brother, who'd become a medical student; my dear little sister; and Gyula, my brother-in-law. Nearly the whole family, that is: absent only was my older brother, Endre, who had long been in Brazil, a doctor in Rio.

By the time we'd come to somewhat from the effects of not having seen each other for twelve years and arrived at 40 Hársfa Street, it turned out that my father had never registered my absence with the authorities, hence I was still officially a resident of the same address, because he didn't think America would last long.

I began my life in Budapest.

Lajos Zilahy had long been home, and on his recommendation a newspaper, *Pesti Napló*, published my novel *Szeretlek – I Love You* in serialized form. Only later did I found out that György Bálint and Aurél Kárpáti were the editors, and when the boss, Miklós Andor, asked Kárpáti if an unknown writer's novel could be published, Kárpáti replied, "No. It *must* be published."

That is how I became a Hungarian writer.

I published not only a novel in *Pesti Napló* but also short stories and articles, and I became acquainted with contemporary Hungarian literature.

But the greatest gift of my life back in Budapest was my friendship with the actress Ella Gombaszögi, which lasted until her death.

Back then, in the mid thirties, there were two or three pinball machines in the New York Café, and I was fond of the game. The first time I noticed them there the machines were occupied, but I kept my eyes on one of them and waited for my turn.

Two huge, middle-aged men were playing on that machine, and as it later turned out, one was Dr. István Bródy, the son of the late author and journalist Sándor Bródy, and the other was Dr. Vilmos Rácz, who was later to become a newspaper editor and even then was an exceptional fencer and dueling authority.

I waited. I asked how long they'd be playing. They reassured me that they had only two rounds left. That became three rounds, then four, and it seemed that never in their lives would they desist. Tired of waiting, I went over to them.

"I've had enough of this trickery. If you don't stop at once, I'll slap each one of you to dust."

The men couldn't believe their ears, and in that critical moment, a muscular, stocky man stepped forth from out of the blue and came over to me.

"I'm Frigyes Karinthy," he said. "Just who are you?" With that, he shoved the two other men aside and the two of us started playing. I was happy. No wonder I'd always adored Karinthy. Now, too, he had descended into the thick of things, like an angel from on high. After playing, I joined him on his walk home to Verpeléti Street, which later became Frigyes Karinthy Street, which, I think, even Karinthy himself had not counted on.

He invited me up to their flat and introduced me to his beautiful, gracious, and smart wife, Aranka, and to their little boy, Ferenc Karinthy, who, like his dad, later also became a prominent writer.

Life was marvelously beautiful. The very fact that everyone on the streets was speaking Hungarian also seemed a cause for happiness, and I could hardly get used to it. In America the din of the street was a cacophony, an inarticulate racket there was no making sense of in the chaos. In Budapest, snatches of dialogue like this struck my ears:

"... and then I said to Lili that ..." and: "... but I still can't put up with it...." And I understood every word.

My friendship with Ella Gombaszögi blossomed, and she introduced me to everyone in Budapest who counted as an actor, a writer, a painter, or a musician. Everyone loved Ella. She had no enemies, for she was as warm-hearted as no one else. She was proud that she could cook remarkable goulash. Not that she could cook much else, but sometimes she had dishes that she herself created.

It happened one day in the Victoria Café—which I frequented a lot with Pista Lukács, Márton Rátkai, Béla Reinitz, and others—that someone at the table I didn't know ordered *körözött* cheese spread. The café served the ingredients separately, and you would mix them yourself. Well, this stranger got down to the task clumsily indeed. Ella watched him for a while, and then sprang up angrily, went over, and made his *körözött.*

"So, you blockhead, this is how you do it!" she said, and left the dumbstruck individual.

Frigyes Karinthy was a Gombaszögi fan himself. "Even if she weren't a great actress," he'd say, "she would be all the same."

Karinthy was a humble genius. Never would he have believed that one day he would become a street and a legendary writer. Never did he have much money on him, though he earned a lot.

One day the two of us happened to be at the front office in a money matter waiting for Andor Miklós, the big boss, when Mr. Láng, the ever elegant, ever calm executive assistant, reassured us that we wouldn't have to wait for long. All at once, Imre Salusinszky, the editor-in-chief, appeared, a briefcase under his arm, and without hesitation marched right into Andor Miklós's sanctum. All that meant was that we had to wait yet again.

While waiting, we discussed whether Salusinszky was a human being. Mr. Láng listened to the sacrilegious conversation with a look of slight disapproval.

Karinthy insisted that Salusinszky was a human being, just a rotten one. I contended that there was no proof of this.

Suddenly the door opened, and the subject of the debate himself stepped out. Karinthy stepped over, and without so much as looking at him, grabbed his bow tie and turned triumphantly to me.

"You see! He has a tie, so he's a human being."

Salusinszky looked at us nervously, as he didn't understand what this was about.

"The bow tie is not proof," I said, "because if we want, we can tie one onto a turkey, too, but that will not make it a human being, just a turkey with a tie."

Karinthy dispiritedly let go of the tie.

"You're right. I hadn't thought of that."

Salusinszky's eyelids were fluttering in terror, and he wanted to make some high-handed remark, but as it was inadvisable to get mixed up into an argument with Karinthy, he clomped out of the room with this dispirited sentence:

"You gentlemen don't have anything better to do."

At first, life was beautiful back home. I kept battering on open doors: The weekly *New Times* asked me to write for them, too, and they published my stories and articles; I worked for another weekly, *Theater Life*; and a play of mine was performed at the Downtown Theater. But that specter called Hitler was already cooking up his plans. He was already the chancellor of Germany, and his shadow was bearing down upon us.

One after another, various fascist parties established themselves in Hungary, but back then we didn't even suspect what horrors awaited us.

The writer-playwright Ferenc Molnár was still in Hungary, with his silver hair and trademark monocle. Every day for about a year and a half he got together with me and Ella Gombaszögi, Adorján Stella, János Kallós, and Lóránt Barabás, who was a newspaper reporter and also happened to be the director of the Andrássy Avenue Theater. Naturally it was always Molnár who led the conversation, and the rest of us reverently listened in.

One little wonderful anecdote of his, for example, was about how in his youth Molnár had wooed, not with much success, the lovely young candy girl at the Omnia cinema. The girl was named Klári, and languidly she sold the candy to cinema-goers, and only reluctantly did she turn her eyes upon Molnár, who for his part was focusing on her with ever more enthusiasm.

"Say, are you some sort of poet or something?" Klári inquired.

"Yes. I'm that sort."

"Alright, then. If you write me a poem and I like it, I'll go up to your place. No one has ever written me a poem."

A few days later Molnár appeared, and after the movie—for Klári, work—they sat down in a café.

"I wrote the poem," said the writer with a smile.

"Good. Show me!"

"No, I'd rather recite it. It's called 'The End of September'," Molnár began, and awaited the laughter—since he was about to read the greatest love poem of the famous romantic poet Sándor Petőfi, a poem that every student in Hungary learns to recite in elementary school. But no laughter came. And so Molnár began:

Down in the valley garden flowers still blooming,
Outside by the window the poplar's still green,
But do you see winter's world o'er there looming?
Already the hilltops a snow-covered scene.

And he recited the whole poem. Klári listened in an increasingly surly mood. Molnár finished and awaited the effect, which was not to lag behind.

"This is a poem? This is nonsense. What's that supposed to mean, 'The End of September'? It's now the middle of November, after all. And what sorts of things have you scribbled down in"—here she was referring to the poem's second stanza—"that I'll leave your name behind for some other guy? Why, I don't even know your name, just that you're some Ferenc, Feri. Get lost. I don't even want to lay eyes on you!"

So it was that Petőfi and Molnár flopped before Klári simultaneously. The story was a tremendous success. Molnár was an amazing performer, but interestingly enough, he invariably told only old stories, because he didn't dare touch contemporary times. One day he was just ten minutes into a long, exciting story when Barabás, who adored Molnár, said with a nod:

"That's how it was. I remember."

Molnár turned pale. He stopped his monologue, and then said, petulantly:

"I can't stand this duet."

One time we were eating in Gundel on a beautiful summer day, and chickens were running about the yard. A young and uncultivated chicken that didn't know Molnár kept loitering about the great writer, who couldn't manage to shoo it away. It kept coming right back, at which Molnár angrily shouted at the bird, "Get lost already, you here, or else I'll order you."

Life seemed beautiful, but the storm clouds were gathering with dangerous speed.

I happened to be at the dress rehearsal of some Molière piece in the company of Ella Gombaszögi, István Békeffi, and Jenő Heltai, when we received word of the Anschluss. Hitler had invaded Austria.

Enfeebled and in shock, the audience fled, and we alone remained for the third act.

Ida Turay was one of the main actors, and afterward she and her husband joined the rest of us as we plodded along to the Belvárosi Café.

Ida was in despair.

"I haven't had a flop like that in my whole life. Terrible! Everyone left the performance!"

Békeffi tried cheering her up.

"But Ida ..."

But he never got past "But Ida," for Ida vehemently interrupted him.

"Let's cut the nonsense! I flopped, and that's that. Let's not sugarcoat things."

By then I'd had enough of the argument, and I stopped Ida.

"Stop! Don't say a thing until I finish!" I began truculently. "Understand it already: Hitler has invaded Austria. With that, we've become immediate neighbors of the Nazi madness. That's why the audience went home, and not due to the show. Do you get it yet?"

Ida understood. Bowing her head, she hissed furiously, "Goddamn Hitler! To ruin a dress rehearsal like that!"

Turay did not know back then that Hitler was not just taking pains to ruin dress rehearsals.

Those who could, started fleeing Hungary. Many foresaw that there would be no stopping the madness. Newspapers were by now hardly writing about anything other than Hitler and Nazi Germany.

Passports were easy to get, but visas were hard to come by.

The situation became increasingly worse. Ferenc Szálasi, head of the fascist Arrow Cross Party, was freed from prison, and his party was stronger than ever.

I resolved to leave the country once again, but that I would not return to America. Perhaps England. They spoke English there, too, and it wasn't far, either. Maybe this madness would end, maybe I'd someday find my home in Hungary, after all.

Yes, but the lines in front of the British Embassy were constantly so long that no one could see an end to them.

I hit upon an idea for my rescue.

Passport in my pocket, I went right in the embassy door as a writer for *Pest Daily*, and asked to speak to the ambassador himself.

Within minutes I was in his office. He was an amiable man, blessed with a sense of humor, and when I informed him that I'd like a British visa, this was his reply:

"But sir, don't you see how many people are standing in line for visas? It's not so simple. It seems everyone wants to go to England. Most of course say they'd go for a few minutes only, long enough to see the Tower and Piccadilly Circus, but I don't exactly believe them. So getting a visa isn't so easy, I'm afraid."

"I don't see serious obstacles. Here I am, here you are, and here are the stamps. Just stamp the passport, and the rest is my business."

The ambassador broke into a smile.

"And how long would you like to stay in London?"

"Not long. I'm thinking forty or fifty years. I'm not so young anymore."

The ambassador now laughed, and gave me the visa. I was happy, because England then seemed to be the country full of peace and bliss and free of Nazis.

With a heavy heart I bid farewell to my parents, my friends, my siblings, and my charming brother-in-law, Gyula, who was more endearing a brother-in-law than it would have been possible to invent.

When we crossed the Channel and the ship arrived in Dover, the immigration office browsed my passport studiously, and then asked:

"How long do you wish to stay in London?"

I recalled what I'd said in Budapest to the ambassador.

"Not long. I'm thinking forty or fifty years. I'm not so young anymore."

The immigration officer nodded.

"You're lucky. That's the same thing you said in Budapest to the British ambassador."

I turned pale. I hadn't counted on British intelligence being so good. If I'd lied that I was staying only for a few minutes, they would not have let me in.

In London my first trip took me to my old friend, Pál (Paul) Tábori, who had a little two-storey house in the heart of the city, four tube stops from Piccadilly Circus, at 15 Stafford Terrace.

There Pál Tábori lived with Kati, his wife, who was likewise an old friend, and with his son, Péter.

He moved me onto the first floor straightaway, and with that, my English life had begun.

Twenty-Three

There are English troubles, too.
Writers write if they're allowed to.
My meeting with the three Kordas.

Life was remarkably beautiful at the Táboris, who were the most diligent human beings imaginable. I couldn't wake early enough not to find the master of the house in his ground-floor study. There he was writing all his works, nonstop.

It was Tábori's recommendation that got me my first job in London. I translated a thick Hungarian medical book into English, and when they wanted to force a Hungarian-English medical dictionary on me, I only laughed.

"I don't think I'll need a dictionary," I said haughtily, but I didn't want to argue, so I took the dictionary. Within minutes it turned out that I wouldn't have been able to even budge without it, for I hadn't a clue as to the English names of the myriad illnesses I encountered, one more beautiful than the other. It turned out that more than one abhorrent disease began with the word "German," as for example German measles. But that was the least of my worries. The greater worry, which I hadn't counted on, was that as I translated the book, I began to notice the symptoms on myself—especially when I arrived at nicotine poisoning, of which the book said that the patient is beset by, among other things, a sense of annihilation. Anxious about having just been annihilated, I immediately lit up a Players, which is a cigarette in England.

No sooner had I finished the translation, for which I was handsomely compensated in British currency, than I got a new job. On Tábori's recommendation I was received by the director of the Pallas Publishing Company, an amiable, sixtyish man, who, as per English custom, began thus before we got to the subject at hand: "With or without?" he asked, meaning with soda or without. He didn't even say "whisky," for everyone knew what this was about.

I turned pale, since I can't drink; I don't like alcohol, and I'd heard nothing but bad gossip about whisky.

Drolly I replied, trembling inside for fear that I might insult the boss:

"Without whisky," I said, and I saw at once that I'd botched up my life. The boss's face suddenly froze, and he stared at me as if at a handful of worms. In despair I tried to smile, but I sensed that this smile of mine hadn't even a trace of the cheer so characteristic of smiles.

"Listen, sir. It's now 11 AM. I've had four whiskies already, and I swore to myself that come hell or high water, not even then will I drink another bite until noon."

The boss's face brightened up.

"Why, that's splendid," he said with a laugh, and drank so much that I myself would have been carried off from the scene on a stretcher.

I'd won the first round.

We then got down to business. I was to write a book of short stories titled *How Do You Do?* about the world's various peoples, wild creatures, semi-wild creatures, and civilized creatures. The publisher would see to it that his slaves would read up on everything at the library and provide me with the raw materials.

I asked for an advance. It turned out that in English this wasn't as straightforward a matter as in Hungarian. "Give me money in advance," I said.

By now, the boss, under the influence of the whisky and of me, did laugh.

"Don't you trust the company?"

"I trust in the company, just not that I'll get by without an advance until I finish writing the book."

I left the press with enough money to rent a flat in Belsize Park: three rooms, all the modern conveniences, and three types of heat (which together ensured that I very nearly froze). I even furnished it with stunningly beautiful furniture. And I had money left over.

I wrote the book, whereupon I got my next assignment: to "appraise" the life of Adolf Hitler. Unfortunately, back then I was not yet able to write about his death, since he was alive.

I knew Sándor (Alexander) Korda from Hollywood, and I now quickly got to know his two brothers: Zoltán, a film director; and Vince, who designed props for Sándor's films.

The true, talented, fanatical director was Zoltán. Sándor didn't like to direct; instead he preferred to secure the requisite finances, indeed, it was he who began producing large-scale British films in Denham.

My first job for the Kordas was a film called *The Four Feathers*, which was written by an Englishman, R. C. Sheriff, though five of us worked on the screenplay.

The film was about a cowardly Englishman who turned out to be braver than anyone else. The cowardly Englishman was played by Ralph Richardson, who, mainly on account of this film, was knighted by the King of England.

There wouldn't have been a problem at all, except that I wrote a play, *Let's Pretend*, for which my dear friend Miklós Bródszky composed the music. Its poems were penned by my savior, the ambassador from whom I'd gotten the British visa in Budapest, and who, it turned out, was a poet when he was not an ambassador.

The piece was performed at St. James Theatre, owned by J. P. Mitchelhill, who had seventeen other theaters in England. In England there are no permanent theater companies, as there are in Hungary, but the actors are chosen for specific roles.

The selection happens like this: the playwright and the director visit other theaters where rehearsals are underway. In short, they become acquainted with the actors as they work and, if possible, they then sign them on for their own play.

That was my undoing.

In one of the theaters, during a rehearsal I noticed a young, spine-tinglingly pretty, red-haired girl. All she had to do was cross the stage and say a few words about fashion. But the director called her back ten times.

"Maud, your voice isn't even audible in the first row. You're muttering. Can't you articulate properly?" This kept up for a while, until finally the director called a break, and we introduced ourselves to the actors. That's how I was introduced to Maud Courtney, whom the director had so many problems with. But I liked her a lot. We got to talking, and to get her to like me, I took the risk: "The director is terrible, Maud. He torments you a lot."

Maud smiled.

"It's not the director who's terrible, I'm untalented. What kind of a playwright are you not to have noticed?"

"I noticed, dear, only I didn't want to say anything. But if you know you're untalented, then why do you want to be an actress?"

"I'm untalented at other things, too. I can't sew, either, but it's here that they pay the most for me crossing the stage. I know I'll never be a Sarah Bernhardt, but life here is entertaining."

I liked her voice, and her figure, and also what she said.

I invited her to dinner. I waited until the end of the rehearsal, when Maud's mother joined us, too. The mother was a red-haired beauty as well, with an expensive car and an even more expensive fur coat. There was no dad, as it later turned out.

We talked, we ate dinner, and we laughed. I liked this girl more and more. I'd long stopped caring what sort of actress she was.

It must have been 2 AM by the time we headed home. The mother offered to take me in her car to Belsize Park.

When I got out of the car in front of my apartment, Maud got out, too, and called to her mother, "I'm sleeping with him, Mum. Bye. Be good."

I was trembling from head to toe with excitement all the way up to the third floor. Red clouds were dancing in front of my eyes. This was unheard of. I dared not even dream of this. I hadn't so much as hinted how much I liked her, though she could surely tell that she had an effect on me, no matter how much I'd tried hiding it.

When I calmed down a bit and began believing that what happened actually happened, we began to talk, for I hardly knew Maud at all.

We got round to the subject of Hitler, and the girl quietly observed, "The Germans are not human."

"And the Hungarians?"

"Not them, either."

I went through all the nations of the world, more or less, but Maud didn't vote for a single one. Finally, certain triumph was at hand, I spurted out, "And the Americans?"

"You can't be serious. Of course they're not human."

It turned out that Maud considered only the English to be human, and when I discreetly alluded to what we'd just done together, she answered, didactically, "That's different. I love my dog, too, and my bathtub and kidney and steak pie. But not even they are people." (Kidney and steak pie is a revolting English dish, a pie with a thick layer of sugar on top. If you cut into it, bloody shreds of meat come squirming out.)

I would have been deathly offended, but figured Maud was just teasing me and waiting for me, the Hungarian patriot, to boil over with rage. But I was so sleepy that I no longer had the strength to get seriously angry.

The rehearsals were well underway, and naturally Maud, too, got a little role: she didn't have to speak for long, but she was gorgeous.

Before the dress rehearsal the theater management held a meeting led by Mitchelhill. The exceptionally manly, forty-year-old boss showered praise upon the men and upbraided the women with revulsion even though they were talented and stunning beauties. For a while I just listened, and then I took the risk:

"You're talking as if you were a fairy."

"Excuse me? That's what I am!"

I was taken aback, but despite the boss's assessment the play was a big success. In the lead was Steve Geray, who had acted in Budapest under his Hungarian name, István Gergyay, with no small accomplishment. Later he took up roles in Hollywood, with less success. And yet this Steve was a really great actor, only that he was so unreliable, so shifty, that it was unbelievable.

On one occasion I wanted to adjust my watch, since it had stopped. I asked Geray, "What time is it?" He quickly covered his wristwatch and said, "Why?"

He didn't even dare tell me the time, for he couldn't remember his previous lie in this matter.

The play was still bouncing along when Geray had to flee London due to certain unpleasant financial matters.

The news from Hungary was increasingly alarming. The country was racing toward catastrophe and couldn't be stopped. I had to renew my passport every six months, which happened with me sending it by mail to the Home Office, and a few days later they would send it back, likewise by mail.

It went this way for quite a while, but meanwhile Hungary issued a new decree, and every Hungarian had to verify his or her identity.

Though every ancestor of mine had been born in Budapest, I still didn't receive the verification, and so the Hungarian embassy didn't extend my passport, which was therefore invalid, and consequently the English could not give a visa.

But I didn't bother much with this, for Maud occupied every bit of my time. I was constantly jealous, not that there was much point in being so, for my dear little fiancée cheated on me left and right. With this fellow or that one. True, not underhandedly, but with such comments as this:

"Be at the Quality Inn tomorrow by two. No earlier, because beforehand I'm going to the hair salon, and then I'm dropping in at the painter I'm involved with, but I'll try to be on time."

I couldn't get a breath. This was a first for me. Was she really saying this to me? This had never happened in the history of the world. Cheating is something a man realizes with dismay, something that turns out, something that is exposed, never something the other person tells you matter-of-factly.

Maud found this completely natural, but it must be said that so did other English. For example, when I complained to an English friend of mine that Maud was cheating on me, he asked, "And what about it?"

He was waiting for me to get to the point. Finally, having had enough of his haughtiness, I asked him what he'd do if he found out that his wife was cheating on him.

"What do you mean, 'found out'? I have."

"From whom?"

"Her. My wife. She always tells me about it. Say, is Bíró a Hungarian name?"

"Yes."

"Well then, with this Bíró too. Supposedly he works at the Hungarian embassy. But she complained that he can't even dance, so it didn't work out. Now she has a Frenchman who not only dances but also does this and that. I'm happy about this, since I like to see that Claire is happy."

Back then I thought that fate had brought me together with some mentally ill Englishman, when I received an invitation to spend the weekend at the home of some illustrious English family. The man was a lord, and his wife was a lovely young lady.

I went with Miklós Brodszky, the composer. The refreshment room was dripping of English ennui, with one word spoken a week and all sorts of alcohol being consumed. The enormous room was heated by a fireplace, which warms you up if you're right in front of it and lets you freeze if you're further off, so I went out to the terrace. There I found the lady of the house completely naked with a gentleman who was not the lord, and they were in a position that made it clear to me that there was no serious need for me here. Thus I headed back toward the refreshment room—just as the master of the house, the lord, came toward me, headed to the terrace. I thought I'd stop him and say something. *Should I talk him out of going out there? It's not worth it, I'm a foreigner in this country, I don't know what's customary; let him go and find out what life is all about.* And so he went. A couple of minutes later he came back and we met halfway, and he knew that I knew, that we knew, for both of us had come from there, and so he spoke:

"What do you say?"

"Well, this sort of thing is unpleasant."

"What do you mean, 'unpleasant'? It's horrible."

"It is in any case awkward," I concurred.

"This is intolerable; it will drive me mad. I can scold her and rebuke her all I want, but I can't manage to get her to wear something on such occasions. She'll get chilled, catch a cold, and die, and then whose problem will that be? Mine!"

But the lady's infidelity could not calm my nerves. The problem with Maud was not that she cheated on me, but what aggrieved me above all was that she didn't comprehend whatsoever what was unseemly about it.

"I've realized something interesting," she said one day. "You're always anxious when I sleep with someone else. Don't deny it, I'm positive."

She laughed and she drank. She loved to drink, and sometimes she got so sloshed she passed out. When we invited guests, she felt obliged to drink, and indeed she got all boozed up and kept saying, drunkenly, "I know you're a German spy, Paul, but not a big deal! I love you."

There wasn't even any defending myself against the accusation of a drunk woman, but it was unpleasant to listen to this sort of thing when the war was already in full progress against the Germans. True, there was a little pause after the invasion of Poland, but everyone knew that that had not settled a thing.

Job opportunities kept narrowing, too. Theaters closed, and foreign citizens were allowed to go about only within a mile of their homes.

I decided to break up with Maud. We lived together in Belsize Park, true, but she had never given up her apartment at the White House.

The big moment came. Maud was lying quietly and innocently in bed, and we were talking. Without so much as a transition I embarked on my big speech, whose point was that I didn't tolerate cheating, it was all or nothing. It would be better never to meet again, I said, because I couldn't endure life as it was. I think it was a beautiful, smart, logical speech. Succinct and open. I awaited the reaction. Maud kept listening all the while, eyes shut, with self-restraint, not saying a thing. But when I looked over, I saw that she was breathing evenly. She had fallen asleep. While being called to account.

Of course, even this was a reply. I understood how little she cared about the whole matter. I shook her awake and told her I couldn't take it anymore, that we should break up, and that she should return to her old flat.

"As you wish," she said and packed her things. All or nothing sounds lovely, but it is conceivable that a person will settle for something or anything all the same.

She left. I missed her unbearably. In vain did I try with other women, in vain did I seek to think of others, the anguish didn't abate. Salty water does not quench thirst, I told myself, and I resolved to be strong, to keep my distance from her, in which case the pain would surely go away.

A few weeks later I happened to be reading something when I heard a key turn in the lock. When she left me, Maud had asked me for a key as a token of remembrance. Now I listened as the door opened, and then there stood Maud, in the foyer. She switched on the lamp, the light adhering tenaciously to her red hair.

"Hello, Paul," she began, "I've come by because I ran about a lot today and got tired. And I'm hungry too. Do you have some food at home?"

I could hardly stand straight from my excitement. I served her courteously and we lit cigarettes.

"You're not angry, are you?" she asked. "As far as I know we're not angry with each other—all we did was break up, right?"

"No, of course not. Why would I be angry? How are you?"

"I'm sleepy. I'm lying down."

Some time back we'd furnished one of the rooms as a 'quarrel room,' and in it was a row bed, so if we got into a quarrel we wouldn't have to sleep in the same bed while we were still rowing.

"Sure," I said, trembling. "There's the quarrel bed."

"*All right*," she said, started to undress, and then lay down. After a bit she appeared again, completely naked.

"It's really boring sleeping alone, don't you think?"

I thought so, too.

In the morning Maud said this:

"Look, we broke up, fine. But we could meet up now and again. And if we meet up, we could go, say, to a movie, and then we could naturally have dinner together, and if we're tired, we could sleep together."

I had to admit that she was right, for we had, after all, broken up.

Twenty-Four

ROTHSCHILD HAS NO MONEY. THE GERMANS EVEN LIE. SCOTLAND YARD IS NOT A UNIT OF MEASURE. IT'S BAD EVERYWHERE, BUT WORST AT HOME.

While reading the Hungarian papers in London, I encountered one horror after another reported by the German News Agency. It occurred to me that a London office should be established from where the Hungarian dailies could get real news. Only that this would require lots of money and serious organizing.

I went to the famous Rothschild investment banking company and notified the main office that I wish to speak with James Rothschild.

I didn't have much hope, but figured I'd give it a try anyway. In the ramshackle, two-storey little house an even more ramshackle elevator took me to the second floor, where I was led into a room. I waited.

The room was full of old paintings, all of them portraying some Rothschild forebear of yore who, kneeling, was giving money to various kings.

After ten minutes of waiting the door opened and—an unexpected turn of events!—James Rothschild himself stepped into the room. That is to say, it wasn't I who had gone in to him, but he who had come in to me. This too was his room. This legendary James was a short man with reddish-blond hair who looked amiable and energetic, and for some seconds I couldn't even get out a word in my surprise.

"Your paintings are wanting, sir," I began the conversation.

"What do you mean, 'wanting'?"

"Well, these paintings show that you gave kings certain sums. But that's not what made your family wealthy. Where are those paintings that show how much you got back?"

James laughed, and, satisfied that he had a sense of humor, I asked him if he knew any Rothschild jokes. He didn't know a single one. I told him one, and he kept asking for more.

Finally I got round to the matter of my visit.

"I would like you to finance a British news agency for Hungarian newspapers. The Hungarian papers are full of German lies."

He liked the idea.

"Sure thing. Go tomorrow to the offices of the *Daily Telegraph* and look up the editor-in-chief, Brigadier General Lawson, and he will arrange everything. You will have an office, a telephone, you can dial up any corner of the globe, and he will also see to your pay."

"I am happy, but—and please don`t take this as distrust—we can simply agree on this without your at least dialing up the editor-in-chief? Perhaps he will pose difficulties. What leads you to think that my office and everything will be waiting for me tomorrow?"

James smiled.

"The paper happens to have become mine," he said unassumingly. I was reassured. Then we spoke for a while longer, and I asked, "How can it be that I am in the headquarters of the world-famous Rothschild banking company, that I have been through the whole building, but I have seen not a penny anywhere?"

"We finance states. In this chair sat Count István Bethlen, too, not long ago. He asked for money."

"And did he get any?"

"Rest assured, he got not a penny."

The next day I introduced myself to the brigadier general editor-in-chief, who gave me a warm welcome. He'd assigned me an office, informed me of my pay, and explained that the ticker would pour out the news, from which I could pick and choose.

From that day on this news appeared day in and day out in the Hungarian papers, always with these words up front: "The *Daily Telegraph*'s news service reports ..."

In light of the war that was underway, we had to show up once a week at the Ministry of Information, where the minister himself gave us a summary of the situation and asked for recommendations.

At one such press briefing I proposed that we release fake news, since the German News Agency was constantly lying, too.

The minister was taken aback.

"What kind of fake news?"

"For example, let's report the names and titles of German pilots who have surrendered and requested asylum in Britain. It's not important that the names be real."

"So you are proposing that we lie. But then what is the difference between us and the Germans?"

Ashamed, I fell silent.

The days became months. I worked for the BBC but not the news agency; I only wrote radio reports. Pallas Publishing came through, too. They published two more books of mine, and if Maud hadn't constantly driven me mad with her strange way of thinking, her drunkenness, and her affairs, life would have been beautiful relative to the circumstances, even though my passport had long expired, through no fault of my own.

I wrote to Budapest to have them verify already that I was a Hungarian citizen, but to no avail.

I happened to be working on a radio cross talk when the buzzer sounded and in stepped an agreeable-looking young Englishman.

"I'm from Scotland Yard," he began. "I'd like to see your passport."

"I can show you, but it won't bring you much delight, because it's expired. It's no longer valid, and consequently the Home Office can't extend my residence permit."

"That's what I was afraid of," said the detective ruefully, at which I blithely observed, "Surely you don't intend to say you will arrest me?"

"Yes, I am afraid that's what this is about, and it is my duty to inform you that starting now you should be careful what you say, because it may be used against you."

I was now remanded, as the British are apt to say. The kind detective accompanied me to Brixton Jail, where there are no convicts, only detainees awaiting trial.

Sparkling cleanliness everywhere. Not a weapon was to be seen, nor did I myself have a gun or revolver with me. Everyone had his own, individual cell, which we had to wash, iron, and keep tidy. There wasn't much furniture, only a closet of sorts, a standard-issue bed, and blankets I never did manage to fold so deftly as to earn the approval of the prison guard.

Every day we got to take a walk and smoke cigarettes, and when I advised the guard that I'm unable to smoke while walking, only while standing still or sitting, he gave me permission to have my cig however I wished.

We were just heading out on a walk one day when a sign posted on one of the calls struck my eye: FURNISHED ROOM FOR RENT.

"Who is the fool who wants to rent a room in here?" I asked the guard.

"You, for example," he said, and already he had transformed into landlady as he now showed me the room, which was beautifully furnished, with a more respectable bed and an eiderdown quilt that looked Hungarian.

"You can rent this if you have money in the office. Nine schillings a week, plus you get a servant who will clean up and fold the bed sheets for you."

I immediately rented the room, paying for two weeks in advance. To this day Britain still owes me eleven schillings, but I don't want to make a diplomatic scandal out of this.

Anyone who needed a separate bath, a pen, paper, or whatever could request a meeting with the sheriff in charge of the institution and who regularly approved such requests.

And yet the sheriff was a stern, spare Englishman with a missing ear perhaps bitten off in his younger years by some nervous prisoner. One had to stand at attention in front of his door, and conversation with other prisoners standing there was prohibited. Thus we spoke silently, at a whisper, as befitting a prison.

One time six of us were standing in front of his door. I was there to ask for paper and something to write with; what sorts of things the others wanted, who knows. Beside me was a kid who couldn't have been more than sixteen years old. His long blond hair hung downward like a girl's, though back then such hairdos were not at all in fashion among males.

He looked so surprisingly little-boyish, so gentle, so kind, that I couldn't begin to imagine what he was doing in here among the prisoners.

"What are you doing here?" I inquired.

"Do you remember the bombing at Victoria Station?"

"Sure. It happened last week. Two people died and many were wounded. But that's not what I'm interested in. What are you doing here?"

"I threw the bomb," he said meekly.

"Have you gone mad? You're a kid and throwing bombs about?"

"I'm with the IRA," he said proudly, "and they entrusted me with this important mission because I'm a minor. I can't be hung. At most I'll get life imprisonment."

The kid saw that I couldn't get a breath from bewilderment, and so he hissed, "What are you so flabbergasted about? Wouldn't you throw a bomb for your homeland?"

"You don't know my homeland. At the moment it is not the sort of homeland to chuck things about for."

The sheriff stepped out and let us into his office one at a time. He listened to each of us and fulfilled the requests. I don't know what the Irish lad asked for, but surely they didn't give him a bomb.

No work was required, but at exactly five in the afternoon the guard appeared in front of my cell.

"Time for your tea, sir," he said, and asked me whether I wished for cocoa, coffee, or tea. With the tea I got a huge slice of bread that tasted better than out in the free world, and corned beef, which I just loved.

During the day it was OK to speak with one's colleagues. Above each man's cell was some text showing what he was accused of.

In the cell beside mine lived an amiable, fortyish man accused of burglary.

"What's your occupation?" I asked.

"Can't you read? It says right there: burglar."

"I thought that was a charge, not an occupation. I bet you have some trade, too, not just burglary."

"Nothing else. I'm a burglar. Last year I broke into Selfridges department store every night. I was cunning, like a cat, but the last time they somehow spotted me and I got caught."

"Every day? I thought burglary was just an odd job. Now and again you break in somewhere, but then you stop."

The burglar smiled indulgently.

"What are you? Your having overstayed your visa in England doesn't say a thing about your occupation."

"I'm a writer."

"And you write once, and then never again?"

"You're right. I can see what you're getting at. And what sort of feeling was it when the detectives showed up and arrested you?"

"Liberating. Sooner or later everyone gets caught. Now I'll get a couple, and then when I'm freed I'll get back to work. But I'll be more careful."

At three in the morning my cell door opened (unfortunately it could be opened only from outside, not from inside) and in stepped a guard. I was terrified. I'd been in the prison for nearly a week already but this was the first nighttime visit.

The guard seemed nervous. After clearing his throat, he spoke.

"How do you like me?"

My first thought was that this poor guard had gone mad. Until now not one of them had thought to ask me if I like them. But that didn't matter just now.

"From what perspective?" I asked evasively.

He took off his cap.

"Look at me in profile!"

"An interesting profile, but first I need to know what this is about," I said, a bit terrified, for I couldn't imagine what he wanted from me, this psycho who so far had seemed completely tame and normal.

"The thing is, you are being freed in the morning. I am the censor in this institution, and I read the letter you received from Alexander Korda. Judging from the letter's tone, you two are friends. I'd like to be a movie actor; I'm tired of being a prison guard, and I thought that maybe you could put in a good word for me with Korda. I'd be happy if I could work in the studio, in Denham. Of course I am thinking of work as an extra or really minor roles for now."

"I will do my utmost, but I can promise you right now that Korda will take care of it."

"It's really very kind of you," he said, and left my cell.

The next day I went free, and when I told Korda about my adventure with the wannabe-actor prison guard, he couldn't stop laughing, and he arranged at once to have a car sent to get the man from his night job at the prison to the studio to be an extra.

Soon my trial date was set. It turned out that the maximum sentence for the crime of overstaying a residency permit in Britain was a five-pound fine.

They took it seriously all the same. There was a judge (replete with a wig) and a prosecutor, and I even had a defense lawyer. Among my witnesses were the world-famous theatrical manager and impresario Charles B. Cochran and the three Kordas, all of whom were cross-examined and according to whom I was not an undesirable alien.

But there, too, was the Hungarian ambassador, who confirmed that until then he had been unable to renew my passport, for the documents attesting to my citizenship had been missing, but meanwhile there had been an unexpected turn of events: it had turned out that I was a citizen of Hungary, after all, for I had been born in Budapest, and every ancestor of mine had first seen the light of day in the aforementioned country.

Though I was exonerated, the sentence was unjust, given that I had in fact committed the crime by unlawfully residing in Britain.

I left the courtroom in triumph, all the more so because Maud was waiting there for me and congratulated me on my lucky release. That was an exaggeration, though, since Maud could not have been called my good luck.

More and more I suffered from being unable to live either with her or without her. In vain I swore to myself that I would break up with her once and for all: when she showed up I faltered, and it began all over again.

I recalled a little vignette I'd once written about a needle that rises up at a tailor's workshop and proclaims that it resents the magnet being the master of the place, that it will no longer put up with the fact that whenever the magnet moves, the needle has to race right over and stick to the magnet, seeing as how it's not the magnet, but the needle, that is the rightful master of the tailor's workshop, for without the needle there would be no tailor and no clothes.

Homesickness plagued me, too, though I knew my birthplace had never less been a home. Hungary had by now completely acquiesced to the Germans, and for all practicality it was no longer Hungary at all. And yet I yearned to go home all the same; for one thing, to finally free myself of this humiliating love affair, and then my parents, siblings, and friends were all back home. It would be best if we died together, I thought; these dive-bombers and the whole of this English war was not my cup of tea. But by then I already knew about the German death camps; I knew that not much good was awaiting me back home. I could have gone to America, too, where I wouldn't have had to start a new life but only resume the old one. But the thought of again living in America made me wilt. I had no desire to do so at all.

It turned out that war or no war, it was possible to go home, only that it was a bit complicated. The boat would take me to Calais, and from Paris I could fly home via Lisbon.

I bought the necessary tickets and informed Maud that I was traveling home.

"Did you buy a ticket for me, too?"

"Of course not. I was, after all, just explaining that it's mainly on account of you that I'm flying away from here, because I can't take your cheating."

"You're always joking. Surely you don't want to travel alone? Say, are there lots of foreigners in Hungary?"

"There, there are Hungarians. There you'd be a foreigner."

"You're joking again. I'm English—how can I be a foreigner?"

She thought Hungary was some British colony where there were natives, too, which nothing could be done about.

With considerable difficulty I talked her out of leaving along with me, whereupon we had a tender farewell and in short order I flew toward home. My trip was urgent, lest I miss the Auschwitz express.

I didn't miss it.

Twenty-Five

I ARRIVE HOME MORE OFTEN THAN I DEPART. BUDAPEST IS NO MORE. DIRTY FRED, THE CAPTAIN. FRIENDS DON'T CHANGE. I DIED IN LONDON; THE REST IS JUST AN ENCORE.

It always takes my breath away when, after a long absence, I see Budapest's Keleti Train Station again. Now, too, I struggled back tears as I laid my eyes on and embraced my family—my mother; my father; my little sister, Tusi; and my little brother, Gyuri, who was a doctor on the side, and not only a member of the family—and we headed home.

I took out a room in what is today the Béke Hotel and was then called the Britannia, on the third floor.

My brother-in-law, Gyula, who was seventy percent goodness and just thirty percent an in-law, helped me with my move and supplied me with all sorts of fatherly advice, summing up the terrible world into which I'd been swept.

My friends, who did not know Maud, barely concealed the fact that while they were happy to have me back, they saw me as a bit foolish for having abandoned England in these grim times and, not even turning my eyes on America, returning to this hell. Not even they knew that the real hell was still ahead of them.

Despite the ever-spreading war I learned that on the day after my departure the Germans bombed the very building in London where I'd lived. There was no basement, and the bombing happened at three in the morning, when everyone was home, and not one among the residents survived.

Fate is unpredictable.

In the Japan Café I found my old friends: Ella Gombaszögi, Sándor Hunyadi, Pista Lukács, and the rest. Jenő Rejtő was writing baldly and diligently on the marble table. He had no apartment; he was at the Japan Café night and day, and there he wrote his masterpieces, such as *Dirty Fred, the Captain*, and every time he wrote a few pages, he raced over to Nova Press and asked for an advance of a few pengős from Dávid Müller, owner of this book publishing company. He then raced over to the Poge, a secret roulette den. There he quickly lost his money and then went back to write some more.

"Come with me," I said. "I'll get you a room in the hotel I'm living in."

He received my proposal indifferently, for he wasn't too enthused about my disturbing his amphetamine-driven lifestyle. (He took uppers to keep from sleeping.) But he agreed, and in no time he'd moved in.

Fortunately, the move didn't take long, since he had no belongings. He was a no-frills sort who bought a new set of clothes only when the one he was wearing shed and shredded off him.

At night we went home together. His room was on the second floor, and there talked for a long time, and then I went up to my room to read and sleep.

A half-hour later I realized with dismay that getting soap these days in Budapest was impossible, and that I'd left Jenő there without soap. He'd wake up in the morning and would be unable to bathe! Horrible. Quickly I threw on my robe and went downstairs to Jenő's room with a few bars of beautiful English soap in hand. I knocked quietly; there was no answer. I pressed down on the door handle. The door was unlocked. Rejtő evidently wasn't afraid of burglars. Nor was he fussy about how he slept: there he lay on the sofa, in his shoes. Naturally his clothes were still on him, his coat carefully buttoned up, as appropriate. He had been asleep, but he awoke to the noise.

"Forgive me, my dear Jenő, but I forgot to give you soap. It occurred to me only now, so I brought it down."

"You've gone mad! To wake up a man for such nonsense!"

I could write for *Pest Daily*, but only as a freelancer, for there was now a Jewish law about this, too. At the literary weekly *New Times* an editor, József Fodor, received me warmly.

"I'm happy, my dear Pali, that you came home, but I don't know if you can work here with us, since according to the decree …"

"Yes, I've heard about it. Let's go in to His Grace."

'His Grace' was Ferenc Herczeg, editor-in-chief of *New Times*, whom I was very fond of even though he was a member of the upper house of Parliament and the rumor was that he was a friend of the regent and head of state, Miklós Horthy. It was also said that he wrote Horthy's speeches, but if the gossip was true, he couldn't have been too busy, for Horthy spoke little and poorly, and rarely used Hungarian words, like *asztal* (desk) and *szék* (chair), he could barely pronounce. Yes, the curse of a German upbringing.

We went in to His Grace, who had more of a say in everything than did István Farkas, the owner and the exceptional painter who was later murdered by the fascists.

Fodor began to stammer.

"What this concerns, your grace, is that Királyhegyi has returned from London, and, well, because of this though he is now home, isn't he because of this it is now the case that …" He floundered the sentences more and more until I helped out.

"What this concerns is whether I can write for *Új Idők*, like before, insomuch as how I count as a Jew, though my mother is a Jew and so is my father, and I suspect that my grandfather is as well."

Ferenc Herczeg pondered.

"A Jew cannot write for *New Times* and never has." He proceeded to name several writers, Jew and not Jew, who had published in the weekly:

"Sándor Hunyadi, Jenő Heltai, Sándor Márai, and Kálmán Csató are all writers. The fact that someone is a Jew is not enough. But if Királyhegyi has written up to now, then he is a writer, and naturally he can continue to write."

Our audience with His Grace ended.

A few weeks later I met up with Ferenc Herczeg in the *Új Idők* building, in the hallway.

"Step into my office, please, right away," he said and strode forward.

I followed him in surprise, since he was not a sociable sort. We never spoke, and you weren't even supposed to speak with him; at most it was permissible to answer when he asked something.

It was a lovely summer. The window of Herczeg's office was wide open.

"The birds are chirping so beautifully," he began. I only nodded, signaling that as far as I was concerned they could chirp all day long, it didn't bother me.

A couple of minutes passed. Then there was knocking the door, and Timár, a staff member, looking panicked and upset, reported, "Your grace! Two detectives are here."

"I don't need even one of them," said Herczeg, and shut the door.

Later the knocking came again, and now Timár reported more calmly that the detectives had left the building.

It turned out that it had been a raid: they had been looking for Jews suspected of being writers.

News such as this, for example, appeared in the papers back then: "Károly Nóti, Béla Pásztor, and other individuals strongly suspected of screenwriting have been interned."

Herczeg had known there was a raid. He had called me into his office because he'd wanted to save me, and he knew they wouldn't dare go into him.

New Times was very gallant, for it paid fifty pengős for a short story while *Theatre Times* paid just twenty.

I also worked for the periodical *Cosmopolitan Novels*, since it paid two hundred pengős for a novella, and Miklós Faragó, the publisher, always threw in at least an extra hundred. It was easy to write such a piece in a day, but you couldn't spend time ruminating or else you'd lose money on the deal.

For the time being we still lived, and every day we were at the Victoria Café, owned by the friendly and warm-hearted Oszkár Alter, and where temporarily poor writers and actors did not have to pay for dinner.

Some ten writers and actors were regulars in our company, including Ella Gombaszögi, but there were lots of tangential members as well.

Béla Reinitz, with his deep booming voice, stridently scolded the Nazis. After his invariable bellowing, though, he would then suddenly doze off. When he awoke, he started all over again.

I was very fond of Ernő Szép, too, who simply couldn't believe that what was happening could be true, and that the Nazis were behaving as befits fascists. He was jovial and he was bald, though in the back he still had a smidgen of hair. He combed that forward and slicked it down to give the impression that he had something to comb.

Though I was one of Ernő Szép's most fervent fans, I was troubled by this aggression he had committed on his hair.

"My dear Ernő," I would say, "why is it that you, who are so smart and so kind, force the issue with your hair? You know as well as anyone that you are bald. Anyone can have hair, it's not such a big deal. I don't understand why you seek to maintain this hopeless illusion."

Ernő Szép smiled meekly.

"If only I was just bald! But I'm bald, old, and Jewish! That's a lot for a man."

We held out hope every day, but from one day to the next the situation worsened. Meanwhile we moved our general headquarters to the Dunapark Café, this at the request of Zoltán Egyed, editor-in-chief of *Film–Theatre–Literature*. He loathed Horthy, Szálasi, and the Nazis vocally and unabashedly, for which they then took him off to Bergen-Belsen, too, but by virtue of some miracle he survived, dying only after the liberation, at the age of fifty, in his sleep.

Pista Lukács was the only one who sometimes asked me, "So, what's with dear little Maud? Has the pain from your wound dulled?"

I had so many other troubles that the wound no longer hurt at all. It was harder and harder to make money, and ever more often I borrowed twenties from my dear brother-in-law, Gyula.

As if I didn't have enough troubles already with the fascists and Hitler, one odious, slippery February day I broke my leg! To this day I don't know how it could have happened, for I'd been pulling myself up onto a tram when I slipped on the platform.

My younger brother the doctor had me taken to the hospital, where the chief physician, Ferenc Czeyda-Pommersheim, also a noted professor, took charge of my care. I listened as my brother conferred in Latin with Czeyda-Pommersheim, and understood at once that my broken leg had to be amputated. My first thought was that this wasn't such a big deal, for I type with my hands, and I'd still have one leg left with which I could do all sorts of things. Then it turned out that I didn't know Latin, that this wasn't about amputation at all. They just set my leg in a cast and had me taken over to a sanatorium.

My friends visited me sedulously in the hospital. Even Countess Margit Bethlen, editor-in-chief of the weekly *Holiday*, came by, bringing with her the thousand pengős they owed me. Needless to say, the paper didn't owe me a thing.

By May, when the German hordes marched into Hungary, I was given an ambulatory cast and, even if I couldn't walk, I could hobble along. But the Germans were carrying out raids even in hospitals, and so my little sister, Tusi, came in to get me, along with my angel of a brother-in-law, and take me away from the hospital, for the Germans were not fond of the sick. True, they weren't fond of healthy people, either.

I rented a room downtown on the first floor of a building at 1 Pozsonyi Street from Mrs. Ullman, a widow. In the same building lived the poet Miklós Radnóti. We often met, but back then I didn't have much of a clue as to what a monumental genius my residence had brought me together with.

Twenty-Six

Minor inconveniences, but that's quite enough. Are the Germans human beings, and are the Hungarian fascists Hungarian?

In terror I sat up in bed. My heart began beating wildly. A cold sweat broke out over my forehead. Someone out in the corridor was ringing the bell to our flat. It was 9 AM on July 20, 1944, so the ringing could not mean anything good.

I lived in a yellow-star house, where at such a time we could have no visitors, because we could go out to the street only at 11 AM. All of us knew that ever since Hitler came to power, we were sentenced to death, only the time and method of execution was uncertain.

But the fear was not constant. Soon it turned out that it was impossible to be afraid all the time, without interruption, for too long. The terror came in waves, and was regularly sparked by some external event or rumor.

Life in the yellow-star house was not merry. By then they'd deprived us of all employment opportunities, and most of us got by on begging or under-the-table work. Writers had the best deal, relatively speaking: they could write under pseudonyms, while actors could not act wearing pseudobeards in their theaters. And then, after March 19, 1944, all life ceased.

Like some heavy, wrathful fog, terror sat hard and numbingly over the country. Everything was prohibited.

The bell rang again, long and determined. *Someone wants to come in.* I didn't have the strength to budge.

Again the ringing, but I didn't open the door. I recalled the German officer at the Britannia Hotel.

When I got home from London, I didn't have a flat in Budapest, so I went to stay temporarily at the Britannia. By then Budapest was full of Germans, with the hotels occupied mostly by them. Indeed, even on the fourth floor of the Britannia, next to my room, there was a German officer, a comely, six-foot-seven young man I often met in the elevator, in the lobby, and in the hallway. I looked at him as if he were a handful of worms, and I would have most gladly strangled him, but I stood barely as tall as his waist.

I usually got home late at night, and as I went by his room I always met with his boots, which were placed out front of the room in lovely German tidiness. The boots were as high as my neck, and were held together up top by a practical belt. I hated these boots and would most gladly have clipped their ears.

One evening I drifted home very late. It must have been three in the morning. Once again the boots were shamelessly standing there completely in the flesh in front of the German officer's door. We had a staring contest. I locked my eyes on the boots from quite close, and it turned out that no matter how enormous they were, they could be lifted with a finger all the same.

Everyone was fast asleep in the hotel. I picked up the boots and headed off with them. I went down to the second floor, looked for the bathroom, and stuffed the boots into the toilet. They were very tall, and in vain did I press the leg part down, so they'd get rumpled up, in vain did I flush several times, the boots simply didn't want to flow down.

In any case, they did lose lots of their original luster. They were now rumpled and sad, and seemed quite forlorn, when I finally left them there to their fate.

By the next morning I'd completely forgotten my little escapade with the German boots, but when I handed over my key at the reception desk on my way out, the chief porter said, "Editor, sir, something awful happened last night."

"What?"

"Sir, a German officer lives here with us. This officer needed to report this morning in an important military matter, and he couldn't find his boots. He had only this one pair, which vanished from in front of his door, where he's put them every evening for cleaning.

"Interesting. Well, and has the thief turned up?"

"No. They didn't steal the boots. That's precisely what's interesting about this. We searched the whole hotel, and at around eleven in the morning we found the boots, half drowned, in one of the toilets."

"Well now, then there's no trouble," I replied ruefully.

"Well, it so happens there is trouble, because the officer is raising a big stink about it. The boots were soaking wet—he couldn't get them on—and he demanded that we catch the perpetrator."

"But why are you telling this to me?" I asked, sensing trouble.

The porter gave an awkward smile.

"Because, sir, you were the last person to arrive home last night, and I thought …"

"You thought what?" I interrupted him combatively.

"I thought you might have seen someone, sir, who took the boots to where we found them."

"I didn't see anyone. Besides, I'm absentminded, and so many shoes and boots are put out in front of doors at night that I don't even notice if one is missing. What's more, I live on the fourth floor."

"That's where the boots disappeared from, which is why I asked you, sir, if perhaps you knew something."

"I don't understand this at all. Who would have wanted to take the boots if not to steal them?"

"Oh," the porter said with a wave of the hand, "lots of people don't like the German officer, and someone probably meant it as a bad joke, but we told the officer not to put his boots out again, since the hotel cannot accept responsibility for them."

"Well, then it's all set," I said, and left the porter there in his woe.

I'd completely forgotten the matter when, a few days later, the German and I arrived at the elevator together.

"How are you?" I asked amiably to throw off suspicion, and I gave the blighted boots on his feet a cursory glance.

The German mumbled something as the elevator took us up, and then we headed together down the hall. When we got to his room, he invited me in for a cognac. Yielding to irresistible compulsion I went in, but I only pretended to be drinking while he drank a whole lot and seemed to be in a bad mood.

We started to talk. It turned out that his name was Hans Müller and that he wasn't a real German, but Austrian, a Viennese toy merchant.

I was a bit relieved.

"Are you married?"

This simple question made the six-foot-seven officer tear up. I couldn't believe my eyes.

"Did your dear wife die?" I inquired eagerly.

"She didn't die. Her name is Ursula. She's healthy and she's lovely. Here is her picture."

The photo showed a strikingly pretty, young blond woman with a mischievous smile.

I looked upon the picture for a while, and then declared:

"Well, then nothing is the matter."

"Sure there is. I adore Ursula and I haven't seen her for more than a year already. Here I am in Budapest; I could fly home to her in Vienna in minutes, but I can't. I've been all over the world in the past year, just not Vienna. And then I hate this uniform, which has ruined my life. I see the hatred in people's eyes when they look at me, because they think I'm the same sort of German as the rest, and everywhere in the world they hate us, with a never-ending hatred burning hot like white coals in a fire. How can I explain to them that I too am bit a victim, that I can't help a thing, that it's not me who sought this horror; how can I explain to these strangers that I too have had all this up to my neck?

"They may hate you people, but at the moment the Germans still have the advantage."

The officer wove a tired hand.

"Force is not strength. They hate us, and all of us will perish in this sea of hatred. Here, for example, are my boots."

"Excuse me?"

"My boots. Nowadays I don't dare put them out front of my door for cleaning. They hate my boots, too, like some terrible symbol. I don't dare leave them on their own, since someone will spit into them or pour soup or scraps of leftover food into them, and one time recently they disappeared altogether. I was in despair. I had to appear that day at military headquarters, and a soldier can't be late, can't cook up excuses like a kid in school. I kicked up a row all over the building and finally, after turning the place upside down, they found them, terribly late and in lamentable condition."

"Sure," I said with a nod, "they were soaking wet."

The German suddenly looked up.

"How do you know?"

"The porter told me. He grilled me, too, asking if I'd seen anyone lurking about near the boots."

"If only I knew who the crackpot was who descended to this."

"It was me."

In that moment, when I pronounced those fateful words, I already regretted it and would have gladly sucked them right back into myself, but it was too late. *Will this German simply shoot me on the spot?* I thought. *He's an officer and a pilot, after all, so he doesn't have to account for corpses.*

The officer cast me a horrified stare.

"You fool, how could you have done such a thing? You couldn't have known who I am, after all. How could you have risked such a thing?"

"I hated those boots," I countered.

"Don't you worry, I won't make trouble, for I understand you, but from now on, be careful: the Germans don't know mercy in such matters."

We talked for a good while yet, reassuring each other that the whole thing couldn't last much longer and that soon there would again be peace on Earth.

The next morning the Viennese toy merchant left the hotel. I never saw him again. He took his boots, too.

Three terrible years had passed since then, the war was still underway, and perhaps it would last forever. . . .

The bell rang again. I limped out to the front door with my cast-bound leg and resolutely opened the peephole.

It was just the mailman who'd been ringing so aggressively.

He was delivering an SAS draft notice, which meant only that I had to report immediately for labor service. The conscription calmed me down. Fortunately, my leg was not in fighting condition, so for the time being I didn't have to fear the army. And maybe by tomorrow the world would change.

The call-up was for the town of Jászberény, on the plains east of Budapest, but I knew that those unfit to travel had to report in Budapest, at the city's command headquarters.

A completely Christian and very friendly, decent, and obliging young man named Szabó lived along with me in the Pozsonyi Street flat at Mrs. Ullmann's. This young man offered to drag me over to the headquarters.

When we finally arrived, I saw that I wasn't alone. The lame, the blind, imbeciles, and the crippled were teeming about in large numbers in the hall outside the office of Lehel Szűk, physician and lieutenant colonel, abject terror on each of their faces.

After waiting impatiently, I found myself in front of the lieutenant colonel's high rank insignia. He was a kindly man, though notwithstanding his ancient Hungarian name he spoke Hungarian poorly. He examined me at length, and then pronounced the sentence:

"Unfit to travel. You must go to Jászberény and there you will be demobilized."

I was taken aback.

"Excuse me, but if I'm unfit to travel, then how should I travel to Jászberény?"

The lieutenant colonel was no longer paying me attention, but had called on the next patient.

I staggered out of the building. I had to travel immediately. Thanks to Szabó, who accompanied me, I somehow managed to wriggle up onto the train. Out of heightened caution I didn't take my backpack. I'd never even had a mess kit. All I had was a little valise, lovely and light, which I'd brought with me from London. Of course Szabó carried this as well, since I couldn't manage to take even myself.

The train was jam-packed with the blind, the deaf, dwarves, imbeciles, and other soldier-designates unfit to travel. With heavy hearts we bumped along toward Hatvan, the first big town east of Budapest. That's where we had to transfer, which would not yet have been a problem, except that a frequent fixture at the station there was one Márton Zöldy, a captain with the gendarmes, who amused himself by rounding up the demobilized and traveling forced-laborers, and shooting them dead.

Fortunately, owing to another engagement, Zöldy happened not to be at the Hatvan train station, so the transfer unfolded without a hitch. The Jászberény train pulled into its destination at eleven at night. We hobbled into the nearby tavern, whose floor, however, was already jam-packed with recumbent conscripts, leaving not an inch to spare.

A young Gypsy man proposed to push me for twenty pengős to another hotel, which was a half-hour by wheelbarrow from the station.

I signed the guy on immediately, and from some place or other he conjured up a wheelbarrow, sat me inside it, and got two Gypsy kids, who supported me on both sides, to make certain I wouldn't fall out of the vehicle, and we headed off toward the hotel.

After a half-hour of bumping along we arrived. Szabó hurried into the hotel, whence, looking sad, he soon returned.

"There are no rooms and there's nowhere to lie down. Every corner is packed with people waiting for enlistment."

The rain began to fall. The Gypsy man was feeling bored.

"Please get out, sir. We've arrived."

"It's true that we've arrived, but you said there would be a room here."

"I said that because there usually is. But now there isn't."

Well, that was true. I was all set to get out of the wheelbarrow when suddenly something occurred to me.

"Say, son, is there a brothel around here?"

"Two of them, in fact," he boasted.

"Well then, drive there."

"OK, but that's thirty pengős, since it's late already."

"Alright."

We set out again, and after a forty-five-minute drive we arrived in front of an aging house. The wood shutters were rolled down. No signs of life.

Szabó knocked on one of the shutters. After a while of doing so, the front door finally opened, and a disheveled, sleepy, grumpy old woman called out into the Jászberény night.

"Who is it, and what do you want?"

"We're travelers, and we'd like to inquire," I replied.

"That's why you wake up someone at night?"

"It's a very important matter. How much does it cost for someone to sleep here?"

"We don't serve Jews."

"I'm not Jewish, and my friend is completely Christian."

"Would it be for a short time?"

"Just for a night."

"Well, then go take a look at the gal in that room, though she's sleeping at the moment."

"Oh, I wouldn't want to wake up the little lady for the world. I'd just sleep here for the night along with my friend."

The madam was incensed at this debauchery.

"Well, what do you think this is here, some hotel? Get the hell out of here."

The rain was pounding down ever harder. I risked it:

"I'd devote a hundred pengős for the night."

"Please step in!" came the woman's now mellow voice. (The mysteries of a woman's heart!) She assigned us a little room with a thin sofa, a chaise longue, which was made for just one person. Fortunately, my friend Szabó was thin like me, but even so, it was more just lying there than it was sleeping we did until five-thirty in the morning, when Szabó headed out to find a one-horse carriage to get us to the draft office.

First we went to the coffeehouse to have breakfast, since it was my monomania that enlistment before breakfast was not a healthy thing. But in the coffeehouse we were met with an unpleasant surprise. The head waiter stated politely but flatly that he couldn't serve Jews.

"I'm not Jewish, besides which, my friend is Christian."

"If you are not Jewish, sir, then why are you wearing a yellow star?"

"This is the latest fashion in Budapest," I said obstreperously. "A lovely color. It's been very popular, lots of people wear it."

"Alright, come with me," he said, and led us into a little room, where we received an excellent tea.

After breakfast we drove to the barracks, where it turned out that the enlistment wouldn't be happening just yet.

"You've got to wait, but no one knows when the doctors are coming," so a kindly foot-soldier summed up the situation for us. Then he added, "In the army, time does not count."

After ten hours of waiting I began to get fidgety. There was no room, only on the ground in front of the barracks, and that's where we stood or sat, and waited. Around six in the evening we decided that nothing would happen that day, and so we drove back to the brothel, where the madam, hoping for another hundred, received us with effusive pleasure.

Again we bargained for another night, on the same old terms. Never has anyone passed a less pleasurable night in a house of pleasure than me with my broken leg during my enlistment at Jászberény.

The next afternoon around four o'clock, Szabó reported, gasping for breath, as I sat on a bench a half-hour's limping from the barracks, that the enlistment had begun.

After several hours of angst, standing in line, and swearing, I wound up in front of the honorable regimental doctor, who, after examining me, allowed me six months' furlough.

Hitler himself hadn't climbed so triumphantly off the Eiffel Tower after capturing Paris as triumphantly as I reported at my little sister, Tusi's place, where the whole family was already awaiting me, saying I'd dodged it for the moment, and in those grim times every moment counted.

I was a free as a bird. Of course, it wasn't as if this freedom was complete. One could only be out walking the streets from eleven to five, and even then it wasn't advisable. People were jostled on trams, in telephone booths, everywhere. Working was prohibited. So was listening to the radio. And talking on the street was perilous, since it was easy to get arrested for spreading rumors.

Moreover, the six months' furlough lasted four days, since four days later I got another call-up, this time to Gödöllő, north of Budapest.

Again Mr. Szabó and I went to see Dr. Lehel Szűk, who again said I was unfit to travel, and so I had to go to Gödöllő, where I would be demobilized.

According to the call-up notice, I had to report at the barracks early in the morning, at eight, and all my life I'd hated waking up early. Laziness: half the secret of health. Amid such conditions we arrived at one in the afternoon in Gödöllő, equipped with divine medical records and a broken leg.

Even at the station it was announced that it would be best if we turned right back, since the enlistment for the day was over, it was a Saturday, and that in the best-case scenario my turn would come only on Monday.

Out of extreme caution, however, with great difficulty I limped my way from the station to the school that had been turned into a barracks.

A few steps short of the school, a young lieutenant came toward me and said, "Sir, it is evident that you are ill. The enlistment is over. We are not accepting new candidates. I see that you have no military gear at all, and you'd have to sleep here on the ground for perhaps three days. Please go in to the barracks and tell the sergeant that Lieutenant Pálosi orders that you be examined immediately and allowed to go home. I am Lieutenant Pálosi."

"I thank you very much, sir," I said, not believing my ears that it was possible to talk to a force-labor candidate in such a humane, kind tone of voice. This angelic lieutenant, who was also a remarkable lawyer, became head of the Pálosi council after the liberation. Pálosi's order was a big success. Within moments I was in front of a doctor, again I was found unsuitable for military purposes, and again I received—this time from Gödöllő, too—an order to report to the Budapest garrison hospital, that I should have myself examined there, and that I should then report again in Gödöllő with the medical finding.

I was happy. Again I'd won time. But winning was never my strong suit, so I reported at the garrison hospital only three days later, where after a long wait I was examined, and received the finding in a sealed envelope.

I opened the envelope and read the doctor's note, which stated that my broken leg had healed and that I was fit for light service. At home I tore this finding to shreds, threw it away, and awaited developments.

But what happened was completely different than what I'd prepared for.

Twenty-Seven

HORTHY LAYS DOWN HIS ARMS. SZÁLASI PICKS THEM UP AGAIN. ÉVA LOVES ME, AND SO DOES BROTHER SURÁNYI, BUT SEVERAL PEOPLE HAVE ALREADY DIED OF THE LATTER.

In these troubled times Éva was my every pleasure in life. She had red hair and snow-white skin, like all true redheads, and I loved her. Unfortunately, by then the miscegenation law had long been in fashion, and Éva was Christian from head to toe, while I, even if I was a bit of a Protestant, counted as a fully legitimate Jew. Amid such circumstances, then, our every meeting was perilous, because on account of Éva, even in the best-case scenario I would have gotten three years in prison. Even so, we met daily, until one day Éva said:

"Hey, what would you say to marrying me?"

"You know full well that's impossible."

"It's not at all impossible. I'll convert to Judaism, and then it will be allowed."

"It would be madness to convert now, when, it seems, they're angry with this religion, which, according to them, isn't even a religion, but a race."

Éva waved a hand.

"It can't be a race, since the law says even those people can be Jewish whose relatives are all Christians but who belongs to the Jewish religion at the moment."

"That's possible, but you surely you can't imagine I'd let someone I love come over to the Jews now, when that doesn't seem at all promising? I wouldn't even wish it upon my mortal enemy to be a Jew nowadays."

A big argument ensued. Éva stuck to her position stubbornly, and finally she said, "If something bad happens to you, I don't want to live, either."

The next day I went to Grossmann, the rabbi, and asked: would it be possible for him to help someone over to the Jewish religion?

The rabbi wagged his bearded head reproachfully.

"What sense would that make?"

"That the individual is Christian, and I'd like to take her as my wife."

The rabbi's bad mood intensified.

"Why don't you find yourself a Jewish girl?"

"Forgive me, dear Mr. Rabbi, but I didn't come for spiritual counseling, just to get an expert's advice on how such things work. There are people who first fall in love, and only then look around to find out what religion the individual is. Perhaps they don't even look around."

"Well, excuse me, but conversion isn't so easy. Ours is not a proselytizing religion. If an individual has serious intentions, she must study for three months with someone who will introduce her to the mysteries of the religion. And then she must take a test, and she can be a Jew only when we see that she has serious intentions."

I managed to get into a scrap with the rabbi in no time, and I left the place happily.

"I'd rather spend sixty years in prison than argue with this rabbi," I told Éva.

"This madness can't last for much longer, anyway," Éva consoled me. "Sound-minded people will rule the world, and then no one will stick their noses into why we love each other."

But the situation kept getting worse. Rumors mushroomed. It was hardly possible to even go out on the streets. Under a new decree you could only go outside to bathe, shop, or go to a doctor, and even that for just two hours a day. This humanity was maddening, that allowed Jews—who had openly been sentenced to death—to "bathe" and to "undergo medical treatment."

Most people didn't even budge from their flats, for they hated the yellow star and feared stepping out into the street. Meanwhile I'd moved from Mrs. Ullmann's and gone home to my parents, lest strangers be moved into their flat. Beyond that, this flat was also officially a doctor's office, since my younger brother was a doctor. In those days, he'd been ordered to be a National Health Insurance Institute doctor in Soroksár, just south of downtown Budapest, so only the office was left of the doctor's office at home, since the doctor lived in Soroksár.

The doctor's office carried the unheard-of advantage of Éva being able to visit me a lot, since though a Christian was not allowed to marry a Protestant, she could drop by a doctor's office if she suddenly fell ill on the street.

Otherwise life generally comprised our being afraid, waiting for deportation, and listening to the BBC. Everything was punishable by death, prison, or deportation, anyway, so it mattered not at all what one was up to.

In the building our every bit of amusement derived from going down to the ground floor each evening after supper to be in fear there, where Mrs. Hirschfeld lived with her sixteen-year-old son, Tamás. Her husband was a forced-laborer, so the kid temporarily held the post of head of household. He walked the streets without a star, risking his life, even during curfew, and brought home the news.

Fortunately, Tamás was friends with the son of the building caretaker, so the danger was less, because Tamás didn't have to fear the caretaker, whom the rest of the residents dreaded.

Among the residents usually on hand for the evening gatherings was Mrs. Seres, from the second floor. She was an intelligent young woman without illusions whose husband was likewise a forced laborer.

The third woman was Panni, who had a lovely four-year-old girl, Zsuzsika, and whose husband was also a forced-laborer, somewhere in

Transylvania. Panni had been moved in with her mother. That unpleasant old woman alone stirred up almost as much trouble as the German occupation, but Panni endured the blow heroically. Shivering with fear both hopelessly and with hope, she sought out the spirits for advice. Via table-rapping and other methods, she communicated with the forces in the world beyond, of whom she would invariably inquire when her husband would come home and how long the war would last. She also often asked the spirits if there would be deportations in Budapest, but the forces in the world beyond always gave an evasive answer to this question.

We'd just been talking about this one evening, quietly, behind lowered shutters, and I conjured up every bit of eloquence I had to explain to my companions how unimaginable this was.

"First, the Pope won't allow it, and beyond that, the Swedish king himself has intervened, besides which, the Germans have other things to worry about these days, and there are no trains, no locomotives, and no people for this purpose."

I already felt I'd managed to reassure the coterie when all at once Panni shrieked loudly and hugged her Zsuzsika tight.

"Did you all hear? Horrible."

We listened in petrified silence. Everyone held back their breath. Outside, the street was completely lifeless. The noise came again. It was as if someone was knocking on the window. I glanced at my watch. Eleven o'clock. It was unimaginable that under normal conditions someone would want to come in at this hour. The knocking could not have meant anything good. We stood there as pale as death, listening, our nerves on edge. Panni's fears were generally unreliable, as they didn't always have gold reserves to back them up. Not long before, one evening the shutters rattled, and Panni harried everyone into a panic, but now I myself heard a dull, ominous noise that did sound like knocking.

I went over to the window to listen. We quickly turned off the light. The knocking came again, louder, forbiddingly, but not from the direction of the window. Panni suddenly broke into a smile.

"It's mother. It must have been her knocking to signal that she's had enough of the talking, that I should go home, she's getting antsy."

"May God strike your mother," I said gently. "She's got to be told not to go knocking at night, because we're nervous."

The next afternoon the electric clock on Pozsonyi Street read one minute past five when an enormous man waved me over to him. I waved back to signal that I'm in a hurry, at which the unfamiliar gentleman stood in my way.

"Round-up," he said, and showed me his detective's badge.

"I'm Jewish. I'm in a hurry, so unfortunately I don't have the time to deal with the round-up, since I have to get home by five."

"It's too late to go home," he said politely. "We're having a round-up to nab those Jews who were out past five."

I looked around and saw those who'd already been caught and detectives who were watching the street with unflagging zeal, catching yet more yellow-starred men and women one after another.

The detective waved a hand for me to follow him.

"Sir," I offered, "it's only just five o'clock, and there hasn't been any trouble."

"It's already too late. That's it."

We headed off. The detective didn't seem hostile, but pitiful. I took the risk.

"Look, sir, you don't know what an unpleasant place you want to take me to, me, who is, when it comes down to it, innocent. From what I can tell, you don't know Dad."

"What dad?"

"My dad. He doesn't like it if I stay out late, nor does he like it when I'm arrested. At least let me run home to let him know to stay calm, there's no trouble, I've only been arrested. You know, nowadays the world is such that dads are anxious."

"I don't care about your dad."

"But he's a very interesting man," I persisted while limping along more slowly. "Even these days he treats me like a little kid. Go ahead and take me in, have me interned or deported. Believe me, I don't care—it's not as if life is merry here these days, anyway—but allow me to first tell my dad."

"Keep your mouth shut. If I were to let you go, someone else would arrest you all the same, since there's a round-up underway."

"I was thinking you might be so kind as to accompany me home, as a detective, come upstairs with me, tell Dad what happened, and then ..."

"Where do you live?"

"Here, by Saint Stephen Park."

We headed off. I knew Dad, and I knew he wouldn't be at all relieved if I showed up in the flat with a detective to report that I'd been arrested, but maybe it would be better this way all the same than if I were to vanish without a word, leaving him there in uncertainty.

"Thank you for your kindness," I said to the detective. "I don't envy your occupation, either, these days."

"Well, but it's better for me than for you."

"I'm not so sure. I'd rather be a Jew caught because he dared to still be on the streets at five than a detective who sends folks to their deaths on account of this."

The detective became downcast.

"Well, you have a point there, you know. Most of us get drunk before setting out on this sort of work, because we too think this nonsense is rotten stuff. It was better before. A man would catch a murderer or a burglar, and then he could slap and interrogate his heart out, since he knew it was about tough stuff. But these Jews, just because they're out walking, it's revolting, it is, but a man's got to make a living somehow."

"I saw right away that you're not like the rest of them. You seem to be a decent man."

We got home.

"Well," I said, "God bless you. I don't want to keep you. I'll go on home now, tell Dad the whole thing, and it would be kind of you if you didn't wait for me. Maybe someone will catch me on another round-up, but for today, at least, let me out of going to the detention center."

The detective went off without a word, and for a while I watched him, with love.

The next morning at nine the doorbell rang. The letter carrier, a young woman, was delivering a call-up notice. She was looking for Pál Királyhegyi.

"You have to sign it," she explained.

"Pál Királyhegyi reported for duty a while back in Gödöllő. How is it, then, that you want him to be in Jászberény too?"

The young lady letter-carrier wasn't interested in the details. She simply wrote on my Jászberény call-up notice, "Already reported," and she left.

The city was awash with frightening rumors, and every rumor seemed true. The Germans had occupied the country. We were all trembling in fear, waiting for a summons to SS headquarters in the Buda hills in the matter of death.

At our evening gatherings we tried to raise each other's spirits, but we no longer paid attention to even our own words.

On a certain day I unsuspectingly went to lunch at my little sister's, and on arriving, I saw that the whole building was aflame, as it were, with excitement. Horthy had laid down his arms! The war was over! No more yellow stars! "Long live Horthy!" came the shouts from both those who'd been moved here by the authorities and the building's native inhabitants. My brother-in-law was a forced laborer, working at United Light Bulbs, but he'd fled home, by chance on this very day. He was brimming with exuberance.

I had arrived together with my little brother, and on the street we saw German tanks four stories high. I couldn't really find it in my heart to be delighted about Horthy's address to the nation. When my little sister asked me what I was brooding about, I said, "Horthy laid down his arms, but the Germans will pick them up again."

Things couldn't go so smoothly. This was already the beginning of the end, but it was not yet the end. Many problems could yet arise from this laying down of arms. Why, in point of fact he had never really laid them down, since he'd never picked them up to begin with. Alongside the Germans, Hungarian arms had not counted for much.

And yet, despite every point of logic, the wave of joy carried me with it, too, in its throes, as on the way home I saw so many yellow stars on the streets and watched as a policeman went up to an old Jewish woman and cut the star off her with his sword. "You won't be needing this any longer," he said, beaming, and looked with satisfaction upon his sword, which until then had not been used to such ends.

That evening, as usual, we went down to Mrs. Hirschfeld's flat to discuss the events. Though in general the residents were enthusiastic, there were many still in fear over the fact that the Germans were in Budapest.

We soon learned that in fact the Germans were not asleep at the wheel, while Horthy had clumsily, ineptly laid down his arms. We learned also that Szálasi, this uninhibited, incorrigible madman lauded as symbolizing "lump-of-earth reality" and the "Great Hungarian Carpathian Motherland," and suffering from an unquenchable thirst for power, had assumed the reins of "power."

Everyone knew that Szálasi was but a puppet in the Germans' hands, but the situation seemed not a bit more reassuring as a result. We took solace in the fact that state radio kept announcing with feverish zeal that fascist-sympathizing Colonel General Károly Beregffy was being urgently sought for treason, but it was harder to take solace in the fact that the servants of the "lump-of-earth reality" began Jew-bashing in a tone that at times would have made even the Germans blush. Szálasi announced that he would "defend" the country from the Russians, exhorting us to persevere, and we certainly were in need of exhortation, seeing as how we were in sheer terror.

By then every sane person knew this was the beginning of the end, that the Germans had lost the war, but they knew also that it was not at all certain whether we would last to the end. While we didn't fret over how the Russians, the Americans, and the British would fare at the hands of Szálasi and his cohorts, it was easy to imagine that they could yet exterminate the unarmed Jews who'd already been tormented to death. The next day the building's front door was sealed off, and we had to sew the yellow stars back on. Those who had some food at home, ate, and those who didn't, went hungry.

After three days of this house arrest, we understood that we had been sentenced to death definitively and irrevocably, only that we weren't clear on the method of execution. Perhaps they wanted to starve us to death, and perhaps the reason we couldn't go out on the street was so the murderers could comfortably occupy the yellow-star houses and not have to worry that at the time of the murders some resident would not be at home. Éva, risking her life, loitered about our building, passing bread, fruit, and other precious items into Mrs. Hirschfeld's ground-floor flat. After dark she could sneak packages in unnoticed.

Unverified reports came in that Jews were mounting armed resistance to the Germans and had killed a few of them. Then there was word of some attempted coup that had likewise been crushed, bloodily so. We knew nothing for certain, only that we were prisoners. The residents sought out each other every minute with fresh news, and the whole building was aflame with agitation as we waited day and night for the Arrow Cross fascists to arrive.

Given the circumstances, I was not surprised when one morning at 5:30 the doorbell rang. *Well then*, I thought, *now everything will soon be over.*

When I opened the door I nearly rejoiced on seeing not unfamiliar murderers but instead only the building's familiar caretaker, who said that there was no problem but that I should get dressed immediately, because the Arrow Cross was taking every man between fourteen and seventy to work. The building had already been occupied by the Arrow Cross and the police, and I had to report for line-up downstairs in the courtyard. Everyone should take along five days' provisions.

For days we hadn't been allowed to go out on the street, so the vast majority of the residents didn't even have enough food to last five minutes. But no one cared about that.

I got to packing.

I was the scion of a famous nonmilitary family; my father had never been a soldier, and nor had my mother or my grandmother, and so I didn't even have a knapsack or work boots, indeed I'd never even bought a mess kit, since I'd trusted that my broken leg was all the equipment I'd need until the end of the war.

My younger brother had some sort of leather jacket, so I put that on.

Mrs. Seres came over from her nearby flat and helped me pack. I'd bought my suitcase in London: it was a splendid, pigskin valise, a reliable British product I could not have imagined ever having to use for such a purpose. Ten minutes later, like a proper lamb, I was in line down in the courtyard, awaiting slaughter.

The Arrow Crossers consisted of a sole, shabby-looking, shivering but rifle-toting young man who in better times must have been a merry-go-round attendant at the city's amusement park. But a real policeman was also keeping "order," prodding the crying, sleepy, frightened people to hurry. The building's Christian residents came down, too, and looked sadly on at the assemblage.

We then headed off toward some suitable place of execution. This early morning procession along the empty streets was not too reassuring, nor could the sight of the rifle-toting Arrow Crosser, the merry-go-round attendant, calm me, and yet I felt liberation and almost joy on being able to be on the streets again: I'd escaped from prison, and no matter what would happen, at least the maddening uncertainty was over.

On the street there appeared ever more groups of Jews surrounded by Arrow Crossers and police, from which I could tell that this was no isolated round-up, but that every Jewish man was being taken somewhere. I was relieved not to see a woman anywhere, as it seemed they'd been let off.

After two hours of walking we arrived at the soccer stadium in Újpest, where an enormous crowd had already come together. Young men and boy with Arrow Cross armbands were keeping guard; miscreants blustered; sometimes a rifle went off in the untrained hands of a fourteen- or sixteen-year-old kid; commands crackled; and the executioner-lads herded the frightened horde toward some as yet unknown destination.

Time passed slowly into afternoon, and yet they didn't give even a bite to eat; for they had, after all, said in advance that everyone had to bring five days' worth of provisions. Night came. They had us line up in military order, and then had us lie down on the soccer field.

From the first minute on I hadn't been able to carry my splendid British valise, so the Lóránts gave me a hand so I'd have some belongings with me. There were two Lóránts. The father was a fifty-year-old onetime army captain with all sorts of decorations, and as such he was a "decorated officer"; and his son, the eighteen-year-old Pali—a strong, lovely kid who'd gone along the road with a dazed look—didn't understand any of it. Not even did we understand completely then just what this was about.

Among the building's residents, in the same line as us, came Pál Leszner, likewise a fifty-year-old man, a landholder, who had also fought in World War I as an army officer, and though he left his wife and two children at home, he complied with the commands without so much as a quibble.

Pál Leszner had everything he needed. Indeed, every last thing that a human mind could think of fit in his colossal backpack, and he even had a splendidly equipped portable "pocket bed," which he spread out on the ground and slipped into comfortably. It was waterproof and warm inside, offering lavish comfort. The rest of us lay down on our blankets and tried to sleep. On waking up after the night spent out in the open we learned that six people had committed suicide the previous night. Later on I often envied these foresighted men, who had chosen a quick death over long suffering.

At dawn, without breakfast or bathing, we headed off on the highway to Gödöllő.

Regular Hungarian Defence Forces men now took over the business from the Arrow Crossers, and under their supervision we marched onward. A plump, bald Jew fell out of line at the very start, at which a Defense Forces soldier gently shot him in the head, and on we went.

"This is an order," he said by way of explanation to a colleague of his, who grumpily adjusted the weapon on his shoulder.

"To hell with them all. These traitors caused the war."

My broken leg still wasn't working wholly satisfactorily, and because we had to go pretty fast, after a few hours I felt that I couldn't take it any longer. My leg was hurting and my throat was parched, my heart was beating wildly, and I had the feeling that my lungs would burst out at once, that I had to stop. But the Defense Forces gentlemen just prodded us on with their rifle butts, and I could still see before me that puddle of blood flowing from the fat man shot in the head. *If I have to collapse*, I resolved, *I'll wait to do so until I can't help it, but I'll go as long as I can stand it.* And mechanically I kept picking up my feet.

Right when the last shreds of my strength had deserted me, the Defense Forces gentleman ordered, "At ease," and then it was OK to lie down on the ground. But it wasn't advisable, since these breaks were short and our journey was hurried, not that we knew why, and then it was hard to get back up again.

The situation didn't seem at all encouraging, but the optimists hoped that they were only taking us for some work, since Szálasi himself had said in one of his radio addresses that during the war he would not allow the Jews out of the country, and that he would "solve" the Jewish question definitively only after the war. Lots of us believed this, including me, not because we imagined that Szálasi had suddenly gotten to like Jews, but because we figured that in bombed-out Hungary and Germany there weren't exactly enough trains for our deportation.

The first night found us on the edge of some village, and we had to lie down by a trench for the night. For my own part, I had never been so much of a nature lover to try this, but arguing was out of the question, so we tried sleeping while swaddled in blankets by the trench. One of the guards announced that anyone who tried to escape would be shot dead pending further measures, so we should watch ourselves.

I wound up in the same "room" as the Lóránts and Pál Leszner, which is to say, we lay next to each other in the cold night.

The next afternoon we arrived in Gödöllő, from where we went on yet again, without stopping, on a forced march, until we arrived in a village named Valkó, a few miles from Gödöllő.

When the exhausted group filed in to the village, the residents greeted us with tears. At first I didn't understand all the sympathy, but soon the mystery was solved. They were crying for Pál Leszner, not us, since the estate they were taking us to was his property, and all signs indicated that he was a good landlord, for the farmhands and other farm workers were fond of him.

One pretty young crying peasant woman wanted to press bread and a slab of roast bacon into Leszner's hand as we filed in, but the onetime master only thanked her and turned it away.

"Be careful, for you could get into trouble, too, for fraternizing with me," he whispered to the woman and waved her away.

By the time we arrived in Valkó, I no longer had anything to do with that wondrous machinery that is my body. I felt no part of my body, and never would I have believed that this degree of exhaustion existed.

They drove us into a barn of sorts that was already full of Gypsies. We could neither sit nor lie down, for there was no room on the ground. All we could do was stand about, without rest.

The space had no windows to keep the wind out, the mice were squeaking merrily, and the fleas were biting with wild enthusiasm. They didn't care that we were Jews. But exhaustion overcame the fleas, and so we soon fell asleep.

The next morning, we were awoken before dawn, at four, when it was still pitch-black outside. Breakfast, bathing, even a means of bathing were out of the question. Instead we got pickaxes and spades, which we put on our shoulders, before heading into the night.

By the time we had crossed the eight-kilometer, terrible road of gulches and slippery slopes to the workplace, it was eight o'clock, and everyone was so tired that they would have preferred to die. But there wasn't time for that.

A thieving murderer of an engineer named Lajkó received us, a rifle on his shoulder. An enormous, fat, strong man with a real gift for kicking and slapping, he encouraged us like this:

"My dear sons, may God make you all drop dead. Here you're going to toil or else you'll rot away alive. The good old days when you used to lounge around are over. I will assign the work, and you've got to do it. If you don't finish it on time, you'll stay as long as it takes for you to finish. None of you should come to me saying you're sick, because everyone's sick, but no one cares about that. Our Hungarian blood kin are fighting on the front, and you will croak right here, the whole filthy, foul lot of you."

I remembered that when I had worked at Paramount as a scene writer, the studio had a motivational speaker who, once or twice a month, would give pep talks to the writers, actors, and technical staff to encourage better work. This guy Lajkó fared with much greater success.

Lajkó designated the place, told us how deep the trench should be, a few specialists explained the work in more detail, and we got to work. I was so weary that I could hardly lift the spade. Pál Leszner and the two Lóránts worked without a word of complaint. The rest of them, too—Vilmos Lóránt, the director; and Dezső Bokor, the Váci Street book publisher—fell to work on the hard earth and dug the trench, which Mr. Lajkó was having us make to defend the homeland and stop the Russians.

It was here, at work, that I met up with Dezső Bokor for the first time since leaving Budapest, and I knew that his situation was far worse than mine, because he'd left his wife and two daughters behind in the Arrow Cross horrors. And yet throughout, through our whole period in Valkó, he endured that spade cheerfully, keeping a stiff upper lip amid pain that would have killed an average ox. He just worked and worked, trusting that he would survive.

I myself quickly stopped digging, since the matter seemed hopeless, and restricted myself instead only to slapping down the dug-up earth with my spade until it was flat.

Even this work was endlessly exhausting, boring, and pointless. I remember our building caretaker's reassuring words by our building door that unforgettable morning when the Arrow Cross dragged us away.

"There won't be any trouble, everyone will work at their own trade."

Well, this Lajkó did not look like someone intent on commissioning me to write a novel, and I didn't think I'd get even an itty-bitty article out of him.

We worked until dark, without a bite to eat, and then we were allowed to go. I feared the return trip more than I had the work. All day long we couldn't sit down even for a moment, because there was no room and they gave us no time. Not that we would have needed a lunch break, as we had no lunch. I couldn't imagine that it was possible to make this hazardous, muddy, slippery, odious journey twice in one day.

It seemed the Arrow Crossers knew better what a man can take, for even while struggling under the constant threat of death, even while slipping, tumbling about, and propping each other up, we still arrived, hungry and dead tired, in our trash can, which was, for the moment, our lodging.

At home, to the boundless delight of the fleas and mice, we fell asleep before we hit the ground.

We got no news from home, writing letters was prohibited on punishment of death, and in general everything under the sun was prohibited. I was allowed only to shiver from the cold in my thin, summer suit, which I'd flung on thoughtlessly back in Budapest.

After three days of filing out to the site, I decided to give up my rank and quit the job even if it meant being shot in the head, since I couldn't take the trek with that spade in hand, not to mention the work.

There was among us a kindly doctor, Dr. Földes, who had been dragged off like the rest of us, and who was authorized to grant one day off in serious cases.

On showing him my leg and explaining that not long ago it had still been broken, I got the day off, which I had to spend helping out Walter, the head chef, and Dobos, the assistant chef.

We got no food, so the work wasn't hard, though on the fourth day word had it that we'd get beans, and word also had it that someone would get hold of a pot from somewhere that we could use to cook for the battalion.

Remarkably enough, this rumor proved to be true. Indeed! On the fifth day we even got meat, beans, potatoes, coffee, jam, and bread. Many cried tears of joy, since they were starting to believe that we would be starved to death then and there.

But the delight was not to last, since along with the food there arrived the Arrow Cross "brothers," who took over command from the Defense Forces.

There were six brothers and Surányi, who was the "people's comrade." Each one wore a rifle and an armband, an unambiguous indication that they were members of the Hungarist Party. We feared the armbands more than we did the rifles, for it was evident that the rifles were a new toy to them, which they didn't quite know how to handle, though the armbands were deadly, since the sight of one could cause a heart attack. The Arrow Crossers chose an engineer, Tibor, as the "battalion commander," making him individually responsible for ensuring that all was in order with the battalion.

Poor Tibor lived in constant fear of death, and this fear gave him superhuman strength, even at the age of sixty, to endure both weariness and torture at the hands of the Arrow Crossers.

I almost felt sorry for these primitive, uncultivated, and incredibly feeble-minded Hungarists, drunk as they were on pleasure, on power, on their rifles, and on being the masters of life and death.

Brother Surányi waved over Tibor, the engineer.

"Youse take orders from me. Anyone who tries anything here is gonna get croaked, 'cause I'm gonna blow a hole right through 'em. In the Hungarist state, maggots gotta work. Shut up. Got that? Anyone who makes a peep gets croaked. Get to work, 'cause I can get nasty too. I'm a good man, but if something's up, I'll get all fiery, and that's that. Get lost, you mangy dogs!"

This speech was a big success, since lots of folks started hiccupping in horror.

It rained on the seventh day, and we didn't have to go out, and it was then that I decided that I would never again dig fortifications against the Russians no matter what. I told Lóránt that I'd talk with Surányi and ask him to give me another assignment, because I couldn't take the walking, especially after a rainy day, when even on dry days this godforsaken village had mud up to our waists.

"You've gone plain mad," said Lóránt. "You yourself can see that this is a beast just looking for an excuse to shoot someone dead. This isn't a human being. You can't talk to him. It's suicide to say a thing to him, and it's forbidden too."

I stepped over to Surányi, who was observing our work in the carrot field across from the barn.

"Brother Surányi," I said, "I can't come out here tomorrow. The thing is, my leg is broken, and besides, I'm still too small for digging, you're not getting much out of me anyway. What's more, I'm a phenomenal cook. So my request would be that you be so kind as to order that starting today, I work beside the chef as an assistant."

Surányi was in a good mood. He laughed.

"I'll let you do it. I can see that you're limping, you filthy Jew, so go be a chef. But if I hear a complaint about you, I'll shoot right through you. Get lost."

I stayed put.

"Say, Brother Surányi, what is your occupation in civilian life?"

"I'm a welder. But now every Hungarist's place is with his responsibility."

"What did you weld?" I pried.

Surányi forgot who I was, and he remembered who he was. He spoke at length about the mysteries of welding, and while I fortunately slept through it, my sole aim was to keep him talking, since I figured it would make him feel good if someone schmoozed with him about his trade.

Lovely days ensued, life became beautiful again. Vili Loránt, the director, escaped, and no one went looking for him. The food got a lot better. We were lodged in an L-shaped yard right next door to the peasants' houses. We slept in the barn behind the houses; the kitchen was out front in some ramshackle wood, village structure; and Walter, the brilliant little chef, acquired pots for cooking.

Moreover, one evening Pál Leszner asked me if I want chicken paprikash.

At first I thought he was kidding with me, but it fast became apparent that the chicken was serious; for the women of the neighborhood couldn't resign themselves to their master's unpleasant situation, and invited him and his closest friends each evening for a lavish dinner. At these dinners there was chicken paprikash, pastry, and all such earthly delights we could imagine, and instead of ration bread we got real, white, village bread. No longer did I have to march out to the work site, either, devoting my life instead to the chef's trade. *Surely the war will end soon,* I thought, *and until then we'll manage somehow, as long as Surányi and the others don't have other ideas.*

With the help of the peasant women we were able to send letters home, too, and got news from home as well. We learned that our loved ones were alive, and that meant more to us than anything. We too were alive, but unfortunately so were Surányi and the rest of them. But we regarded the latter as only temporary.

News spread that the sick would be taken home to Budapest on wagons to be examined, and if they really were sick, they could stay home for good.

"If I'm taken to Budapest to be examined," said a stationery merchant named Kondor, happily so, "no bad can come of it for me, that's for sure. I have optic nerve atrophy, and it's certain I'll go blind. This can be determined easily, and then I'll be a free man again. I feel sorry for you healthy fellows."

The mood was sanguine, and there was good news to be had even from the front, for we could already hear the rumbling of artillery off in the distance.

"Maybe just a few more days," we heartened each other, "and all this will be over with. Even if Germany holds out for a couple more weeks, no doubt the Russians will liberate us a lot sooner. They're almost here."

At three in the afternoon Surányi arrived with his six-member team.

"The sick should line up by the pigsty with all their gear—they're going home to be examined."

Kondor and the others were brimming with delight.

"You see?" said Kondor. "These are human beings, too. If someone is sick, they don't make him work." By way of encouragement he added,

"You come, too—with your broken leg they'll kick you out for sure." And hurried to the barn to gather his belongings.

Just then I happened to be peeling potatoes, and I didn't move. For one thing, I didn't trust the Arrow Crossers; for another, I was in no mood to go home. In actuality it couldn't properly even be called home, for, after all, what would I do there, in the locked-down building surrounded by streets crawling with Arrow Crossers? Here I could get through this, I figured, and maybe Valkó would be liberated before Budapest.

While I was pondering this, the sick—six of them—were already standing at attention, blissfully, in front of the pigsty, and as I glanced over, I saw the Arrow Crossers fling their weapons off their shoulders as Surányi began to speak:

"Mangy dogs! While our blood kin are fighting on the front, you want us to set up a sanatorium for you here? Dogs!" So he concluded his short speech. With that, the weapons crackled, and from up close several dozen shots were fired upon the sick.

Meanwhile I just sat there on the barrel peeling potatoes, not believing my eyes or ears, waiting to wake up from this nightmarish vision, thinking, *this can't be, this can't be true.*

Bleeding from several wounds, Kondor, the stationery merchant with optic nerve atrophy, kneeled down and begged the executioners, "I'm not sick, I got here by mistake! I want to work! Long live Szálasi! I'm healthy! Don't harm me, gentlemen!"

But he spoke to the murderers in vain. They just continued shooting, and Kondor fell completely silent. The vicinity of the pigsty was awash with blood.

Still unable to believe what I'd seen, I only kept peeling potatoes and looked at the dead men, who a minute earlier had been laughing and full of hope, indeed, they had been certain of freedom.

Dobos, the assistant chef, was shaking all over and his teeth were chattering as well.

"We're done for, we're done for, they'll shoot everyone dead, we've got to escape, we've got to hide in the cornfield, we've got to do something, good God, I'm diabetic, they'll find my syringe and insulin, they'll realize I'm sick, they'll shoot me dead, too, they'll kill everyone." He just kept it up until Walter, the hard and brave little chef, snarled at him: "Quiet. Stop shaking. They won't kill everyone. Not everyone will die. I have a wife I adore, and a little girl I love more than the world, and I'm still not afraid. It will work out somehow. If we've got to die, we'll die. There's no need for fear. Fear is worse than death."

Meanwhile I noticed in terror that a postcard belonging to little Pali Lóránt, the elder Pál Lóránt's son, was lying on the ground. Had the Arrow Crossers found that card, it would be all over for the Lóránt kid. Correspondence was punished with death. The postcard was smeared with blood, but the address was legible. Pali had written to his mother that he was always thinking of her, reassuring her that things would be better, and asked for food.

He'd given the card to Kondor to have him drop it in the mail in Budapest. If someone else were to have found it, I knew, the Arrow Crossers would shoot Pali Lóránt dead.

I tore the bloody postcard to tiny shreds and buried it along with Kondor.

That evening the Lóránts got home from work scared to death. Not only had they already heard of the murders, but they had also gotten word that Surányi and the rest of them had visited the other barns and farmsteads, too, and had executed the sick everywhere. They were afraid that the Arrow Crossers had found Pali's postcard and that it was all over with.

I could barely calm them down. I had to tell them a hundred times what Pali had written on the card before they finally believed me that I'd destroyed the evidence of the deadly sin.

The next day it rained. We didn't have to march out. Of course they still had the wake-up call at dawn, for they didn't want us to completely soften up from idling.

An order came that at eleven everyone had to line up in the yard with all their gear.

I figured the Arrow Crossers wanted to rob us, which they'd already done often with forced-laborers, and so I'd given most of my money, my cigarettes, my tobacco, and my cigarette paper to one of the stalwart peasant women for safe-keeping.

Leszner and the Lóránts had likewise handed over most of their money, but they took their cigarettes with them to line-up.

Exactly at eleven Brother Surányi arrived, together with his brother executioners, and gave the following speech to the battalion:

"Jews, listen here. Everyone hand over their valuables, money, fountain-pens, pencils, cigarette cases, and flashlights to battalion commander Tibor. If anyone keeps something all the same, we'll shoot him dead. So he is responsible for the whole filthy bunch. In a word, then, hand over everything. Put your backpacks in front of you, and the brother will check them."

One by one we had to pass by the table set up in the yard, and everyone put their money and all other assets on top.

The robbery unfolded without a hitch. After a while, once lots of small change had piled up on the table, Brother Surányi, beset by a fit of generosity, declared:

"Sums less than a pengő need not be turned in."

The conscientious brothers then proceeded to search all those who'd been robbed, but as it turned out, everyone had behaved "properly," turning over everything *voluntarily*. Wedding rings also had to be pulled off.

The robbery over, Brother Surányi ordered me to help compile the "inventory," since "everything has to add up."

Naturally no one took the inventory seriously. Everyone knew that, at most, Surányi would have to divvy up the money and valuables with his executioner-colleagues, and I myself knew little about bookkeeping, so the inventory included items like this:

"Several objects that seem to be of gold, including watches."

We completed the inventory in no time. Having conveyed his utmost satisfaction, Surányi then ordered us to dig a cesspool in the woods behind the yard so we wouldn't steal the day away without any work, because in a Hungarist state this sort of thing didn't fly.

Blessing the good nose that had led me to deposit my belongings in advance with the Kovácses, I ran right over there for cigarettes once Surányi and the others left, hardly able to wait to light up. I also brought some for the Lóránts and Leszner, who had nothing left, for smoking cigarettes was punishable by death.

But back then, everything was punishable by death, so it was not possible to pay too much attention to the question of which death applied to what and whom.

That night I lay down blissfully among the fleas on the thin layer of straw and smoked my Chiubek cigarette blissfully in the dark, when suddenly I heard footsteps and the rattle of weapons, and my faithful Arrow Crossers stormed into the barn armed with flashlights.

The blood froze in my veins, as did my hand with the burning cigarette in it. I didn't dare put out the cigarette in the straw, fearing both that the motion would give me away and that the straw could catch fire, so instead I stretched my hand out far, in it, the burning and smoking evidence. The flashlights zigzagged about until a strong beam finally landed on my face. I knew this meant death. Three seconds passed, and the light suddenly went out. The church bell was ringing in the village, which meant only that there was an air raid.

The alarmed Arrow Crossers fled the crowded barn. Had the air raid been delayed even by a second, I would not be among the living. I'd always known that smoking was a deadly habit. But in those dark days even living was. So I didn't have time to fear each and every little thing.

There was among us a strikingly handsome young boy who couldn't have been older than sixteen. His name was László Boldog, and though *boldog* is Hungarian for "happy," he didn't seem all that happy. He cried a lot, and it was really hard for him to resign himself to the fact that he was Jewish. At first he'd been an illegitimate child, born to a Christian mother, but his biological father was Jewish, and though at first he didn't bother much with his son, when he once met up by chance on the street with the mother and the kid, the boy was so winsome and lovely that the dad married his former lover and legitimized the kid. This boy, who had been born and raised Christian, now converted to Judaism. And so the unhappy little Happy legally counted as fully Jewish. Spade over his shoulder, he slogged the daily twenty kilometers to the worksite and back and dug all day with diligence to avoid Lajkó's kicking and castigating, dragged himself through the bottomless mud, and every day he was happy simply to be able to somehow trudge "home" to the barn. One day his foot got to hurting so much that he couldn't stand on it, and Dr. Földes gave him a day-long exemption from duty, which meant only that he didn't have to head out to the worksite, but he could help with kitchen duty.

Around three in the afternoon we happened to be busying ourselves with the kitchen work when, suddenly and unexpectedly, like a plague, Brother Surányi arrived with his ever-present little rifle.

Quite by chance the boy, at the moment when the brother came into view, was not busying himself but sitting on an old stump and crying, since he wanted to see his mother in a certain matter.

On seeing the slacker, Surányi screamed so loudly that my heart stopped beating.

"Get over here, filthy Jew!" he began gently, at which the boy got so scared that he started hiccupping and couldn't move, like a rabbit meeting up with a giant snake.

Surányi took this as disrespect.

"Are you deaf, too, you mangy dog? Can't you hear when I scream, 'Get over here'?"

Walter, the hard and brave little chef, ran over to the kid and stood him on his feet.

"I humbly report to you, sir, that he is sick, and can't stand on his feet."

Surányi laughed.

"He can't?" he said, and flung the rifle off his shoulder. "I'll count to three, and if by three you're not here, you mangy dog, I'll put a hole right through you!"

He counted to three. The boy was as pale as the wall, but he could neither speak nor move, but only waited for the shot.

"You get lost!" he yelled at the chef, and, lowering his rifle, stepped closer to the boy.

"What are you called, you piece of trash, who refused my order?"

The kitchen, where I was working, was a step away from Surányi. I took a chance: "Please don't be angry, sir. He is not refusing anything, it's just that he's still a child, and he's a little timid."

"Shut up," said Surányi, turning toward me gently, and already he was standing up close to the kid.

"Don't be scared of me, you bunny, you. I'm not a bad man, just when folks make me angry, and then of course I shoot. I ordered you to say what you are called."

"László Boldog," the kid groaned, and on hearing this unusual name, Surányi burst out laughing.

"So then, you're happy. Well, glad to hear."

The little kid, too, tried to smile through his tears.

"Why didn't you go out to work, you louse?" Surányi kindly inquired.

The child pointed to his foot, signaling that he couldn't speak. The order had been for him to stay home, since his foot hurt.

Surányi laughed, and what happened next seemed more horrible and unlikely than being shot dead.

Throwing his rifle back up onto his shoulder, Surányi raised a hand. He caressed László Boldog, who fell into a crying fit. There was no stopping his tears.

"Take him in there, to my room," the party servant said to Walter and me with a wave of the hand, and we helped the kid into Surányi's room, the onetime lodging of the distillery director.

Surányi then ordered us to leave the room, and he remained there alone with the kid, with whom, as later turned out, he fell hopelessly in love.

Surányi no longer let the boy go out to the work site; instead the boy stayed in the kitchen, though his main responsibility was cleaning Surányi's room, and he also had the right to polish Surányi's boots. At first not even Surányi understood, not even he believed, what had happened to him.

He showered László—Laci—with chocolates, choice bites to eat, and cigarettes.

The hapless boy became even more unhappy from Surányi's love than from marching out to work on fortifications.

"I'm so afraid of him I can't even sleep. He locks the door and kisses my hands. He cries, and says God has struck him with me. I think he's gone mad. What will become of us?"

From then on Surányi visited the kitchen often, and always summoned little Laci in to his room. In our presence he chided him and cursed at him for not polishing his boots well enough, but it was apparent from the sound of it that the coarseness no longer had gold reserves to back it up.

From Laci I learned that we would soon be taken away from Valkó. Not even he knew where: all Surányi had told him was that the Jews were to be taken somewhere else, but that if Laci went, too, he, Surányi, that is, would die of it.

This didn't seem like such a serious threat. We were all hardened by then, and when it came down to it, we could bear the thought of Surányi dying from his love.

Laci was in despair.

"I'm really afraid of the journey—these Arrow Crossers can't have anything good in store—but I'm also afraid of staying with him. That's worse than death."

I was unable to give the kid advice, but it was Surányi, anyway, who decided in the matter.

One afternoon, amid a storm of swearing and cursing, he came to the farm, already shouting Laci's name from afar.

"Be here in the yard in ten minutes, you rotten maggot, with your backpack, 'cause I'm gonna blow your brains out! I got a complaint about you, and I'm taking you to Budapest, you scum. But I can let you in on it now"—he kept shouting—"that you won't make it back here alive."

Little Laci did as he was told, but his whole body was shaking as he secured the straps on his small, beat-up backpack.

From this I knew that soon we would be leaving. I was sorry to be leaving Valkó, for no matter how bad the situation was, we were surely being prepared for something even worse. Here, at least, you knew your murderers.

On Tuesday we learned that early Wednesday morning we were headed for a destination unknown. Together with Leszner and the Lóránts, we deliberated on escape, but we couldn't decide. I reassured Leszner, "You're the only one who could stay here. The peasants know you and love you. Surely they'd hide you if you asked them to. The Russians will be here soon now, judging from the sound of artillery fire in the distance. Maybe a few days of excitement, and you'd be rescued."

Pál Leszner waved a tired hand.

"I don't want to bring trouble on others. Several of the locals have offered to hide me, but I'm not used to hiding. That trade has to be learned, and there's no time for that now. I doubt they'll be taking us to Germany, since there are no trains, and besides, Szálasi said he wants to solve the Jewish question after the war. Until then everyone will work in the country for the Hungarist state. Come what may, I'm going with all of you."

A lawyer, Emerich, who lived in the same building as us, said, "It can't be all that bad, since they could have killed us here, too, if they wanted to. They must be taking us to work somewhere. And that can be endured."

That afternoon we didn't go out to work, and we were in a fluster and without information. The air was abuzz with contradictory bits of news, each one worse than the last. I was busying myself in the yard when a wagon appeared.

Emerich spoke up: "I think it's Arrow Crossers coming with guns. Maybe they'll kill us right here and now."

When the wagon got closer, I saw that it was full of women. I just felt my limbs go numb. I recognized one of the women as Éva.

The wagon was coming straight toward us. A brother with a Hungarist armband was driving the horses. Éva noticed me from afar. She jumped off the wagon. My arms were so heavy that I could hardly embrace her.

"Éva, how did you get here?" I stammered.

"I got permission, as an Aryan wife. Don't worry about it. I brought you all sorts of things."

She opened her haversack and showed me what was inside. There was all sorts of food and lots of cigarettes. She even brought matches—who knows how many. She didn't know that each one was punishable by death.

We had to bid a quick farewell. The Arrow Crosser was hastening Éva to leave: "Let's just get going, because there'll be trouble."

Éva vanished with the wagon and with the other women. Had I just dreamed the whole thing? But the treasures were in my sack.

Twenty-Eight

Life in cheerful Germany is sad.
Everything is forbidden, even living.

On Wednesday night at eight we got the order to depart. No one escaped. We were weary and apathetic. I still worked in the kitchen, but the others had walked twelve miles every day to the work site and back, and returned half-dead from exhaustion. Walter cooked them a splendid bean goulash, but no sooner had they downed the dinner, which was simultaneously breakfast and lunch, than we had to leave.

We walked all night: semiconscious from weariness we plodded forward toward a destination unknown. At dawn we stopped somewhere, and one of the Arrow Cross guards ordered us to line-up on the street beside a fence.

A sergeant who looked like a sergeant announced that those with Horthy waivers should step forward. Many did so, including my friend Bokor, the publisher, and the sergeant scrupulously studied his documents in the gray of the dawn. He tore up most of the waivers, including Bokor's.

We were certain that after marching all night we'd rest somewhere or other, but we were mistaken. The matter was urgent, but though they did give a ten-minute break every three hours, that did more harm than good. We trudged along from Gödöllő toward Budapest, and news spread in the column that we would work in some factory by Budapest.

Along the way we slept under the open sky, wrapped up in blankets, but this sleep wasn't too refreshing, for the "Hungarian lump of earth" was too hard for sleep, the weather was on the cool side, and it often rained for no reason at all.

The Lóránts and Pál Leszner were all the happy owners of Swiss protective letters, indeed, their families had somehow managed to send them their *Schutzpass*es, but for the time being they could not reap the advantages, for there was no official forum to release them. Our lives passed in the company of arm-banded Arrow Crossers and guards who had never heard of Switzerland.

I begged the Lóránts and Pál Leszner to feel free to escape, for with the bona fide documents they now had, no trouble could befall them. The monitoring was lax, and when we arrived late at night at the brick factory in Óbuda, on the northern outskirts of downtown Budapest, all they would have had to do in the pitch-black was to jump aboard one of the trams, and they could have gone on home. But they didn't go. They waited for the official body, anyone, to release them according to regulations. But, by then, forums and regulations had long gone out of fashion.

I too could have fled, but I didn't believe that I would have fared any better back home. I thought of the arm-banded brothers, of identity checks, and of death, which didn't seem so horrible, but then again, it didn't seem desirable enough, either, to go rushing after it. It was my conviction that fleeing from trouble wasn't a good idea, since you might run right into it.

A shudder of terror often passed through me when I thought of my closest family members, friends, and acquaintances, but I was incapable of rising up against my fate. I knew that it was a real and rare miracle when the bad wins its just punishment and the good its just reward, and when patience does in fact bring roses. It is far more common for a sly conman to steal a whole bed of roses in a matter of moments, and I knew also that the gazelle is a gentle, grass-eating, innocent creature, and that despite all rumors to the contrary, it isn't even Jewish, but the lion eats it nonetheless, roaring angrily on top of it. So too I knew, to the extent that gossip about such lions came my way, that there was hardly a lion that had a guilty conscience over the torn-up corpse of a gazelle.

There were moments in the course of the journey when I regretted my fatalism and I couldn't imagine that I would have gotten into a worse situation in Budapest or during an escape than on this trip.

Likewise troubling was that they'd completely stopped feeding us, hence we were left to be wholly self-sufficient. This "self-sufficiency" comprised mainly begging, for we'd been relieved of all our money and valuables well beforehand.

Along the highway were boards nailed to trees, which read:

"J---'S ROAD"

It was at the first such board that I began suspecting that the walking would lead to Germany. Nor did I like how they arranged our lodging. In the period before the deportation I'd heard a lot about the Jewish question; there was even talk of solutions in reply to this question that in reality didn't exist and wasn't posed by anyone. And yet I never heard a thing about the lodging question, whereas it sure did exist. Nature is lovely, no doubt about it. Even my distinguished colleague, the great romantic poet Sándor Petőfi, adored it, but it was a bit boring to pass every blessed night in the open, on the edge of ditches, under the thoughtful supervision of gendarmes.

When we lay down I would have liked to go on; when we were going I could hardly wait to reach a place of rest. A man is never satisfied with his fate.

The rule was that the forced marching lasted from dawn to late at night. We got very few "rest breaks," and even they were endlessly exhausting, because most often we could only stand in place in the mud. We could neither sit or lie down on it.

In Budapest we were joined by women deportees as well, which was utterly depressing even though the women were much better at putting up with the walking, the bad treatment, and going hungry. Behind me young women even sang as they marched, in pitch-black darkness, when hungry, when for my part I could barely drag myself along.

The worst was perhaps that men and women had to relieve themselves in front of each other, and the guards could laugh boisterously and make witty remarks in the matter.

Begging worked splendidly. I was the most flexible of anyone in the group: since the Lóránts were carrying my bags, I was able to easily jump out of line and press my way into peasant homes for bread, jam, and other earthly delights they happened to be handing out.

The peasants acted with great decency. In one of the houses, for example, without any lengthy explanation, I got a slice of bread as huge as a millstone, with some sort of braised beef on top that must have weighed two pounds. It was all so delicious that I was giddy with happiness, and I thought to myself while sharing the bounty with the Lóránts, that this meat and this bread had been worth being born for.

I also saw that life, even this life, could still harbor lots of good, since my capacity to appreciate only grew and every little trifle could now bring me joy. Moreover, amid the feverish rapture of begging I didn't even think of where we were going and why. I cared only about the present and to not have to go hungry on top of the marching unless absolutely necessary.

Of course not even begging came for free. Stepping out of line was strictly forbidden. To do so was to risk being shot dead or beaten dead by the stalwart and dutiful guards.

One time I found a thousand-year-old, weeping old lady in a peasant house who explained that she was lamenting for the Jews, since they were being taken away to be killed, and God would punish everyone for that.

"May I have a bit of bread?" I inquired, since there wasn't enough time to cry.

The old lady cut an immense slice of bread, spread it with jam, and handed it to me.

"What do I owe you?" I asked. Aside from courtesy there was nothing to my question, for I had not even a penny to pay her with.

"Owe? You don't owe a thing, sweetheart," said the old lady, who started to cry anew. "We're the ones who owe you. Just take it."

I took it. But it wasn't easy, because as I tried returning to my place in line, one of the Arrow Cross guards noticed not only the bread and jam but also me, and from afar he held his rifle above his head as he ran toward me.

The custom at such times was that the person being pursued, ran, and the guard, who was well fed, young, and eager, ran even faster, usually caught up, and kept beating the pursued with the rifle butt as long as he or she was moving. But if the guard was bored of the protracted but entertaining beating, he simply shot the individual, for the guards, under order, did not have to account for the dead. The only important thing was that the number of people delivered tally with the number that set off. Whether the guards would hand them over alive or dead to the next gendarmes or soldiers was of no consequence.

The foot-soldier ran toward me, and my blood froze, but then something occurred to me. I waved with feverish excitement to the soldier to come faster, at which he broodingly slowed his pace, not understanding why I was hastening my being beaten dead. But I just kept excitedly waving him closer, calling him ever more impatiently to come, and when he was right up next to me I voiced a harried whisper:

"Disappear fast, and don't ask questions!"

The flustered guard didn't even think to beat me, but instead took his place behind the line and went back to marching along with the rest of us. A half-hour later I looked back and saw that he was still there, still marching, still chewing over the strange enigma.

That's how I escaped getting beaten dead the first time.

The days passed. My legs, my sides, my shoulders, and my lungs hurt from the constant walking, and I couldn't get used to sleeping in the open all the time, indeed I often envied the shepherds, who supposedly liked it.

The Lóránts, Pál Leszner, and I often spoke about how nice it would be to sleep under a roof one more time in this life and to at least see a bathroom from up close. No longer did we even remember what washing every day was like, sometimes shaving and having breakfast in the morning.

Close to the Austrian border, in the town of Mosonmagyaróvár, we finally managed to get under a roof, but we later cursed the moment when this madness took hold of us, and we wept for the good old days when we still slept calmly under the open sky in torrential rain.

Sleeping under a roof happened like this: the gendarmes slapped us into a sort of granary, crowding together so many people that we could stand only tight up against each other, and then one of the gendarmes howled, "Lie down!" and locked the door on us.

At first we couldn't even believe this unexpected turn of events, and then we realized there was nothing we could do, and so we tried to make room for ourselves somehow all the same. Of course this was no easy matter. Most of us were already collapsing from exhaustion, but it wasn't even possible to collapse, since there wasn't even room to stand. Only to lie, stand, or sit on each other. Many suffocated, and many were crying out in pain. Nothing could be seen in the pitch-black darkness. The women were sobbing and screaming. But the shut door did not move.

All at once, through the hellish chaos, I heard someone yell my name. I yelled back, though I couldn't even imagine what someone would want of me now, when in this situation it wasn't exactly in my power to get anything done.

In the pitch black a young man stumbled over to me, wading across everyone in his path. It turned out to be my nephew, one of the Himmler boys, and he handed me a Swiss protective letter made out to my name. Éva had sent it.

We headed on the next morning at dawn. Ever since setting out from Valkó we hadn't met with any sort of official body, but many claimed to have heard that at the border everything would come into order, for a high-ranking Hungarian officer and a high-ranking German officer would be waiting for the deportees there, and they would send only those to Germany who didn't have protective letters.

At the last stop in Hungary we were told that if by chance we had any valuables with us, we should hand them over, even if not officially, for the Germans would take everything away from us, anyway, and it would be better if Hungarian pengős remained in Hungarian hands. Many obliged in the hope of being able to fill their canteens with water. Their hopes were only half-realized, for while the gendarmes did take the pengős and other valuables, they didn't give water, since they hadn't gotten an order to do so.

After an eleven-kilometer walk we finally reached the border, where indeed a high-ranking Hungarian officer and a high-ranking German officer were both waiting for us, and they decided our fate.

The Lóránts had gotten there before us, and as Pál Leszner and I walked along we were happy to see the Lóránts sitting off to the side with their few belongings on a little island, an island of bliss, waiting to be sent home. It turned out that decorated officers and their dependents would be allowed to return. My heart started beating wildly. Now it was certain that there was hope, for both Pál Leszner and I had protective letters, and Leszner, moreover, was a decorated officer.

But on getting in front of the German officer it turned out that my protective letter had no success at all. Looking at the Schutzpass, he said a coarse, unmistakable one-syllable word and tore my protective letter in two, and with that, my protection had ceased.

He likewise shoved Pál Leszner back in the line and the procession headed off toward Germany.

I didn't even have time to be surprised before our feet were on German soil. Pál Leszner whispered to me, "In the best-case scenario all this means is that we'll be liberated six months later than if we'd have stayed home."

Beside me marched a strikingly handsome, appealing teenager with a rifle slung over his shoulder. He couldn't have been more than fifteen. I felt sorry for him having been forced to be a soldier so young. The soldier-boy knew German and Hungarian equally well.

"Got money?" he inquired.

"I have seventeen pengős," I said politely. I had that much with me because someone had given it to me while walking, asking me to take care of it, figuring that the chances of it not being taken away from me were greater, since I was small.

"Hand it over."

"Now, while marching?"

"Now," he said, and his rifle jerked menacingly on his shoulder.

I never was a tightwad: I gave him the money, at which he took my gloves, too, and then stepped over to the man walking beside me—a woeful fiftyish man who looked to be a veteran and was made of tougher stuff than I.

"I've got money, but I'm not handing it over. Not my gloves, either. There's no regulation for this."

In the next moment the boy raised his rifle and shot. The man bloodily collapsed and tried to speak. The child opened fire. He shot three times, at which the victim lay motionless on the ground. The SS kid said insouciantly to the machine-gun-toting adult who ran over at the crackle of gunfire, "The scumbag wanted to escape. *Saujude*."

The older SS guy nodded, and then snarled at the group:

"Faster! Wake up, filthy scum!"

We marched on in terror, and no one bothered with the dead man. The SS kid stepped up to his next victim. From this point on he fared with enormous success, though I could not help but marvel how he could hide all those gloves and the money.

After a few more hours of forced marching we arrived at the train station. We were happy to see a train for the first time in so long. The walking was over, it seemed, and finally we could travel by train. I had to admit that the Germans were, after all, more decent than the Hungarians. Here, everything was much better organized. We got into the train cars, which were quite orderly and clean, with bona fide seats. True, I began to get a bit anxious when I noticed that they were squeezing at least eighty people into each car, but I was relieved to see that before departure the Germans were distributing food among us. They distributed bread, cheese, margarine, and sausage in fairly large quantities. It was unlikely that they were taking us away to kill us if beforehand they were lavishing so much food upon us.

The congestion, the general despair, and the uncertain fate of my loved ones weighed down upon me with horrible force, but the worst was that for the first time in my life I was traveling without knowing where the train would take me. The least they could have done, I thought indignantly, would have been to tell us where we were being taken.

Night came, but the train sat motionless on the tracks. Two young SS guards stood in front of the car. Soon it turned out that they knew Hungarian splendidly. They were Swabians, or ethnic Germans. At night they exited the car, locked it, and left us to ourselves.

Only then was it truly apparent how little room there was. Heaped on top of each other, we tried lying down in the most impossible positions. I trusted that because I was little, I wouldn't be in anyone's way.

I tried lying down on the floor on some unfamiliar backpack, and curled up in as teeny-weeny a ball as possible, but there was in our group one Dr. Klein, a physician, who, it seemed, had gone mad, and he kept shouting that he must be called "chief physician." This would not have been such a problem—though it was unusual for someone in a situation like this to insist to this degree on his rank; but the bigger problem was that this hapless doctor was obsessed with the thought that if he broke my leg he would be able to sleep calmly. He always found me in the dark, and with expert movements he tried breaking my left leg in two. Only a few weeks earlier, the bones in my right leg had more or less fused, and I was in no mood to have the same thing happen with my left leg. In vain did I try to talk this crazed doctor out of his plan. With religious zeal he rose every ten minutes from his lair, felt about for my left leg, and tried to break it.

I kicked and I struggled, and fortunately the doctor was already in frail condition at the age of fifty, so in the morning, after many heated battles, my leg was still whole. But sleeping was impossible, and the train still hadn't left.

By then everyone had gone half-mad from lack of sleep. The luckier ones did get a couple coins' worth of sleep, but even if they did manage to lay their heads on someone's belly, you couldn't talk about long-lasting, serious, refreshing dreams.

For two days the train just sat there before, long last, finally heading off. By then the more cunning among us had eaten everything and lived from thievery. Once in a while a voice would cry out that someone had stolen his remaining bread, but nobody cared.

We got no water, even though thirst plagued us all terribly. Before then I'd known thirst only from novels, and I never would have believed that it can cause such torment. This torturous journey lasted six days, until finally we arrived in Auschwitz.

Auschwitz back then was just the name of a place, without any negative connotations, and most of us had never even heard of it.

Along the way the SS now and again had us throw the dead out, but even so there was very little room. The goofy doctor lasted all the way to Auschwitz, but not for a moment did he give up the thought of breaking my leg in two. He was calm by day, but as soon as night fell, he got back to work. He even tried gentle persuasion, whispering into my ear in the quiet of the night like a lover:

"It will be better for you, too, believe me. Sacrifices must be made for the common good. Let me break your leg, then we'll all have enough room. Don't be so stubborn. Believe me, I know this sort of thing, for I am a chief physician."

Fortunately thirst really got the better of him, and by the third day the old zeal had left him.

Auschwitz is a bleak, ugly place. The SS herded us behind some sort of barbed-wire fence, and the gate between the two towers closed. No longer were we paying attention to a thing. We were weary and lethargic.

Dawn was breaking. We'd been standing in rows of five for hours on the *Appellplatz*—the roll-call place, that is—until finally something happened.

Dr. Mengele arrived, though none of us yet knew who he was. He was a remarkably appealing, tall, strikingly handsome, well-groomed man. With gentle blue eyes he looked sadly upon the jaded crowd. From what we understood, we were being selected for work. He went down the line, and amiably, as if he had no power, in what seemed more a humble request than an order, he said to people:

"To the left, please. To the right, please."

When he got to me, he seemed to hesitate. "How old are you?" he inquired.

I told him, whereupon he said, apologetically, "To the right, please," and gave me a gentle kick.

The whole thing was not frightening, just deadly boring and tedious. I felt that this standing in line in the cold would never end.

After quite a while they herded us into some stark, hideous space, where we got dinner: *Dörrgemüse*—a mishmash of dehydrated and bitter vegetables—and bread. One spoonful was quite enough of the vegetable stew; not even with the best of intentions could it be eaten.

The next morning at four we were beaten awake with rubber clubs and had to run out to the Appellplatz. Thus began another pestilent, meaningless round of standing about for hours, which ended with us getting breakfast. We got a surprisingly good, pulpy soup and more bread.

On the Appellplatz I got up my nerve and addressed a handsome, six-foot-seven SS stripling:

"Excuse me, sir, I don't know the ranks here, but I'd like to say something."

He gave me an encouraging look. "Say it."

"If you've called so many guests here who in actuality didn't want to come, and there's not enough room, either, as I can tell, you could at least let us bathe. We took a long journey and we're dirty, so a little bath would be really good.

The SS lad laughed.

"Don't bother with bathing. Our guests arrive through the door and leave through the chimney. Don't worry about the rest."

This declaration didn't reassure me, either, but three people who'd heard what the SS stripling had said to me, believed him, and immediately embraced the high-voltage barbed-wire fence.

The next day at dawn we marched back out to the train station, and soon we were again on the road toward a destination unknown.

Once more there were eighty of us in the train car, but now we traveled in better circumstances. This was a bona fide, pleasant cattle car strewn thickly with straw. The chief physician who'd always had a problem with my leg had been sent to the left by Mengele, but back then I didn't yet know that "left" meant the crematorium or, rather, the gas chamber.

Spiced with plenty of hitches, stations, and air raids en route, the journey took four days in all. We arrived in Buchenwald.

We didn't even have to throw out the dead along the way, only at the last stop. There the women disappeared, leaving only the men and the boys.

It was only a few steps from the station to the camp, and men in convicts' uniforms were at work everywhere we went. We saw no SS soldiers. In the camp we were received by the familiar barbed-wire fence and towers, but here the two towers were more imposing, and they were connected above the gate by a bridge.

Again we stood about for an infinitely long time with our backpacks on until finally we wound up in the bath house. By now, after Auschwitz, everyone knew what "bathhouse" meant. But no one was afraid. We were tired and apathetic, wanting to get over everything, the sooner the better.

Before the bathing we had to leave all our clothes and our backpacks in the storeroom, and we headed to the bathhouse completely naked. We knew this was death. I was silently ambling along with an old actor-friend of mine, when I noticed his body was covered with rashes. Drawing on my incomplete medical knowledge, I asked, "Say, don't you have syphilis or something?"

The actor waved a hand dismissively.

"Come on, who cares?"

But it was interesting, for it quickly turned out that we'd been taken not for execution but to a real bathhouse.

In a room, prisoners cut our hair and shaved us—everywhere. We stepped in the actual bathhouse completely bald. I noticed that the barbers were conspicuously careful with hair and beards, but I was too tired to ponder this German peculiarity.

First we had to step into a tub stinking of disinfectant, and then we got soap and washed under a warm shower. This shred of cleanliness after so long felt terrific. I washed myself at length and with enthusiasm, completely using up the soap that had been allotted me.

After bathing we were lathered up with some stinging and stinking disinfectant, and then we had to walk out naked for a good while in the cold air until we again wound up in a closed space.

It was some sort of storeroom. Everyone got a number that was on a rectangular linen rag. This was on mine: 75505. This, I held tight, naked, until we arrived in the next long space, where, again, it was prisoners who handed us various items of clothing. I got a little jacket, trousers, a cap, and a pair of wooden slippers with thick soles.

The jacket was tight and tattered, and the trousers were just twenty percent trousers and seventy percent rags, the rest being buttons. There was no word of underwear and socks. We then threw on our rags, and headed out into the rain and mud until we arrived at a tent bearing this text: Zell 5. After herding us in there, they commanded us to lie down.

Lying down didn't go smoothly. The tent was divided into stalls, and we were crowded in so tightly that once again we could lie down only on our sides, hating each other due to the constricted space.

But the situation was much better here, since we lay on straw and got blankets, too. There was one blanket for every two people. The space seemed clean and insect-free. Pál Leszner and I held hands tight and took care to be sure we wound up next to each other. By now he was the only treasure I still had from my previous life.

The boss of our tent, Zell 5, was a Ukrainian prisoner who dealt out soup and bread to everyone. A single spoon per person comprised our entire arms cache for eating, but soon it turned out that soup represented the entire repertoire of German cuisine, and so a spoon was enough for it all.

I was hungry, but I didn't trust the soup. Exaggerated caution led me to taste it all the same, whereupon it turned out that even from a Hungarian perspective I was face to face with a first-rate bowl of goulash soup. The German empire had filled the one-liter billycan to the brim, and I could not recall ever having enjoyed a dinner as much as this first Buchenwald soup.

Soon it turned out that life in Buchenwald was tolerable. We mainly ate and lay on the floor, with the exception of during *Appell*. The one unpleasant thing was the Appell, the roll call, which meant having to get out twice a day, once before daybreak and once toward evening, on the Appellplatz, where we had to stand at attention, motionless, for four or five hours straight, until an SS junior officer arrived to take the data from the prisoners and count everyone, and if the numbers matched, we could go back to lie down.

There was a cinema at Buchenwald, too, which I was awfully scared of, for it was in that space, which had in fact formerly been a cinema, that we got inoculations, which reassured me on the one hand, terrified me on the other.

It was reassuring that we were being inoculated against typhus and all sorts of other illnesses, because I figured they didn't want to kill us, if they were taking such good care of our health, but it saddened me to see that they were constantly recruiting volunteers for inoculations. Anyone who volunteered to get inoculated by the SS doctors was promised *Nachschlag*, an extra half portion of soup.

If they asked for ten volunteers a hundred raised their hands, for only the first batch of soup was strikingly good, the rest were languid, with hardly any potatoes, and everyone stayed hungry. Such volunteers then never returned, which raised some eyebrows, but back then I didn't think anything bad, because only much later did I learn that those hapless fellows were used for experimental purposes, and that they were experimented with until they died.

Many died during the Appells—those who could not stand the cold without underwear and socks and who could not stand motionless for hours at a time. But the Appell was sacred, and disturbing the dead—those who fell out of the line—was forbidden. Only after the Appell did the *Heftling*s gather them up.

Soon we learned what the secret was of us not being made to work. Buchenwald was in fact a distribution center from where slaves were taken to forced labor.

A week later Pál Leszner was taken away to an unknown location. A German civilian foreman selected the crew. He chose Pál Leszner and left me behind. At that I volunteered for work, begging the Germans to select me, too, since I wanted to be together with my friend. The Germans shoved me back into the line.

I would gladly have strangled that headstrong, rat-faced German, for then I didn't know that he had saved my life. Pál Leszner died there, in that *vernichtungslager,* where the poor man had been taken.

Twenty-Nine

EATING SNOW IS UNHEALTHY IF YOU GET SHOT AT MEANWHILE. BENEDEK IS ALL DANCING AND DECORUM. YOU NEED TO KNOW HOW TO SALUTE.

Two weeks later I was taken from the tent to a genuine wooden barracks, where I saw a stove from close up for the first time in a long while. There we slept in beds, bunks, and there was straw under us, so, in a word, it was pure bliss.

We only had to watch out for our wood shoes, because at night the prisoners stole them off of each other's feet. The Germans didn't hand out enough of them, and yet shoes were important, because without them the prisoner would soon die.

Three weeks had passed in Buchenwald when one day I too was finally chosen for work and assigned to a batch of prisoners taken for labor.

I got new clothes, new wood shoes, underclothes, and even a brand new sweater. I began taking delight in life again. Some already knew that we were being taken to Niederorschelbe to work in the airplane factory.

The day of departure arrived. At daybreak, bread, cheese, and wurst were divvied up between us and the gate of the Buchenwald prison opened up. The SS guards accompanied us with rifles pointed at us until we reached the train. It seemed they were afraid of us, though we hadn't bothered a soul.

Here once again two young SS men watched over us. One of them knew Hungarian remarkably well. It turned out that he was a Swabian from the outskirts of Budapest, and Imre Ráday was his favorite actor. When someone told him that I was a writer from Budapest, he couldn't stop asking me about Ráday.

"What kind of person is he in real life? Do you know him personally?"

The train lumbered along toward yet another German destination. Once again they gave no water, and though it was winter and the cold was ungodly, thirst tormented us terribly. I inquired with the Ráday-loving SS soldier:

"Wouldn't it be possible to get a little water?"

"Forbidden. The order is not to give water."

"I'll talk to you for hours about Ráday if you let me out to lick snow."

Lovely, appetizing snow shone white all around me, and our train had been standing in place for hours, since the tracks were not in order.

The Swabian SS soldier slowly cut a big piece of wurst with his pocketknife.

"You can go out, but then I'll shoot into you."

"Can't you just shoot to the side?" I inquired, since the thirst seemed unbearable.

"Then I'll smash in your head with the rifle butt," the boy said, smiling, and hit me on the back with the rifle butt in jocular but vigorous fashion.

And so I gave up the idea of licking the snow, though never in my life had I ever found food so appetizing as I now did all that lovely white snow on the hillsides. I recalled Dad, who had sent the maid back five times with the pitcher of water asking her to run the tap a bit more, because the water wasn't cold enough. I recalled America, where I had spent so many years and where I could now be living free and without a care. When I was in the process of heading to Budapest from Hollywood, in my hotel room in Chicago ice-cold water flowed from a separate tap alongside the hot and cold water, a tap fashioned solely for drinking.

Consolation came by telling myself how much water I'd drunk all my life, between sentences, not even paying attention, and sometimes even when I wasn't thirsty—so why was this nonsense worrying me now?

The train stood still. The snow sparkled desirably all around brilliantly white. We were in the Bavarian Alps, and it was impossible not to delight in the beauty of nature. *This Germany is lovely,* I thought. *If only it weren't so hideous.*

On the fourth day a colleague of mine, a certain Mittelman, fortunately stole my remaining bread and cheese from my pocket at night. It couldn't be proven, though, since in all his guile and wile he ate it immediately in the dark. This theft did have the advantage that starting then, the thirst didn't torment me as much, for I remembered that good, cold, fresh water truly tastes good only after eating.

The train spent more time standing still than moving, and even when it was moving, it was just barely jolting along, so we made the six-hour journey from Buchenwald to Niederorschel in five days. It was inhumanly cold, but it turned out that not even this weather helped against thirst, so the superstition that water is truly important only in the dog days of summer proved to be just that.

When the train stopped for good, we saw that we again had another couple of corpses, but the bulk of the troupe, though broken, arrived at its new station in relatively good health.

Niederorschel, in the very center of Thüringia, is an awfully beautiful little town. Already awaiting us at the station were the SS boys, who drove us in a forced march to our new workplace. After a forty-minute march over unbeaten paths we arrived in some little village amid ancient, one-storey houses and well-fed, enormous Germans.

No sooner had we gone a half-hour past the village when there loomed ahead of us two towers of the sort we were already familiar with from Buchenwald. We stepped through the gate between these two towers, and so began the concentration camp, densely surrounded by barbed wire.

After the SS carefully counted us, we were transferred to other German soldiers, who entrusted us to a lead prisoner, a kapo. The kapo was a kind-faced, muscular, fortyish man, a German who, it quickly turned out, had spent the last ten years in captivity, and the prisoners who'd been there for a while whispered that he was a good man but that sometimes for no reason he got edgy, and at such times he was combative for no reason, like all Germans.

We marched up to our room, where they counted us again, then the kapo stood before us and gave us the following speech:

"Friends! I am the kapo, which means only that your lives depend on me. I arrange the eating and every other thing. You yourselves can't speak with or have any contact with the SS sentries. If you see any German soldier, remove your caps immediately and greet them with respect. Of course they won't accept your greeting, but don't worry about that. They'll beat dead anyone who doesn't greet them or doesn't remove their cap. Here you'll do just fine, actually—only those of you will die who want to. If you stick to the rules, you'll be alright. This is the best concentration camp in all of Germany. If you have any problems, because you'll have plenty of them, to be sure, turn to me in confidence: I'm a prisoner, too, your friend, and if at all possible I'll help you out. The food here is very good. You won't get the bread, that trash mixed with soybeans, like in Buchenwald, but regular, civilian, German bread, which is outstanding. Everyone gets the same size helping. But there's one thing I'll warn everyone about. German scientists have determined that with the calories we get here it's possible to work and, indeed, to stay alive, but at most for six months. If something happens in the meantime—I think you know what I mean—then we'll live, maybe. If not, we'll die. So if I catch anyone filching even a morsel of food from anyone else, I'll beat him dead. *Abtreten*."

The speech was not too reassuring, but the six-month deadline was. The work was not bad, but on the first day, especially since Christmas was approaching, we worked for sixteen hours straight, to get used to the pace.

Soon it turned out that the camp wasn't such an unbearable place. Instead of the abominable German army bread, here they gave regular, civilian bread, which was indeed outstanding, and generally the food was unbelievably good. On investigating the matter, I discovered that the camp cook was a portly Czech prisoner who conjured up the meals out of virtually nothing. There was no salt, the core ingredients being just cabbage and potatoes, carrots, and, on rare occasions, beets, and out of them this fat genius created his culinary marvels, yes, I even kissed the back of his hand one time when I happened to cross paths with him in the hallway, as I had no other currency to pay him. Though he tolerated the kiss apathetically, the next day he waved me over and allotted me a little extra soup.

Christmas was approaching, and all of us anxiously awaited the Holy Night, for rumor had it that we would then get a double portion of bread and supposedly meat as well.

Although I did not put too much credence in such rumors, even talking about the matter felt good, because hunger or, rather, starvation, was by then such that aside from liberation no one was interested in anything but eating.

During, before, and after work we daydreamed for hours about stuffed cabbage and beef and ice cream and chocolate and other foods that we'd heard of and perhaps even tried at times in our previous lives, but whose existence we could no longer seriously believe in. I myself was obsessed with the idea that if I was freed, in one sitting I'd eat six liters of goose drumsticks, roasted. Because after all the soup, I could no longer even think in any unit of measurement other than liters.

Finally Christmas arrived. We expected a bit of extra food, but what we got surpassed even our wildest dreams. The portly little Czech genius of a chef had really outdone himself. He cooked a heavenly rice pudding, with real milk and real rice, and there was another sort of soup, too, some sour, lunglike work of art, and we got three helpings of bread, fresh bread, and beyond that, each of us got a quarter pound of beef and twenty-one pieces of boiled potatoes with a triple-size portion of margarine.

There was a frenzy of delight in the barracks. After dinner a young man came by to visit me from the other room and timidly said, "Um … I heard that you … that is … wouldn't you trade bread for the beef?"

I couldn't believe my ears. The bread we'd gotten was good, to be sure, but we wouldn't have dared even to dream of beef. Everyone knew that Christmas didn't happen every day. Why did this barmy young man want to trade his beef?

"How much bread do you want?" I said, trying to sound him out. With his dirty little hands he showed how much. The price for the meat seemed quite cheap. I quickly cut off the piece of bread as agreed, lest he should change his mind. He grabbed the bread, of which at the moment we had plenty, and I immediately ate the second helping of beef, but my curiosity was stronger than my bliss.

"Tell me, young man, why did you trade the infrequent meat for the frequent bread?"

Warily he leaned to my ear:

"It's not kosher, and we mustn't eat *treif*."

I was shocked. Not that I really expected the Germans to add kosher slaughtering to their to-do list, but that in this place in such circumstances someone should care about this fact, well, I hadn't counted on that. Moved by this nearly maniacal nonsense, I took the risk:

"Say, I don't suppose you have a lunatic friend, too, who doesn't regard the meat as kosher?"

"Sure I do," he said, beaming, and in no time he'd run off and then returned with yet another cut of meat, which I likewise happily traded for bread, secretly blessing my Protestant faith, which is not as strict with me and allows the consumption of nonkosher beef. True, any religion that could have forbade me this pleasure in exchange for dry bread and salvation in the afterlife would have had to be quite a religion.

At table five, where I ate, an amiable, intelligent young student named Elias sat beside me, and squeezing in on the other side of me was an incredibly thin, middle-aged man.

"Please be so kind as to make a wee bit of room. I'm very thin." So he said to the two of us before introducing himself: "Benedek."

"What is your profession in civilian life?" I inquired.

"I'm a teacher," said Mr. Benedek with self-respect.

"What field?" I pried, since I liked precise answers.

"Dance and etiquette, on Klauzál Street," he said, and with a deft motion he hid his dentures in a little aluminum container, since they got in the way of eating.

Benedek, the dance and etiquette teacher, did not shine at work, true, but he was a genius when it came to trading and stealing various foods. This thin little man bought on credit, too, saying he'd pay later, but he didn't, because he was unbelievably gluttonous. Those who worked outdoors could constantly steal potatoes and carrots, which did much to enhance the sustenance of the whole barracks.

We traded in two types of currency. The most important and most valuable was bread, for which you could get anything. The other stars, on par with bread, were cigarettes and tobacco.

At first we got ten cigarettes a week or a pack of tobacco every two weeks. Many did not smoke or else quit smoking in the interest of life, which is to say, more bread. There were yet others who had been in the camp for longer and had been stockpiling more and more tobacco under their pallets.

In the most advantageous position in this respect, as I've already mentioned, were those on an outdoor work crew, or *Aussenkommando*, for potatoes and carrots were stored in hoppers they had the opportunity to steal from. The stolen raw materials could then be traded for bread or cigarettes.

The folks who worked on the *Ausserkommando* were those who declared themselves to be day laborers, farmers, or members of some similar occupation, figuring that the intellectuals would be executed anyway. In contrast, the doctors, engineers, writers, and businessmen were retrained as skilled laborers. This meant only that we could toil away in workshops, thanks to the *umschuling*, as the Germans nicknamed school.

The penalty for sabotage was death. This bit of common knowledge was communicated to me many times a day by my "master," a German worker who looked like a combination of Laurel and Hardy, who trained us with German thoroughness. This master was a kind, well-meaning man, and a bad word from him could cost each one of us our lives.

We talked a lot, which was forbidden, but the scant SS contingent was unable to check whether it was training or idle chatter that was underway between prisoner and master.

One time, between two rounds of drilling, I took the risk.

"Say, dear master, what is sabotage, actually?"

"Quite simple. The drill, for example, amid today's circumstances, is irreplaceable. The work almost solely comprises various types of drilling. Anyone who deliberately breaks a drill, dies."

"And if they break something else?

"They'll die then, too."

"And if they don't break it deliberately, but the drill just breaks?"

"Then they have to report it to me—the master, that is—and there won't be any trouble."

This was a great relief, for I already understood enough of the trade to know that all I needed to do was hold the electric drill at a certain angle, and it would break like a toothpick. I even trained a beginner colleague of mine about this fact, with huge success at that.

The little Éliás, who kept losing weight but was one of the most skilled workers, always broke his drills when bored SS soldiers were watching him busying about. On such occasions he immediately reported it to the master, who, though grumbling, promptly issued another one to the kid.

I grew fond of this Hardylike master.

"Say, master," I inquired, "Is it true that in Germany there is no longer any pastry at all?"

"A lie! We have all we want. We have everything."

"I'd only want to see one," I said, without a hint of complaint. "Ever since we got here, we haven't even seen any fruit or pastry. A strudel or something similar must be a lovely sight."

The master growled at me to quicken my pace.

"*Los! Los!*" he said, leaving me there. An SS soldier appeared in the far corner of the factory. It just happened to be the canine-accompanied corporal, the lone soldier of ill repute in the whole camp. He limped, since a bit of his foot was missing, which was why he got light duty, but he couldn't resign himself to that little deficit, and he found fault in everything. Actually he had nothing to do with the factory itself, only supervising the work outside was in his scope of authority. He happened to look inside the factory only as a courtesy, to warm up, and to find someone to beat up. He came closer, and waved over little Éliás.

"You were talking, you scum!" he hissed, and meekly dabbed the boy a few times on the face, whereupon the boy fell down. Then he stopped bothering with the boy, who stood up and hobbled back to his work station.

"I just noticed that you limp, too," I said to Éliás.

"Ever since Mecklenburg. Things were bad there. We had to lug sacks of cement, and meanwhile we'd get beaten. And the German shepherds tore lots of us apart. One of the soldiers broke my leg," so he said, languidly, reaching for the drill. "This is a very good place. Heaven." Presumably the kid hadn't gotten a religious upbringing, which is why he had an erroneous conception of the real heaven.

The next day my master brought two pastries.

"Eat them fast, and be careful that they don't see you," he whispered, and hurried off in a huff.

I gave one to Éliás, who cried as he ate it. He was still young, and he really missed sweets.

The scarcity of cigarettes tormented me to no end. We hadn't gotten even a drag since getting here. The kapo and the two assistant kapos were smoking all the time, and the soldiers had enough cigarettes, too, the sight of which only ratcheted up my desire.

After the pastry, Éliás relaxed completely.

"I have two packs of cigarettes," he said.

I got dizzy. Even out in everyday life I prized luxury items more than necessities, but here I would have given half of Germany for a cigarette, with half of Austria thrown in for good measure.

"For sale?" I asked nonchalantly, but my knees were trembling.

"For bread."

We sealed the deal in a matter of moments. Éliás had the right to cut as much from my bread every day as he saw fit until—as he saw it—he was paid for the two packs of cigarettes.

At lunch I got the cigarettes. I'd never felt as rich in my life. The first pack wasn't even yet empty when, miracle of miracles, we officially got one-and-a-half packs of tobacco along with cigarette paper.

The master arranged to have me and Éliás each get a one-mark bonus as exemplary workers, and for that money we could get cold beer or mussels in mustard sauce at the canteen.

Of course, such mustard-laden festivities were rare, and by then we had gotten out of the habit of having such foods. Poor Éliás, who saw mustard as food: for weeks he was sick from this honor bestowed upon us, for which we were so envied.

Life was beautiful, and I was almost happy. I was satisfied with everything except for going hungry all the time, and I felt that if it went on like this, the whole famous deportation would prove to be but a passing adventure I'd someday tell stories to my grandchildren about. Here, only those died who wanted to or who had singularly bad luck. Even the starvation was possible to get used to, and I trusted that the Reich had less than six months left, and we'd be freed.

The news from the fronts was pleasant for us, everyone knew of something and the mood was hopeful, though the old staff sergeant, the barracks' commander, did his level best to discourage us.

One cold winter day we filed out onto the Appellplatz, where the old staff sergeant personally examined the heads from a hair-cutting perspective. He hated hair, and the moment it grew on someone even a bit, he immediately took action and ordered it cut. Only the Germans could have hair.

We welcomed the inspection cheerfully, and while our vanity hadn't rebelled in a while, the sergeant noticed that we were in an unusually good mood, and he growled at us.

"You must have gotten news from the front. But don't be too cheerful, you scoundrels, because no matter what happens, we'll have enough time to exterminate you from the world. It's striking, how many people are alive who are not German. They are completely superfluous. Got that?"

This little speech made me really happy, for I figured it must be going quite badly for the Nazis if they tell us, too, and whether we're to live or die, something would happen soon.

But the days passed, and nothing happened. Only the pace of the work slowed, for somehow there wasn't enough aluminum in the factory for processing. And the finished wings were languishing out on the field beside the factory, since there was no way of shipping them.

One day my boss sent me to another wing of the factory for tools. A narrow path led there, a thick wire fence on both sides. I didn't like such assignments, since it was bitterly cold, and I was capable of feeling splendidly cold in my ragged coat in the course of this short, ten-minute footpath.

Halfway there was an SS soldier standing guard while laughing off the cold in an ankle-length fur coat. Resourceful Germans had cut a little gate in the wire fence, which was good to allow a soldier to step into the factory ground anytime and beat anyone he chose.

I'd just reached the midway point along the path when I heard the soldier's voice.

"Come to me."

The blood froze in my veins. This "Come to me" couldn't mean anything good. The soldier had a rifle, I had nothing.

I went closer.

"Pardon?"

"Do you have a cigarette?"

"No."

"Tobacco?"

"No."

"Are you hungry?"

"Always."

"You'd like bread, right?"

"I'd like it very much."

"Look here," he said, and the lining of his fur coat flashed, and in it, as if in a soft nest, lay a whole loaf of heavenly, civilian bread.

"Lovely bread."

"If you have cigarettes, you can have it."

"Look, sir," I said, because I was unfamiliar with the ranks, "I'm really scared of you. You are a German soldier; I am a Hungarian prisoner. I'd give you all I have just to relax you. I just mentioned that I'm hungry. You can believe me, since I'm not the lying sort. But I have no cigarettes or tobacco, and even if you crucify me I won't have any."

The German lad had black hair, seemed likeable, and was strong. He looked more Serbian than German.

"You haven't got any cigarettes but the bread would be good, huh?"

"I could do a lot with the bread."

"Here, it's yours," he said, handing the whole big loaf through the little gate. I wept. *Surely this will turn out to be some sort of German prank*, I thought. *He'll let me take it, and then he'll shoot me as I leave.* But I didn't even care about that. All I was thinking was that I could never be so happy ever again. I grabbed the bread and tried squeezing it under my little coat. I left. I forgot to thank him. I only lurched, dizzy, toward the other wing of the factory.

Later I looked back. The soldier was trudging languidly about in the snow, not bothering with me.

I could hardly wait to get back to the other part of the factory and tell little Éliás the state of affairs. When I cut a big piece of bread for him, first he quickly ate it, and then he couldn't believe it. He just stared ahead, and when the bread was gone, even then he kept mechanically swallowing.

"These Germans aren't bad guys," he said. "May God strike them all dead," he added, from which I understood at once that his adoration was just temporary.

A twenty-year-old, amiable, brawny guy named Löwinger, who'd mastered the trade of accompanying the dying, lived better than any of us in the camp. His trade saw him shadowing this or that frail old man who obviously wouldn't last long. He had to hold up the man, help him into bed, and help him out to the Appellplatz, because the man was just wobbling along, and the dying invariably began when the poor man lost his appetite and couldn't even eat the little food still portioned to him.

Of course out of gratitude Löwinger got the leftovers, bread, and margarine, and sometimes he had two or three patients at the same time. And even though the dying had seen death so many times from up close, no one could believe in his own death, which had no precedent.

Löwinger did not restrict himself to alms, however. He stole, too, as much as he could—and he was able to steal a lot—and without batting an eyelid he stole from the Germans, too, because he didn't believe he'd be punished.

One time he snuck off from his work site, blending into a throng of workers out on the fields, and he tried sneaking back to his work site with a heap of stolen carrots.

But, alas, the carrots bulged out from under his coat, and right at the gate he came across an SS man with a dog, a soldier who, amazingly, did not beat him dead. He seized the stolen goods and gave him a bit of a thrashing, but let him run.

We had a fellow prisoner named Mittelmann whom everyone loathed. This fiftyish, constantly gabbing, medium-size twerp was a deportee just like us, except that he was ever making a fuss about the work, nothing was good enough or fast enough for him, and if anyone snarled at him, he immediately went to the kapo or the nearest SS soldier to complain, which of course usually had unpleasant consequences.

The kapo hated him, too, but was obliged to investigate his complaints. This Mittelmann was an odious, pushy fellow. I don't know what he might have been in his previous life, but here he practically took delight in the sea of hatred surrounding him, splashing about in it blissfully, like a fish in water.

This Mittelmann really loved beets, which were quite an event at the camp, since we rarely got any, and when we did, in precisely measured servings.

We each got two of these boiled German monotonies, which I invariably gifted at once to Éliás, who, like most others, was a beet aficionado.

One beet-distribution day someone stole Löwinger's helping, which many saw as the hand of fate, but the kapo found out and began an investigation. Soon enough they found the stolen beets in possession of Mittelmann. Denying it was hopeless, since under no circumstances could a man have a double helping, and Mittelman had committed the enormous mistake of storing away his own helping in the hope that he could later trade it for bread.

The kapo began beating Mittelmann slowly, calmly in front of everyone in the room, and only on noticing that he didn't stop did we realize that he was beating him dead. When he fell to the floor from the punches and kicks, he yanked him up and went on beating, with German tenacity, without a break. When Mittelmann was no longer stirring and it was evident that he was no more, the kapo stood up straight and said:

"I'll beat dead every thief just like this, as you've seen. This man was a murderer, because he knew full well that he mustn't touch another's food. So be careful...."

The speech was short but effective. Everyone was struck by the whiff of death. We could feel that we were in Germany.

The last day of the year arrived. Most of the German workers didn't even come to the factory. As for us, we got larger portions of bread and margarine.

The kapo reassured us that we'd all spend the next New Year's Eve as free men.

"It's absolutely certain that the war won't even last a year longer. Be strong, for freedom is closer than you think."

The work progressed half-heartedly on that day, but on returning to the barracks we saw that we got a better dinner, or soup, that is, than usual. There were optimists who thought to discover shreds of meat in the soup.

The new year began. The news from the front was ever more exhilarating, and the pace of work in the factory was ever slower. Even the blind could have seen that there wasn't enough in the way of raw materials and that the Germans were increasingly grumpy.

The food got worse, too, and the portions of bread shrank day by day. Rumors were flitting about that we would be taken away from here, since due to the frequent air raids, undisturbed production was possible only in an underground factory.

We were terribly scared of being sent away from Niederorschel, because by then we knew that this was the best concentration camp in all of Germany.

But January passed, and nothing happened. The days passed in uniform ennui, and we spoke constantly only of food.

From thirteen to seventy, every age group was represented at the camp, but no one cared about a thing other than eating. Not a word was said about women; at most we sometimes mentioned our families, but no one really believed anymore that any of our relatives could still be alive. News never reached us, and our former lives somehow became completely implausible and unimaginable, and we believed it to be only a dream that we'd once lived in the land of freedom of men and freedom of food, where we ourselves had determined our choice of soup.

Dr. Feiner, a tall, muscular, forty-year-old chemical engineer I was very fond of, always used to daydream that if we were ever freed he would go to the market and buy a whole kilogram of potatoes, take them home, boil them himself and, in utmost secrecy, eat them together with an entire loaf of bread. Yet others were such optimists that they still believed in stuffed cabbage, chicken paprikash, and fruit, and, moreover, there was a surprisingly large contingent of pasta aficionados.

At lunchtime I happened to be holding a presentation on bologna for my audience when the master sergeant, the barracks' commander, came by. I cast him a listless stare but forgot to greet him, for I didn't know him personally, we'd never talked.

Greeting was mandatory, and the Germans took it very seriously. We had to stand at attention and remove our caps when we saw a German.

The master sergeant looked at me once more. He couldn't believe his eyes. I still hadn't greeted him, and I had no idea why he was staring with so much agitation. It dawned on me only when he struck the cap off my head and began shouting wildly. The others numbly watched the scene, which came to a close when the boss waved a hand for me to follow him, and so I did.

He took me into his room, a spacious, well-heated space furnished with a writing desk and a typewriter. I stared longingly at the machine. Since leaving home I hadn't so much as seen a typewriter. I recalled my little portable Remington, which I'd left back home and which the Arrow Cross had by now no doubt already executed, for the poor thing was a Jewish machine.

I also thought of our building caretaker, who'd said no trouble would befall us, that we'd only be working and that everyone could continue to ply his own trade.

How lovely it would be, I thought, *if this old sergeant were to desist with this hopeless quarrel about the greeting and let me write a novel or play on the typewriter, which is, after all, only aimlessly ornamenting his room.*

But the sergeant began slapping me. He seemed quite agitated, the veins swelling on his temples and his face purple with rage, and I began getting worried about him. It seemed that this wretch might have a stroke at any moment, and then I'd be executed for murdering a sergeant, which was strictly forbidden in Germany.

I watched this poor old sergeant as he beat me. He was a blue-eyed man who looked like a warm-hearted grandpa, the sort I'd help across the street if I saw him in civilian clothes. Maybe he no longer had the strength or he didn't want to beat me seriously, but I hardly felt his blows, only his shouting annoyed me.

"Forgive me, sir, for interrupting, but allow me to observe that I was never a soldier, so I didn't even know that here I'm supposed to greet you with my cap, since the Germans aren't in the habit of returning greetings. Believe me, it wasn't discourtesy on my part but, rather, overenthusiasm."

"What sort of overenthusiasm?" he inquired even as the veins swelled on his forehead and temples and his hands trembled.

"We were talking about foods, and the mention of chicken paprikash was overwhelming. I'm sorry you got so worked up. At your age, sir, such bursts of emotion can be harmful."

Pause.

"Yes. I've got this godawful temperament. I fall into a rage right away. But fundamentally I'm not a bad person. Only when someone riles me up. And you were the third one today who didn't greet me. So I've even got to write a report about the poor discipline at the camp."

I kept silent.

The sergeant sat down at the machine, inserted a sheet of paper with his unpracticed hands, and began to type. But he got stuck at the outset. I would have given his life to be able to go over to the typewriter and write on it. Anything. A letter to someone, an *a* and a *b* and a *c,* some exclamation marks, anything to once more have my hands on a typewriter. The situation did not seem hopeless. I gave it a shot.

"There's a problem with the machine. I'm a professional. I'll fix it, if you wish."

The sergeant looked up at me.

"What were you before?"

"A writer. I typed a lot at one time. I learned the trade."

"Well, I don't mind. Take a look to see what's wrong."

I was worried he'd hear how loudly my heart was beating. I caressed the machine like a hussar does a horse. It was a German machine, but a typewriter all the same.

I took a good close look.

"It's jammed," I said, though I'd seen from the start that nothing was wrong with the machine.

"Well, just work on it here, in the room. If you ruin it, that's sabotage. I hope you know what the punishment is."

"Death," I said meekly, sabotage expert that I was.

"You don't have to go back to work. You'll work here, on this machine. You'll be done in a week?"

I turned pale. Should I lie to him? There's nothing wrong with the machine. *It would be heavenly, instead of that horrid drilling, to spend a week in complete security, in the sergeant's sanctum, in the immediate proximity of the typewriter. And if some German expert comes in and determines that the machine is faultless, that it's just the sergeant who has a jam?* My hesitation lasted for but a moment. It was best to be forthright. I had to lie.

"I can fix it in two weeks," I said. "But I'd need a new ribbon, too," I added to distract him from the two weeks.

He nodded. "I'll have a new ribbon brought from the city. You just work diligently."

He began to head out before stopping in his tracks in front of one of the closets, whose door he opened with a key, took out a whole loaf of bread, and gave it to me.

"This is for you. The others don't have to know about this."

"I am truly grateful, but I would have an audacious request."

The sergeant smiled.

"*Los.* Out with it."

"Dr. Feiner. Chemical engineer. A very talented man. I would like to divide this immense loaf of bread with him. I've gotten out of the habit of big meals, and he could really enjoy the bread. He speaks German impeccably. And he's always hungry."

The sergeant yelled so hard that I nearly collapsed.

"I'll have that scoundrel brought over. Then you two get to work, or else I'll trample both of you to smithereens."

Five minutes later the kapo brought Feiner, who was deathly pale with fear. A minute later we were left there on our own.

Feiner could hardly get a word out on seeing both the bread and me.

"You're still alive? The boys said that animal beat you dead."

"Of course not. We had a very pleasant conversation."

"From the way he screamed at me, I figured he was taking me to be hanged. What's this about?"

"Eat. This here is our bread."

Feiner fell upon the bread.

"We need to fix this machine."

"Right. But I don't know anything about it. I'm a chemist."

"You're crazy. The machine is fine. We'll fiddle away with it for two weeks."

Feiner's tears fell as he ate.

"Why are you crying?"

"Of course I'm crying when it's so warm in here, and I've been working on an *Ausserkommando*. I hope the sergeant doesn't die while the machine repair is underway."

The sergeant didn't die, but a far more unpleasant thing happened.

Two days later they drew up a list for a march. Most of us at the camp had to travel somewhere, because the provisions were getting worse and worse, and there wasn't any work. I too was assigned to the march.

For one last time we got an out-of-this world cabbage soup, two whole loaves of bread, cheese, margarine, and horse-bologna, and without delay we were heading off to the train.

Everyone was worried about the trip, because rumor had it that the Hardylike master had selected only the poor workers and the old. But one couldn't know the truth, for there were also good workers and young men among us. Little Éliás came with us, too, and not only was he young but he also counted as a good worker. Feiner, too, was assigned to join us.

Thirty

EVEN AT DEATH'S DOOR CARROTS ARE STOLEN.
EVERYONE GOES FASTER THAN THEY CAN.
DURING WORK I UNEXPECTEDLY STAY ALIVE.

The journey began with the train standing still with us in it for two days. Some said it was because air raids had damaged the tracks, and some didn't know a thing. The train stood still. A cold wind blew in the open door of the cattle car.

Guarding us were two SS boys, one of whom spoke Hungarian impeccably, seeing as how he was Hungarian. They seemed like well-meaning fellows and didn't much bother with us.

After two days of standing about the train started. Out of courtesy I called over to the Hungarian SS kid:

"Where are they taking us, sir?"

"To the death camp."

"Finally some good news. And how long is the journey?"

"Hard to tell. There's a war on."

Of course I didn't believe the death camp, because I was thirsty, and at the moment nothing else interested me. One can be unbelievably thirsty in winter. And in summer too.

A quick succession of many stations followed, and our godawful train, if at all possible, stopped, and at every station there was a faucet a meter from our noses, but the canteens and the mess kits remained empty, because the order was that water taking wasn't allowed to those aboard.

On the third day the train stopped.

Though I already knew the German prohibitions against drinking and the law forbidding even the licking of snow, still I tried to talk the amiable, Hungarian-speaking SS kid into giving me at least a gulp of black coffee from his canteen. He didn't even answer. I tried everything. I got him to talk about his family. He told me his mother had been blinded in some accident, and his father, poor man, had fallen in the war, and now he was the apple of his family's eye, for although he had one more sibling back in Hungary, in a certain town called Soroksár, that was only a girl, and as such didn't count.

My heart sank, and I even forgot about the water. I thought of my younger brother, who was a National Health Insurance Institute doctor in Soroksár, of all places, and who had perhaps treated this boy or his blind mother, and who had no doubt by now been murdered by the Arrow Cross.

They'd wanted to deport him right from Soroksár, but he talked the gendarmes out of it, explaining that because he was a Budapest resident, he deserved deportation from there. They admitted that he was right, and let him go. Since then perhaps he too had wound up in Auschwitz or Buchenwald, and I was scared of looking at the unfamiliar, ragged prisoners, lest I should accidentally see him among them.

The slow, torturous journey was into its fourth day. Dr. Feiner was traveling in a sleeping car with me, and the SS boy had even gotten us straw, which is what Dr. Feiner was lying on apathetically. The little Löwinger kid was so thirsty that he even forgot to steal, but we got no water.

By the fifth day even stealing provisions would have been impossible, for the Germans had planned only for a two-day trip, and it seemed that they'd forgotten that there was a war going on, and that in war the length of a journey is uncertain.

I was no longer hungry, just thirsty, but getting water was completely hopeless. I remembered that when I lay in the sanatorium back in Hungary with my broken leg, how irritated I'd been that the nurse had not let the water run for long enough to make it nice and cold, and that in America, from where I'd always longed to go home, how lackadaisically the waiter at the Ritz-Carlton had placed a glass of ice water before me, and how I'd tasted it absentmindedly at best, not even paying attention to the precious water. I remembered how much water I'd frivolously wasted in my life, and I resolved that were I to live, I would care for each and every drop.

On the seventh day we arrived in Halberstadt, a lovely little town with clean, ancient houses, inns, and clean, healthy people.

For a long time we stood aimlessly about at the station, tortured by hunger and thirst, frozen blue, waiting for some arrangement to be made, until finally a German soldier arrived and we started off toward the camp.

After two-and-a-half hours of walking we arrived in the village of Langenstein, beyond the town border. From there we kept walking along unbeaten paths until finally we glimpsed the two towers that were the same in every German concentration camp. The towers were equipped with revolving machine-gun nests so as to nip in the bud any thought of escape.

Again aimless hours passed with the Appell, which was an indispensable feature of every German concentration camp, until finally, counted and diminished in numbers, one hundred twenty-seven of us were herded into a little room that was numbingly cold, though perhaps at one time it had windows, too. It still had a space.

There we were left on our own. After a while we got a bit of bread, margarine, and lukewarm, watery carrot soup in which two little, transparent shreds of carrots were floating aimlessly about.

The shrewder among us drank the soup and stashed away the carrot shreds for harder times. I myself wasn't shrewd, worried as I was that my more artful colleagues would steal the carrots out of my tattered pockets.

For two days nothing happened. I was already starting to get hopeful when, on the third day, we were ordered off to work.

I wasn't concerned for myself, for I was an outstanding skilled worker, the Germans' pride and joy, yes, it was with me that they wanted to win the war, which is why they'd brought me here.

At four in the morning we awoke on the scant layer of straw strewn over the ground. We spent an hour with breakfast and line-up until we could finally head off toward some work site. Of course, breakfast, which comprised some black coffeelike swill, was not delivered right on time. Most often we'd already left by the time the barrels filled with the hot liquid arrived, but by then it was too late. No one bothered to ensure good service.

The camp's longtime residents said the workers get soup at noon, too, and a larger portion of bread, because we were engaging in hard physical labor in an underground factory.

Such news raised our spirits, but along the way they plummeted again. It turned out that the SS soldiers wanted us to proceed on the road somewhat faster than possible. They prodded the group to hurry with rifle butts and billy clubs, and those who fell over, whether on their own, because the road was bad and walking in those cumbrous wooden shoes was hopeless, or because they'd been knocked on the head by a rifle butt, were immediately beset by four or five SS soldiers who beat the individual with wild enthusiasm until he could no longer move. Most unpleasant was the fact that most of us had ragged shoes, and they didn't provide shoelaces. While the shoes themselves must have been made at one time of exceptional wood, their soles had the tendency to flake off.

Over squelching mud, hills, and poor, rocky roads we hurried to work, so by the time we reached the factory gate my fancy for the whole of Germany had completely faded; and that's when the worse half of the journey began. The factory itself had been blasted into a huge mountain, and a pitch-black, long tunnel led to the actual plant. The airplane factory was complicated by a quarry, and the mining carts that were constantly going back and forth on rails, carrying rocks, disturbed our marching a bit. Many were trampled by the wee but spunky carts, many got their legs caught between the tracks, and many simply collapsed, only to be trampled by the others.

On reaching the far end of the tunnel we had to run to the assembly place, where we were assigned to work. Here, a German clerk received us, reading our numbers in a strange dialect from some sort of book. Anyone whose number was pronounced had to step forward. The clerk was a huge, well-fed, strikingly strong, large-handed, large-footed German who deemed it natural that the deportees knew or, at least, understood German. And yet many understood not a word other than those of their mother tongue, and anyone who didn't spring forward from line immediately on hearing his number had a ruined day ahead of him, because the number they wore on their chests allowed the clerk to immediately determine who it was who'd contravened his order.

In the best-case scenario the clerk would beat and batter the guilty party only with his fists, but a *vorarbeiter* (foreman) or two from among those who were constantly roving about usually gave a helping hand, and whose sole serious business comprised egging on the recalcitrant prisoners with beatings.

Based on my profession, I was assigned to the warehouse, which, as would turn out, meant life insurance.

The work in the warehouse involved puttering about: we had to sort through the various parts, light bulbs, needles, washing powders, textiles, and hardware, and during work the boss, who was called Müller, didn't bother anyone.

This Müller—a short, spectacled, kindly German, personally selected his colleagues, and when that happened, he gave us the following speech:

"Prisoners! Only doctors, lawyers, engineers, writers, and businessmen can work under me. I demand precision and conscientiousness. Those who do good work will not have any trouble; bad workers will be let go. Dismissal means certain death, since anyone I send packing will be assigned to an *Ausserkommando*. That means only that you need to transport goods arriving at the station to the factory. You may leave. *Abtreten*. Let the work begin."

Not that I understood why transporting goods from the station should be deadly, but I had neither time nor the occasion to interrogate the dear little German in detail.

I began my operations in my new field of work.

I tried to sabotage as much as possible, but it soon turned out that this was unnecessary. The work was completely meaningless and aimless, anyway. Various goods had to be carried from one place to another, and then returned to where they'd come from.

Meanwhile the SS soldiers, the *Vorarbeiters*, beat everyone constantly. It took me days to understand that the emphasis here was not on building airplanes: the plant was a true-to-form death factory, where nothing mattered except that the forced laborers should die slow, painful deaths.

And yet the rumors concerning the midday soup proved true. At noon we get not only thick, tasty soup but also a slice of bread, the same sort of normal, civilian bread as the Germans.

I spent the first day carrying an enormous light bulb from one place to another, and then taking the same bulb back to its base. No one bothered with the point of it. All they saw was that I was industrious, and aside from Müller, who made only rare appearances, as it was cold in the factory, no one knew what I was doing and why.

At five, work ended and the Appell began. We were counted, and then, prodded along with billy clubs and rifle butts, we were driven back to our lodging between the two towers.

There was no time, occasion, or place for bathing. My hand was the only part of my body I could see, but it was so filthy that I didn't even recognize it.

The second day, for "punishment," the noontime soups ceased. Instead we were led out to push train cars under the supervision of SS soldiers. This pushing of train cars was a dangerous trade, for many fell under the train and many died of beatings.

A furniture factory owner from the outskirts of Budapest, whose family name was Székely, wound up along with his nephew in the same room as me. The boy was fourteen years old but doing the adults' work. On account of his looks and his smarts, one of the guards grew fond of him, and secured him a good position in one of the heated rooms, and, since he was a child, he also got *nachschlag* – extra soup. Using bricks and other odds and ends, the uncle fabricated a stove in the room, and out in the yard we gathered dry twigs to conjure a little heat into this icy hell.

All of us partook enthusiastically in collecting wood, and we were proud of ourselves, but the next day the camp leadership confiscated the stove along with the wood.

At night, when we got home from work, we had to wait so long for the cold, thin, sour, carrot soup and for the bread and margarine, that it was eleven by the time we got to bed or, rather, could lie down on the cold straw. We could then sleep as much as we wanted until four in the morning, but not even sleep passed completely undisturbed.

Indeed, the Germans had come up with a game called *Augen zu!*, which saw them yelling their tops off as they burst into the dark bedroom around two in the morning, turning on the light and roaring, "Eyes shut!" Of course everyone opened their eyes in terror to see what was going on, and most didn't even understand, and those whose eyes stayed open got beaten silly with billy clubs and bludgeons.

Anyone who survived to morning did so by virtue of a miracle, and then the beating began anew. Both the kapos and the *vorarbeiters* did the beating, so hardly anything was left for the SS soldiers.

They beat us during morning wake-up, though everyone sprang up at the shout, *Aufstehn*! And they beat us at the Appell, though everyone stood properly in line, and they beat dead anyone who was "faking it" by daring to report that they were sick.

Those who were weak in the morning and couldn't go to work were beaten dead. The rule was that you had to report that you were sick a day in advance, and if the illness was confirmed, then in the most serious cases the prisoner-doctor had the right to grant three days' *Schonung*, or sick leave. Those who could no longer even move were taken to the *Revier*, or the hospital, where the guards waited for them to die.

The sick received smaller portions of food, so most people preferred to accept being beaten dead than to starve to death.

We were most afraid of the clerk, who assigned us to work every day, for he was strong and merciless and he loved beating. Sometimes he began with a seemingly trivial slap, and then when he warmed up to it, psyched up for a good beating, he went at it and didn't stop as long as the individual was still moving.

Those who dodged the clerk had some hope of staying alive that day.

I began to believe that this was a death camp on seeing that in three weeks in that room where one hundred twenty-seven of us had arrived, just twenty-one of us were still alive. The rest starved to death or got beaten dead.

There were often "lice inspections," which were completely pointless. The inspection would consist of our having to strip naked in the room, whereupon the deportee-doctor would check our clothes from a hygiene perspective. Since we'd all been lice-infested for a good while, the results never caused even a bit of surprise.

It would have been easy to disinfect all of us, but there was no command to this effect. For my part, I kept reassuring my colleagues that we would most certainly be disinfected, since we were constantly in close proximity to Germans, and it was in their interest not to get lice-infested from us. But later it turned out that my prediction did not come to pass. And so the only medicine that could be used against lice was scratching, but during work they forbade even that, since they didn't want us stealing time with nonsense that didn't advance the cause of winning the war.

Langenstein was a dreary place, and I couldn't even imagine getting out of there free and alive.

Only sometimes did I get a little taste of the *Ausserkommando*, when lots of goods arrived or when lots of goods had to be transported to the station a half-hour away.

At such times everyone was called upon, even those who worked in the warehouse or other places, and as soon as we stepped outside the factory gates, the SS assumed command of the forced laborers.

I once overheard an older SS guard who looked like a family man boasting to a comrade that for him even ten billy clubs a day aren't enough, since he breaks all of them on the prisoners' backs and heads.

From the trains we had to transport hopelessly heavy and slippery goods over steep roads amid constant blows.

With great difficulty March arrived, but it was colder than all the other winter months combined. It was an odious, German March, and I pined for death, for I knew that life now comprised nothing else but the pointless lugging of heavy objects, being beaten, starving, scratching, and the endless Appell at dawn each day, from which one by all means had to die.

One morning four o'clock wake-up came and went. We got up only at six, and that day there was only line-up, a clothing inspection, and slapping, but no work.

Rumor had it that the end was near.

The next day they ordered us out to work again.

But there was hardly even any work for show, as the factory had ground completely to a halt, so everyone was led out to the *Ausserkommando*, and starting then I got a different outside assignment every day.

The first outside task involved us walking down to Halberstadt at dawn and digging trenches under the supervision of German civilians. My commander was a lanky German peasant who was tireless at beating. With an iron pitchfork and a stick he beat dead those he singled out.

He climbed down into the trench I was in and showed me what to do.

I'd never heard that pitchforks could be used for digging, too, but he showed me. He pressed the pitchfork into the earth, and in one deft movement he flung an immense amount of dirt out of the trench.

I could hardly even lift the pitchfork, that's how weak I was. I explained to him that for such work you had to be strong, young, and an expert, and that I was little, lice-infested, and hungry. He should just go ahead and beat me dead, let's be done with it, he could even take his pitchfork with him, as far as I was concerned.

The German peasant hardly paid me any notice. Peering out of the trench, he saw a thin French kid who had paused while working. Grabbing the pitchfork from me, the peasant rushed at the boy. By the third blow the French boy had stopped moving.

Somehow the day passed without me getting beaten dead, whereupon I reported that I was sick. But the doctor determined me to be healthy, though I could barely walk.

The next day they marched us out to the quarry. This work was even worse than the business of ramparts and trenches.

We had to toss impossibly big rocks in and out of train cars. Meanwhile we had to push the loaded train while grabbing on to what we could on godforsaken roads, amid a hundred thousand possible deaths. For example, we had to cross a slender little bridge whose left side was flanked by a tall, straight cliff, while the right side was furnished with a six-storey gaping gorge, its bottom strewn with sharp rocks. Nowhere a railing.

The SS soldiers amused themselves by leaning up against the cliff wall and, with their exquisite, strong boots, kicking into the prisoners, who somersaulted head first into the deep, where the sharp rocks tore apart their bone-withered bodies.

I crossed the bridge apathetically, almost nonchalantly. By then I wasn't afraid of death, for it had been some time since I'd had a life they could have taken from me. The SS could deprive me only of the Appell, the beatings, the starvation, and the lice, and perhaps some ever-fading ray of hope that barely flickered in me. I was incapable of either being happy or feeling fear.

Before me went R., who was my roommate at Niederorschel; and behind me an eighteen-year-old boy, Gottesmann, who had volunteered for the death camp, since his father had been enlisted, and he didn't want to let the old man go alone. Being strong and young, he helped his dad a lot during the daily marches, which he endured better.

The dad had been assigned to an *Ausserkommando* and was beaten dead the first week. The son became a gaunt, eerie image of his former self, but he proved tough.

When he reached the SS boys in the middle of the bridge, he looked at them in terror and started off. One SS kid gave him a heel kick, and Gottesmann plummeted in a wide arch into the sharp rocks below.

I looked indifferently into the lovely blue eyes of the SS kid and went forward. Another SS soldier raised his foot to kick me down beside Gottesmann, but it seemed that the game no longer amused him. He let me pass.

I felt no pleasure at all.

The next day I wound up in the factory again.

By then I was really bored of all of Germany, the war, and my own life. Everyone I loved had died away around me. Taking pity on me, one SS soldier let me take enough water into my canteen for lunch from the hot water faucet maintained for the Germans.

I took the risk of addressing him:

"This is very kind of you. There's no better lunch than good, hot water."

I spoke only so that at least I wouldn't have to work meanwhile, because I was exhausted and so tired that I could have fallen asleep while walking. The SS man asked, from an immeasurable height, "Where are you from?"

"I was brought here from Budapest."

"Do you have anyone back there?"

"My father, my brother, my friends."

"You only *did*. In Budapest, everyone's croaked." *Alles krepiert*—that's how he put it in German. "We scorched the whole city. You can go, then."

So everyone had perished. The SS soldier had surely lied. *He's a murderer, a bandit, and a Nazi—why shouldn't he be a liar?* I brooded. *Not everyone's died. The law of numbers doesn't allow for everyone to die. I haven't died, either, and here it really is impossible to stay alive.*

By then I'd been playing a game in my head that went like this: If I could choose, who would live and who would die? It was impossible that my entire family and all my friends would pull through this horror alive. But also that everyone would die.

If my dad would die…. He's the oldest. May my little brother, Gyuri, my little sister, Julika, and her daughter and my brother-in-law live. Dad is the oldest. That doesn't work. Dad never hurt anyone; he dedicated his whole life to his family and gave us his every penny. No, he shouldn't die. If Gyuri would die, my little sister should live, she's got a daughter she has to raise. And if my brother-in-law No, my brother-in-law shouldn't die, since he was only good to everyone, helping where he could. Ella shouldn't die, either, she's my best friend. Instead, maybe Éva could die, she's still young, with a life ahead of her, or maybe Zoli Stób who was always good to me and paid me a terrified visit in the sanatorium when the Germans invaded, and taught me what to do, and who was then soon captured and sent to a prison camp on the city outskirts as a leftist newspaper reporter? No, he shouldn't die, either. Gyuri, too, should stay alive. So, Ella should survive. Gyuri and Tusi should die, Dad should stay alive.

I couldn't get my mind off this game; I was thinking of it all the time, and I was scared I'd go mad from it. I couldn't reach an agreement with myself, since I absolutely insisted on Pista Lukács surviving, too, for after Ella he was the friend I was fondest of. No, surely I couldn't let Pista, that plump, angelic fellow, die. I wasn't a murderer.

I remembered various trifles concerning Pista Lukács. Though he was a lazy man, he got up at the crack of dawn for my sake but didn't even show up for a meeting when I could have helped him out. Back when we first became acquainted, when I didn't yet know his famous, kind, husky voice, he phoned me one day:

"Is this 185-432 talking?" he asked.

"Yes."

"Pál Királyhegyi's flat?"

"Yes."

"Mr. Pál Királyhegyi is on the line?"

"Yes."

"Wrong number," he said, and hung up. For some minutes I walked about the flat, confounded, brooding. *What could the mistake have been?*

No, I wouldn't let Pista die.

What should I do? It was a maddening game, but I couldn't escape it. At night I dreamed of them, and at dawn the Appell began from the start all over again.

By now only a trace of the prisoners at the camp still worked inside, in the factory. The others went out to work either at the quarry or some other place nearby. Again I was assigned to some digging project, but by then I was in really rickety shape, barely able to drag myself along, and I knew the end was near when the young Löwinger kid sidled up beside me.

"Hey, old man, if you die, can I have your remaining bread?"

"Of course you can. Just don't let me collapse on the road."

"And you'll give me your margarine, too?"

"I will, just lend me an arm."

We got out to the field, which was then overrun by SS troops. Before the morning was out, before my eyes, the Löwinger kid was beaten dead, since he'd been mishandling the spade.

I dug the lousy German mother earth wildly until finally lunchtime came. Again I'd stayed alive.

Sitting on some piece of rail, I was chewing my dry remaining bit of bread when a sad-faced SS trooper sat down beside me.

"What's wrong?" I inquired in German.

"May they all rot in hell," he replied in Hungarian.

I was overjoyed to hear this familiar curse from back home.

"You're complaining? You're the master of the world. An SS guard. You can't top that. What's your complaint? Maybe I can help."

Not that I trusted my ability to help, given that I had rather little authority, but he went on complaining, probably just out of a desire to express himself, which is very strong in all people.

"The food is bad. We're starving. And there's no tobacco, either."

"Sir, don't kid around. You people are starving? Sir, you are with the SS. Do you know what this uniform means?"

"It's not worth a rat's ass. I don't even know German. They dragged me off from my village, dressed me up in this costume, gave me a rifle, and then they said that if I don't like it they'll shove me in here among all of you."

"Listen here. Where are you from?"

"Somogy County. A pox on them."

"So. Go to the nearest peasant house, but now, right away. You needn't talk much, for even the Germans get the jitters on seeing this uniform. Go into the house and don't even say hello, give a hard stare and say "*Eier*." That's it. That's all there is to it. Your hunger will be gone in no time."

The Hungarian peasant brooded, then shook himself off, stood up, and left. Ten minutes later he returned, loaded up with bread and eggs. He was beaming.

"This here is yours," he said, extending the bread and two eggs to me.

A cold shudder of excitement passed through me. I hadn't even seen an egg in almost six months.

"These are raw eggs. What can I do with them? You can boil them in the kitchen."

The Hungarian peasant, Péter Balogh, from Somogy County, boiled the eggs and sought me out that night, during dinnertime, in my lodging. He had me summoned outside, where he secretly gave me the two eggs, hard-boiled. I wept. Because he gave salt with them, too.

Thirty-One

EVEN AS YOU'RE BEATEN DEAD, YOU'VE GOT TO BE SECRETIVE. PLEASURE, TOO, TAKES STRENGTH AND NERVES. PINEAPPLE IS FOOD, TOO.

The days passed, and I didn't care about anything anymore. Least of all, about life. In the dim light of dawn, during morning line-up, someone stole the cap off my head, which meant that my shaven head could get as drenched as it wanted to, but no longer did I care about even that. I'd thought the watery carrot soup couldn't get worse, but it turned out I was wrong. I could barely drag myself along the cold, slippery road, and yet by virtue of some miracle, at dawn each day I headed off and arrived, more than that, I was still alive by the time we got to work at some *Kommando*, in the fields or the quarries.

One day, when I saw that I was near the wasting away end of wasting away, and that only the adverb "completely" stood between me and perishing, I reported to the camp doctor, a Czech, who gave me three days' sick leave. All that meant was that I didn't have to go out among the murderers, but instead I could stay there among them. Of course the Nazis didn't give illness for free, either. They always found some work suitable for the sick alongside cleaning and sweeping. At times one had to lug rocks from one place to another, for no reason at all, and at other times one had to carry logs, to ensure that we would not soften up entirely amid the deluge of idleness.

On the second day of my sick leave one of the young ruffians shoved me into a line-up even though I showed him my pass confirming that I was temporarily relieved of service. It was six in the evening, so I knew they were taking me off to night duty somewhere, and I barely even resisted. I'd heard terrific things about night work, when even the executioners were sleepy and so not paying so much attention to their victims.

I was surprised to see—insofar as one could see at all in the half-light of dusk—that we were being taken to the factory, where there was hardly any work anymore. Somehow I managed to make it to the tunnel entrance, but the tunnel itself—if this is possible at all—seemed darker at night than by day, and a few yards in, I stopped short. It seemed that the little train was coming right at me, except that it was dark, too, as in some unlikely moment of delirium, and besides, I could barely drag myself along.

Having noticed my hesitation, the *Vorarbeiter* gave me a few kicks to get me going. All I could do was wonder, for I could no longer feel pain. How he managed to strike me in that pitch-black tunnel, I will never know. But by then I cared not even about the train, nor about the rocks, which, had I stumbled on them, would have meant certain death. I just walked blindly ahead in the clammy darkness.

It was a fifteen-minute journey until I finally saw faint lights glimmering in front of the factory.

After line-up the *Vorarbeiter* assigned me to wagon work, which meant having to unload impossibly heavy and slippery sheets of iron from the flat wagons in the factory.

Within minutes every one of my fingers was bleeding and I couldn't feel my body, but still I tried lifting the plates with another person. Working beside me was Weisz, a compact little fellow who, though he was already pushing sixty, was incredibly tenacious and smart, worked zealously, and kept cautioning me that I didn't have the enthusiasm that unloading iron sheets by all means required.

Alas, it wasn't only Weisz who noticed this. All at once, from out of nowhere there appeared an immeasurably tall and strapping SS soldier in a beautiful uniform and with a thick billy club in his hand. He too found my pace too slow, and he bore down upon me with terrible force. The first blow caught my shoulder, paralyzing my hand, so by then it was out of the question that he might goad me into quickening my pace.

But this SS guard isn't paying attention to the work so much as to the beating, I thought. With that thick billy club, he kept hitting me without even aiming.

And then something unprecedented happened. My tenacious and compact companion, Weisz, paused in his work, stepped over to the SS soldier who was busy beating me, and spoke up.

"I'm sorry to bother you, but my friend is slow because he is sick. Actually he shouldn't have been marched out here at all. Please look at his *Schonung* pass."

Even Weisz himself was frightened by his boldness, but he stood right there awaiting a reply.

"*Los!*" snapped the SS soldier, striking Weisz with his billy club twice between the eyes, leaving him tottering. But he did not fall. He just went back to the iron sheets.

The SS boy calmly resumed the beating. I'd often seen this since I'd started to work here at the extermination camp, and I knew full well that this was not a case of punishment but a case of being beaten dead.

The executioner kept beating me and didn't stop. And it seemed he didn't want to stop, either, as long as I remained alive.

I sensed that I had only moments left, and in that dispiriting instant something occurred to me. I called out to my murderer.

"Listen. I'd like to talk with you."

The billy club froze in the hand of the SS guard. He couldn't believe his ears. This wasn't his first case of beating someone dead, and the victims could only whimper and beg for mercy. No one was in the mood for a conversation on such occasions.

Heartened by my success, I continued.

"It's important. It's urgent."

"What do you want to say, you piece of trash?"

"I can't tell you here. It's a secret."

Lying there all bloody though I was, I could see his eyes glimmer. He must have figured I had some intriguing conspiracy to reveal before I died.

He let down the billy club and pointed to a nearby room.

"Go over there. Talk."

"I can't stand up anymore," I replied. "Carry me."

The giant SS boy snatched me up with two fingers—I must have weighed about a quarter pound back then—and took me to the other room. He closed the door behind him.

"So! *Los!* What's it you want to say?"

Every last bit of me hurt from the beating. With my fist I tried wiping away the blood trickling into my eyes. I lay there on one of the worktables, struggling to gather up what strength I had left to lift my head. The SS murderer gently placed a hand under my head.

"*Los!* So, what did you want to say?"

"Listen, sir, I don't know what your rank might be, but that's not even important just now. I've already died. You've beaten me dead. In my former life I was a writer, and I was always more interested in the story than my own life. Tell me, what is it that drives you? Why are you angry at me? Why have you beaten me so wildly? What pleasure do you get from me dying?"

The SS boy laughed.

"Are you crazy? This is my job. We make statistics of the dead. I've got to exterminate my quota. But I could just as well beat someone else dead. I don't really care who it is. Today I happen to be tired, and in case you didn't know, we get two extra cigarettes for every death. Know what? So you see who I am, I'll take mercy on you. It doesn't really matter."

"You can't take mercy on me anymore," I replied, "because I've already died. I can't even move because of your beating. When the shift is over, toward morning we'll go home, and anyone unable to march down the road will get beaten dead, anyway."

The SS boy pondered for a moment, and then decided.

“I’ll give you two prisoners and a wheelbarrow. They will push you home now, before the shift ends, and then you won’t have any trouble. I’ll have that brave little friend of yours who stood up for you accompany you. Or should I beat him dead? It’s really hard to get cigarettes….”

I managed to talk him into having Weisz help take me back, and I was still alive to a certain degree when I was helped into the room and lay down on the lice-infested straw.

Lying down wasn’t good, though, because no matter how I positioned myself, I was touching my own bones. It turned out that I was too thin even to be lying down.

The next day no one had to go out to work. On the third day I overheard it said that the SS guards had vanished from the towers. That day for “punishment” no one got even a spoonful of soup. We must have done some mischief.

On the fourth day the SS disappeared completely and a white flag was fluttering on each of the two famous towers of the concentration camp.

By then rumors were circulating that the Americans were really close, but I didn’t believe them. I’d heard so much good news already in Germany, and the situation always just got worse.

But it was true that the SS guards had disappeared, and a German political prisoner named Adler, who’d been a teacher in his former life, took over command of the camp. The beating ceased.

The Russian deportees broke open the locked storerooms, and everyone got plenty of soup. They also got potatoes from the hopper.

But, now, more people were dropping dead from eating than from the SS guards. A doctor friend of mine among the deportees explained to me that starvation renders the stomach and bowels paper thin, and they become useless.

I was lethargic and lice-infested. The injuries I’d suffered while being beaten were still smarting. I couldn’t even raise my left hand.

I could feel this was it, the end: I was able to itch, but no longer did I have the strength to scratch. I pined for the good old days, when I’d still been enthusiastically scratching and had believed in a better future.

The German political prisoner promised a double helping of soup to those who helped take the dead from the room out to the yard. In earlier times, as a shrewd businessman, I would have jumped at the offer, but now not even that could inspire me. True, the dead were unbelievably thin, so it couldn't have been hard to take them outside, but I had to forgo the double helping of soup. Not that I understood why the individuals had to be separated in the first place, for by then all of us were dead. What sense did it make to be carrying each other?

At first I sensed only a wave of unintelligible jabbering around me, and I didn't even pay attention. I tried opening my eyes only when the first white-uniformed American soldier triumphantly stood above my bed of straw, brimming with youth and health, with a bona fide, burning Camel cigarette hanging from his mouth.

I felt no pleasure at all.

Pleasure takes strength, and I no longer had enough energy in me to say even a word. I vaguely remembered that I knew English at least as well as I knew Hungarian, for I'd lived a dozen years in America, had written books in English and films in English in Hollywood, and America was my second home, but now I couldn't force myself to greet this unlikely miracle that had dropped out of the sky, this American soldier with a Camel.

My brain was still working, though: I would have liked to tell him how good it was that he'd come, now, at the last minute, just like in a Hollywood movie he might have freed from evil an innocent, kindly, lovely, lice-infested typewriting gal, me.

But I couldn't even whisper. I was dying.

So this is what that famous "dying by withering away" feels like, I thought. But I felt no fear at all. Fear takes strength. As does pleasure. And heartbreak. As does everything. No, they are not mad, all those people the world over who have breakfast, lunch, a snack, and dinner—lest they should die by withering away, like me and others who've been condemned to death.

No longer was I of sound enough mind to understand that it wasn't necessary to talk much to the Americans, who knew everything.

Gentle, strong hands lifted me and put me along with many others into a truck, which then stopped with us on Horst-Wessel Strasse, at the military hospital.

Not for a moment did I faint, I was just weak. I saw American soap that was whiter than snow; with that, we were bathed. I saw the white delousing powder we were disinfected with in a tent in front of the hospital, where they also burned the rags I'd had on and gave me brand new underclothes and then took me into the hospital on a stretcher, covered me with a light but warm American camel-hair blanket, and fed me.

Not soup. The era of German soups was over.

The first meal I got from the Americans after a thousand years of soup was pineapple! While I recognized it from years earlier, never would I have thought that I would meet with it again in my life.

There were mirrors in the hospital. It took quite a while before I recognized myself in that bald old wreck looking back at me. There were bags under my eyes that had formed from all the fluid, bags I'd never seen before, and my legs were swollen.

Three days later I was able to speak with the American doctor, who asked me to translate for my companions that they should strictly abide by the rules, and not to eat more than what they were given.

"Tell them that you folks are not hungry, but starved, which is a big difference. That means that the feeling of hunger does not stop after eating. It will take at least six months before you can eat normally again. Anyone who eats more than allowed to will surely die."

I translated the doctor's words into every language, but the vast majority of my companions listened with disinterest and could hardly wait for all the empty babble to be over. They ate, and they died.

It was easy to get more food than was allotted to you, for there were lots of dying people who no longer ate at all, and they gladly handed over their portions to the rest of us.

I wound up in one room with little Élias and two strangers.

I spent hours explaining to Élias the disadvantages of eating, until he finally understood. And he survived. He was seventeen at the time. By then he was just wobbling, and had nothing earthly left on him.

By the time I slowly came to, it turned out that the Americans were handing out not only food but also eight cigarettes to each of us with religious precision each day. The medic explained that we mustn't smoke more, because we were still too weak.

But out of caution I smoked Élias's allotment, too. He wasn't interested in cigarettes, because he was young; he cared only about chocolate, because it was sweet.

In the hospital I learned that the war wasn't over yet, since the Japanese were still fighting. My angelic American sergeant, a certain McCormick, also told me that Roosevelt had died. I wept for the president as if he'd been my own father.

Not only was the food unbelievably good, though, and not only did I get cigarettes, but every day I read the American newspaper *Stars and Stripes*, from which I learned of the latest events.

Every time I took that paper into my hands I had to choke back my tears, that's how overcome I was to know that even if I were to die soon, I had at least lived to see this. That, after so long, I could read a real paper. That tasted even better than cigarettes.

Only a week later did I notice that there were American women in the hospital, too. They functioned as nurses. I'd forgotten that there was more than just blood, filth, grime, and SS guards on earth, but also—very rightly—women, too, who could be lovely, kind, gentle, and sweet-smelling.

One of those American nurses regularly supplied me with American magazines too.

Meanwhile we were weighed and examined four times a day, like newborns, and I overheard one of the American doctors who didn't know I spoke English say to his colleague:

"He probably won't make it. But we've got to try everything."

As for me, ever since seeing myself in the mirror I knew I couldn't make it, for those skinny little nothings that had once been my arms, my feeble legs, and my sunken, rickety chest could not be slapped back to life, not even with pineapples.

Nonetheless, in three weeks the Americans led us out to the yard for exercise.

For me, the exercise meant being helped down the six steps and then, leaning on two people, walking around the yard almost once. Then, with panicked urgency, I staggered back to the certainty of the bed, where walking around was unnecessary.

It was heaven, this hospital where the doctors and nurses did everything humanly and superhumanly possible to somehow keep us alive. And this wasn't easy.

So caught up in the throes of liberation, we were, that many of my companions fled the hospital to live free lives. Among us there was an Italian man who ate everything he could, and despite my telling him that he needn't eat and drink the aspirin and vials of medication, he remained unedified: he stole wherever and whatever he could, and it seemed he hadn't even heard that there was such a thing in the world as medicine, for he saw as food the contents of even the sternest-looking bottles of medicine, and swallowed everything indiscriminately. There was no getting through to him. I was certain that this compulsion of his would kill him. But he survived.

Thirty-Two

There is no time for regret. Ursula laughs, I don't know why. I walk on the train. The past haunts.

After six weeks of eating I asked the American doctor to let me out of the hospital, since I already felt healthy and strong.

Of course this was an exaggeration, as I could only trudge along, but on the one hand, I wanted to get home to Budapest already, and on the other hand, no matter how kind and warm-hearted the Americans were, this hospital was a prison, too, with planned meals served on precise schedules, lights out, and discipline befitting a military hospital.

I wanted to walk on the streets, to come and go aimlessly amid the freedom of food, setting my own schedule, to slurp of the freedom that was more precious than anything else.

The doctor said he would let me go together with Éliás, who was likewise burning with impatience, and who'd regained his strength far faster than I.

For the journey we got a German worker's uniform that was clean and brand new, a pair of real leather shoes instead of the wooden boots, socks, and an SS cape stripped of its insignia, not that ranks had ever interested me much, anyway. And so I felt almost happy. The only thing that bothered me unceasingly was that I hadn't yet managed to get even a shred of news from home. Germany was completely cut off from the outside world: one couldn't even dream of telephones, telegrams, or letters.

Halberstadt itself was in sorry shape, too. More than half the city was completely destroyed, with burnt-out trams lying about on the streets, and not even the firewalls remaining of most buildings. As I learned, the Americans had called on the city's leaders to surrender before the carpet bombing, and so they began bombing Halberstadt only when the Germans gave them no choice.

But this city never had grown too close to my heart, and so I shed few tears over its destruction.

Our first order of business was to find some sort of housing. On recommendation of the American doctor, we dropped in at the Halberstadt girls' high school, where former deportees were lodged.

The director of the girls' school, a former German deportee, got us a room with beds in minutes, and issued food rations right away as well.

The food was outstanding, and though I was exhausted by the time lunch ended, impatience drove me to go for a walk along with little Éliás.

After only a few steps my feet took root in the ground in terror. There, coming right toward me, glowing with good cheer, was the camp's sadistic German clerk, wearing the uniform of the former prisoners.

With my shaky legs it would have been hopeless for me to run after him, so I greeted him with a friendly smile.

"How are you? I'm so happy to see you!" And meanwhile to myself I damned that international custom whereby the police are never nearby when you need them.

The situation was completely hopeless, since the Americans got about only in their jeeps and in planes. They didn't go about on foot.

But still. A miracle happened. I'd spoken hardly a few words with the murderous German clerk when an American MP jeep pulled up beside us and asked me for directions.

With a smile I replied in English:

"I'm actually not in a good mood at all. I'm smiling just out of slyness, because this German standing beside me is a murderer. He beat many people dead. What can be done with him?"

The American jumped from the vehicle.

"Consider him arrested. You'll come with us, too."

The German clerk anxiously asked me what happened, what the problem was, and where they were taking him, whereupon I reassured him:

"These are military police. I told them you're a murderer. They'll interrogate you."

The German was sulking. He didn't want to recognize me, though I'd gotten a whole lot of slaps from him a few weeks earlier.

In the jeep I told the MP this much more: "Just to be clear, this German is not my personal enemy. It's just that he's a mass murderer. There are many living witnesses who saw him beat people dead. This boy with me is also a witness. We were deported together."

"I believe the two of you," said the American officer. "No more witnesses are needed. Was he with the SS?"

I nodded.

"What will become of him now?"

"We don't torture anyone. The order is to shoot all SS dead."

The Americans took in the German clerk, interrogated me along with Éliás, and then I never saw the German again. He disappeared somewhere.

Ten of us shared a room in the girls' high school, but life wasn't sweet through and through there, either. We had to go at a set time to get our soup, which was remarkable, with plenty of meat. They even gave coffee and as much bread as we wanted. And yet I still wanted to change the situation. I resolved to look for new lodgings.

In fact, soon Éliás and I did manage to find a real, true-to-form home right out of the good old days, without military discipline and soups. Our landlady was called Frau Rose, and she lived with her husband and seventeen-year-old boy in their own little house, in which they rented us a room. Back then in Germany no one much cared about money. It was impossible to spend more than one hundred marks a month, anyway, because practically all you could buy was what was available for ration coupons, and there wasn't much of that.

The former deportees had it good. Anyone who knew his way around a bit could acquire all sorts of things with or without coupons, and for Frau Rose our being deportees was a good recommendation.

"The Germans are in very bad straits just now," explained Frau Rose. "People hate them. And yet my own husband was in Buchenwald, because he is a communist."

We got to know her husband, too, a smart, fiftyish German who berated Hitler every chance he had.

Through the Americans we brought home lots of food, and Éliás kept getting rounder and couldn't stop eating. We regularly visited Halberstadt's biggest meat factory, where we got as much as ten kilograms of meat at a time, which is not even to speak of various cold cuts.

Out of gratitude Frau Rose cooked and cleaned for us, and in exchange for the food we procured she sometimes gave us each a pair of socks, sometimes a shirt, sometimes some other item that was priceless and impossible to find in Germany at the time.

At the meat factory we got the meat under the table, without ration coupons, but at regular prices. The factory owner had a strikingly beautiful young daughter, Ursula, and we never left there without her stuffing Éliás's valise to the brim with all manner of meats.

One day on getting home, happily loaded up with our usual multitude of raw materials, we found our beloved landlady in tears. I felt terribly sorry for the poor woman, who was crying like a downpour, and we couldn't stem the flow. Finally, through much difficulty, it turned out that her husband had been arrested.

"Imagine, the Americans arrested him here, in the house—my husband, who suffered through Buchenwald, whom the Nazis had wanted to kill. I can't believe it."

Since I knew English, she begged me to go to the American commander and find out what happened. The American's didn't know German, she reasoned, so surely they'd confused her husband for another

Rose, for that was a common name in Germany. "For the love of God, do something," she said, "because he won't survive this."

I hurried to city hall, which was where the American headquarters was. After a few questions I learned that the officer responsible for Herr Rose's case was in room 11.

I clomped ardently into the room.

"Sir," I began, "a great injustice has occurred here. Or a mistake. This Rose …" But the officer raised a hand for me to stop.

"Who is that Rose?"

"My landlord. He's innocent. He was in a concentration camp, at Buchenwald. He hates the Nazis."

The American smiled.

"Is this certain?"

"Dead certain."

"Well, if you please, here are the Rose files. In German and in English. Look them over, and if you then see some injustice, Herr Rose will immediately go free."

"So he's under arrest at the moment?"

"Naturally. Go ahead. Here are the files."

I began studying the Rose case files. It turned out that he was one of the earliest Nazis. He'd been an agent provocateur who'd made a living regularly informing on people. He'd been in Buchenwald, too, for a few days so that as a faithful comrade he could listen in on political prisoners' conversations. He'd sent many men to their deaths.

I thanked the American officer for the information.

"I think my dear landlord, Herr Rose, is in the right place."

On the way home that evening I kept pondering, *Is it possible that every kind, gentle German is, at least at the bottom of his heart, a mass murderer?*

Frau Rose received me with tear-worn eyes and an agitated expression.

"Did you speak to the Americans?"

"I did."

"And? What did they say?"

"Frau Rose, rest assured, if your husband is innocent it is completely certain he will be freed."

At this reassurance my landlady fell to weeping yet again. She already knew that evidence of Herr Rose's innocence would never surface in this lifetime.

Later I overheard someone say he somehow got himself shot dead, because evidence of his innocence never did surface.

The flame of revenge flickered in me only faintly, though, for I was still rickety, and I was tormented by the total news blackout that went on despite the liberation. We knew nothing about Hungary, and after the rapture of our first meals we now thought in terror of our long-lost loved ones.

My life wasn't worth a dime, because I could still only shuffle about rather than walk, but I'd already begun to feel, if uncertainly, the rapture of freedom.

With German grit Frau Rose soon resigned herself to the fact that her only husband would never return home, and she adored us, since we furnished her and her son with all sorts of earthly delights. We acquired the bulk of them from the meat factory with the help of the American authorities, from whom I'd received a document in both English and German according to which every business was obliged to serve us with all sorts of food out of turn. The Germans abided by this with the same religious zeal they complied with every command.

I met often with Ursula, the daughter of the owner of that Halberstadt meat factory. At first we exchanged only a few words, since I was still far from being able to again sense the difference that emphatically exists between men and women, but even so, at first I saw Ursula primarily as German, though she was a very pretty young girl, and with her dazzling youth, her milky white skin, and red hair she reminded me of Éva. Redheads were always my destiny.

On one occasion, we got a conspicuously large amount of meat from the factory, thanks to Ursula's intervention. Éliás proved too weak to carry the load, so Ursula offered to help.

Having me haul something, too, was out of the question, since even carrying myself was a burden.

There wasn't even a trace of any vehicles other than American jeeps, so we just ambled along on foot.

Out of courtesy I asked Ursula, "Say, Fraulein, were you a Nazi, too?"

Ursula nodded solemnly.

"Of course. All of Germany was Nazi. We lived under some strange spell, and those who weren't Nazis died. I am nineteen years old, and ever since I can remember, all I heard said was that Hitler is the greatest. Everyone worked and everyone fought."

"What did you do?"

"I was a telephone operator at SS headquarters. It was a very interesting and instructive occupation. Every single member of the SS was sentenced to death, actually, only that the date of execution was uncertain."

"Why would they have been sentenced to death?" I asked, taken aback.

"Because everyone was spying on everyone, and even a shadow of suspicion was enough to sentence someone to death. It happened, for example, that one of the SS sergeants went home to his village for two weeks on vacation. He took his revolver with him. Back home he wasn't allowed to be in contact with anyone but his father. When he got back from vacation, his colleagues were waiting for him, arrested him, and executed him within minutes. He shouted a bit that he was innocent, that he hadn't done anything, and he died without knowing what he was accused of. I, as a telephone operator, knew exactly what had happened. Back home he'd given his revolver to his father so he'd have a weapon "in case something happens." The father boasted about it to his best and only friend: strange things would be happening in the near future, he said, but he already had a revolver that he got from his stalwart son, an SS officer. The best friend immediately phoned headquarters and reported the incident, and with that, the fate was sealed of the SS son of the loose-lipped man."

"And didn't you feel sorry for the SS soldier who was shot dead?"

Ursula shook her lovely head.

"There was no time for that. Even my own life wasn't worth a pfennig. I could never know when I too would be executed for some real or imagined crime."

"But you said you were a Nazi, too. Are you still a Nazi?"

Ursula smiled.

"Surely you don't imagine that a real Nazi would help a former slave of the Germans in any way? I said I didn't have a choice. But I never did believe in the craze about race and German superiority, and I hated Hitler. I said only that we all lived under some strange spell. But I always knew that violence was not power, and I also knew that people generally don't like being oppressed. In my view there was never a difference between one person and another, but no matter how much I'd now like to make what happened not happen, it's not in my power to do so. I feel sorry for the Germans, too, for I too am German. We sinned a lot against humanity. We'll pay a heavy price."

I listened to Ursula more warily and coolly than I would have otherwise, due to my experiences surrounding Herr Rose, but the girl was irresistibly sweet, and I never was one to hold a grudge.

As long as she's helped carry the heavy meats all the way home, I thought, *it's appropriate to invite her up for a little coffee.*

Ursula accepted the invitation, made friends with Frau Rose within minutes, and within further minutes ousted Frau Rose from her own kitchen and cooked dinner herself. She was a much better cook than Frau Rose.

After dinner we talked for a long time, and Ursula left for home only at five minutes to ten, whereas being on the streets after ten was strictly prohibited.

We agreed that the next day she would come by to visit us in the early afternoon.

The next day I felt very weak, so Éliás went out on his own for the usual daily rounds of shopping, and he said in advance that he would get home later than usual, since he didn't know German, and though Ursula was a sweet girl, he preferred not being in her presence.

Ursula arrived with German precision. She brought a whole lot of stuff with her in a huge, elegant suitcase—all sorts of clothing including shirts and socks, handkerchiefs, and other things one couldn't buy back then in Germany for any sum of money.

"Reparations," she said with a smile as she painstakingly laid out all the expensive stuff, which I had to accept, since I missed them very much.

The days passed, and Ursula became all the more indispensable. She was smart and accommodating. No longer could I even imagine my life in Halberstadt without her. It was very good to trudge about in the increasingly warm German summer while leaning on her strong young arm.

Ursula chattered and chattered, saying she wanted to come with me once transport was back in operation and I was able to return to Budapest.

"I'd like to get away from here," she said, and I froze in place. I turned pale and my forehead went clammy. Coming toward me slowly, casually, was that pitchfork-wielding German peasant we'd all suffered from so much and who for unknown reasons had forgotten to beat me dead while I'd been digging ramparts.

"This here is a German murderer," I said to Ursula.

The girl nodded.

"I know him. I know where he lives."

Halberstadt is a small town, and so I believed that Ursula did in fact know the German, but just to be sure I looked around to see if an American soldier was about. I trusted them more than Ursula. But there wasn't a soul nearby.

The pitchfork-wielding murderer looked at me listlessly and greeted Ursula before ambling on, a thick cane in his hand.

I could tell that he hadn't recognized me.

On the way home I shared the story with Éliás, who likewise remembered the man and was in despair.

"Surely Ursula won't give him away. She's German, too, after all."

But Ursula told me the murderer's exact address, and I happened to be brooding over what to do next when unexpected guests arrived.

Pál Királyhegyi

I had a friend I'd gotten to know in the girls' high school—Boldizsár was his name, and back in Hungary he'd been a burglar, and for all sorts of wiles he got a total of fifteen years in the penitentiary. Convicts had been taken to Germany for forced labor, and that's how we crossed paths. In the high school he shined as a chef and procurer of goods. We became friends. Boldizsár was a six-foot-seven Hercules, who suffered through the whole concentration camp with his best friend, a certain Tihamér, who on account of various crimes had been sentenced to death, and clemency had seen him taken to Germany, where he then went free along with the other convicts. The two of them were inseparable, and though they didn't know a word of German, they stayed true to their pasts.

Tihamér was a sweet, gentle lad, and in an unguarded moment he let slip that back home he'd been accused of a fatal robbery, but that "it didn't go down exactly like that."

I was a bit afraid of them, because they had strange habits. For example, Boldizsár loved bicycling but didn't like seeing bicycling Germans. In consequence, one day when I happened to be with him and he saw a bicycling German on the street, he flagged him down and said this to him in Hungarian:

"You German, I'm now taking your bicycle, and you can go home on foot."

Boldizsár did not believe that there were sound-minded people who would not understand reasoned, straightforward Hungarian words.

The German made some high-handed comment in German, whereupon Boldizsár, who did not like big words, pushed the German off the bicycle and got on himself. The German flailed and bellowed in protest, and then an American jeep on patrol happened to come by and the driver began asking questions in English. I went about explaining to the American in English and to the German in German, and to Boldizsár in Hungarian, so in the end I didn't even know what language I was speaking in.

The American driver gave the German a belligerent look-over. Boldizsár insisted that he'd had just this sort of bicycle back home, and no doubt the German had stolen it from him. The American patrol chief didn't believe it, but still gave Boldizsár the benefit of the doubt.

"The German has bicycled enough while this man here was a deportee, so he gets the bicycle." Thus came the decision, and the German acquiesced. He even tried to smile, for Boldizsár looked very strong. And that, he was.

From then on Boldizsár wouldn't have parted from his bicycle for all the treasures in the world. He even slept with it, for as he said, "There are lots of thieving Germans around here."

On one occasion Boldizsár asked me to go with them to city hall, where IDs and ration coupons were being handed out, so I could help them with their case, too, in English and German.

All would have been fine, too, except that Boldizsár and Tihamér were bored at city hall as they sat there in silence in the room under a huge mirror. All at once I heard them start to speak behind my back.

"Hey, Tihamér, this is a very nice mirror. We should steal it."

"Yes, but who is going to carry it?"

"You're not lazy now, are you? The two of us can easily carry it home."

"OK, let's go," he said, and in no time they unhooked the huge mirror from the wall and took it back to the girls' high school, where it was universally admired by all its residents, consisting of former deportees.

This was the kind of man Boldizsár was. He too had worked under the pitchfork-wielding German, and so was also angry with him to a certain extent.

I proposed reporting the man to the Americans, who would see to the rest.

Boldizsár grumpily scratched his head.

"We shouldn't go dumping on someone at the authorities," he said. "And then maybe the gal is just lying. It would be better if we first go see if our man really does live there. And maybe you were wrong, and he isn't really the one we're looking for."

Ursula agreed to lead us to the pitchfork-wielding murderer's home.

Soon we arrived in front of a delectable little house. Ursula led the way, followed by Boldizsár, Tihamér, Éliás, and me.

The pitchfork man himself opened the door.

"This is the pig," said Boldizsár, firing off an ardent punch to his face. Tihamér wanted to give a kick, but Boldizsár held up a hand, saying, "Once I finish with him." He then turned to me.

"You just keep speaking to him in German so he knows what it's about."

In one deft motion the German sprang outside and took hold of the pitchfork lying about by the door, raising it high and wanting to bring it down on Boldizsár's head.

But Boldizsár jumped suddenly away, and the pitchfork ran into the ground as Tihamér stepped on the hand of the German, who bellowed in pain.

From the start I could tell that no matter how strong the German was, he didn't stand a chance against Boldizsár. By the third blow he was already staggering, and a thin trail of blood glowed red at the edge of his mouth. There wasn't much more for Tihamér to do. Boldizsár kept beating and kicking the German until he stopped moving, and then poured cold water on him and went about reviving him, since he wanted Tihamér to partake in the beating, too.

But this did not come to pass, for just then an American jeep pulled up in front of the house. Four fresh American MPs jumped out.

Boldizsár turned to me.

"Say something to them."

"Gentlemen," I explained, slightly exaggerating the incident, "this here is a German murderer who beat dead many of my fellow deportees before my eyes. All of us here are witnesses. We wanted to capture him to hand him over to the American authorities, but he resisted. He tried stabbing my friend with the pitchfork."

The Americans saw through the situation at a glance. In a matter of moments, they bundled up the bleeding, unconscious German and threw him into the jeep.

They wrote down our names and addresses so we could bear witness against the pitchforked German, and then they rumbled off.

Boldizsár jumped up onto his bicycle.

"Sorry, Tihamér, for my being so greedy, but that pitchfork made me lose my temper." Turning to me, he added, "If there's more such work, you can always count on us."

We didn't waste any more words on the matter. Tihamér jumped on his bicycle, too, and he and Boldizsár rode off.

Ursula, Éliás, and I ambled home in silence. I didn't understand Ursula's behavior. Never before had I believed more in the mysteries of a woman's soul than I did in the secrets of a man's. I'd been convinced that there are only people, who sometimes do incomprehensible things. But this German girl's behavior took me aback. I couldn't imagine what it was that drew her to me, that had inspired her to give up a German to us, a German who was just like the rest. When I questioned her about this, Ursula only smiled.

"Reparations," she said, locking arms with me, since I was staggering.

I understood her behavior even less, though all my life I'd always been interested above all else in why someone does something and less in the action itself.

No matter how I considered the matter, I didn't get it. Ursula nursed me, cooked for me, took care of me, encouraged me, and reassured me that transport would soon start up again and I could go home, and that I'd forget the whole nightmare that Germany meant.

She behaved as if we'd been husband and wife for a long time, whereas I hadn't even kissed her yet.

I took the risk of asking:

"Say, Ursula, why are you behaving this way with me? You talk of reparations, but that explanation doesn't suffice. It's not as if you alone can resolve what happened against the world. All of Germany would be too little for that reparation. Tell me honestly what's driving you, why you're bothering so much with me?"

Ursula gave an embarrassed laugh.

"Are you crazy? Why, haven't you noticed that I'm in love with you? I want to go with you to Budapest."

She fell into self-conscious silence.

I kept prying.

"Don't lie, Ursula. Not that I've ever been overly vain, but this bald wreck, this broken, sick man that I am, cannot be loved. I haven't gone nuts."

"First of all, you're not bald, it's just that they shaved your hair and it hasn't yet grown back out. You're not ugly, you're just convalescing. You'll be strong and healthy. I love you."

"I'm sorry, Ursula, but I don't believe that. I'm not going to lie. Nothing interests me except getting home one last time. I can't take home a German girl. I'm too old for you. Even if I get better, which I don't think I will, not even then will I last for more than another year or two. Who knows what illnesses I contracted here that I don't even know about? There were times when sixty of us ate from one mess kit. It happened that a boy with tuberculosis who could no longer eat gave me his leftover soup. It's impossible for me to get healthy."

"Do you hate me because I'm German? That's impossible. You can't be like Hitler was. There are no Germans, only human beings. Back home you don't have to tell them I'm German. I speak Czech pretty well. We'll say I'm Czech but my German is better, since I left Czechoslovakia as a child."

I didn't answer. I fell to pondering. But soon enough I brushed aside my thoughts concerning Ursula. *It doesn't matter. She's good to me, she's sweet, and she's beautiful too. I don't care. As long as I can get home somehow.*

Weeks passed, and the weeks turned into months, but nothing happened. At first there was word that government-organized transports would get underway, but then we realized that that was but a dream. I began getting stronger, but I still couldn't take on a solitary endeavor. The journey was long and uncertain. We were in Thüringia, in the middle of Germany. Éliás was bored to tears of having Ursula around, and was burning with impatience. Plump and strong, he often declared that he could even go home on foot, but that he'd wait until I too felt strong enough for the journey.

The Germans, under American supervision, began rebuilding the bombed-out train station. But it all seemed hopeless, and I recalled half-forgotten tales from the previous world war, tales of Hungarian POWs in Russia who'd been able to flounder home somehow only after long years.

In wartime various governments are capable of going all out, of sacrificing astronomical sums to transport soldiers, but after a war is over no one bothers about those marooned in foreign countries.

It was on July 20 that I first heard that trains were leaving from the station once again, but only on July 25 was I told, at the station, that the rumor was true, that real train tickets could be purchased at the station's ticket window.

I was giddy with joy. I told the news to Ursula, who did not share in my enthusiasm.

"I know about it, too. But the most expensive ticket they sell costs forty pfennigs, which means only that there's no transfer once you get forty pfennings' distance from Halberstadt. Besides, in all of Germany it's forbidden to be outside past ten o'clock, which means only that you can't even walk, since the occupying forces will shoot dead anyone without warning who is out after ten at night."

I told Éliás what this was about, but he was so excited that he didn't bother about the details.

"The train is running. We've got to go and not sit here overthinking it."

I would in fact have gone, but I was still terribly rickety and didn't think I could bear the predictable burden of the trip.

Another week passed. By then I'd given up imagining that I'd ever again be in the same condition I'd been prior to my German excursion, and I resigned myself to the fact that after a five-minute walk I had to lie down, dead tired. This would be my life. I thought of Heinrich Heine, who lay for eight years in his famous "mattress grave" back in the mid-nineteenth century and still wrote such lovely poems.

Éliás's excitement was contagious, and when I imagined that I could again walk the streets of Budapest, even after 5 PM, without a yellow star, freely, and see my family, or at least those who remained, as well as my friends, and that I could again write in Hungarian, well, the impatience that took hold of me was such that I felt I could crawl right home on my belly.

The next day, armed with Éliás, I went to the American headquarters and obtained two travel documents to Budapest.

The same day I paid visits to my old sources of procurement and got a whole lot of cigarettes and canned goods from my American friends. In silence, Éliás packed the suitcase we got from Ursula.

On seeing the mad desire all over me, Ursula wept, but no longer tried talking me out of the journey.

"Go ahead. But you'll turn back, anyway, since they're not letting anyone leave. If you reach the border of the American zone, the Russians won't let you go on. You should wait, but I suspect I'm talking in vain. Leave, and when you see that it's hopeless, come back. Don't be ashamed if you need to return. Turn around. It will be much easier for you to wait here until the time comes when you're much stronger and there's regular train service again.

The train left at 6 AM. Ursula was at our place by 5:30 and accompanied us to the station. I sensed that I must have seemed a bit ridiculous when I bought the two, forty-pfennig tickets to the next station, a half-hour away.

It was only through Ursula's teary eyes that I saw that the departure could be taken seriously too. The German girl gave me an envelope containing, she said, a self-addressed postcard.

"My address is on it. By all means, write, and even if you don't want to correspond with me, at least let me know if you've arrived somewhere."

But I could no longer pay attention, since I was giddy with joy. The train arrived. It was a real, true to form, German train without SS men, and I had a ticket in my pocket, which is to say, in the pocket of the clothes I'd gotten from the Americans.

There was quite a scramble, but thanks to Éliás's youth and cleverness we managed to get seats. As soon as the train departed and Ursula vanished on the horizon, I took out the envelope in which she'd put the self-addressed picture-postcard.

That's when I noticed that the envelope was sealed. I tore it open.

Inside the sealed envelope was the self-addressed picture-postcard, two five-hundred mark banknotes, and a letter.

I know you won't write no matter how good the postal service will be. Take care of yourself, and accept this sum in reparations with as much love as the happiness with which I am giving it. Ursula.

The forty-pfennig ticket quickly ran out. After a half-hour of jolting along we arrived at some terminus whose name was still German. We climbed off the train, inquired, asked about, and learned that, all told, we had to walk seventy kilometers to the nearest place where we could transfer to another train.

At first we tried getting a horse and carriage, but we soon had to admit that this was hopeless. And so we set off on the journey, map in my hand, afoot in the scorching German heat.

When I began getting exhausted, Éliás reassured me:

"We've only got to walk another sixty-nine kilometers to the train."

While I was swallowing the German dust on the road, America came to mind. I thought of my life in Hollywood and my friends there: Yelena, Karcsi, and others. Karcsi Vidor would have no doubt taken me all the way to Budapest with his car. I remembered that in Hollywood we'd gone on long, aimless excursions, which consisted of having to wake up at eight in the morning, getting into the car, and racing along for six to eight hours so as to arrive in some other, unfamiliar city. There we rested, though we weren't even tired, before then rumbling back to Hollywood.

Almost every day we drove three hours from Hollywood just for a whiff of the heavenly fragrance of orange blossoms in the groves on the outskirts of Los Angeles.

What's become of them? I wondered. *Are they still alive? When it comes down to it, after all, it's possible to die of natural causes, too. But it would be nice to live long enough to get one more letter from Zoltán Korda or my other friends, from whom I've already gotten so much good in life.*

We made the seventy-kilometer journey in five days, living with German families along the way. Everyone was friendly, readily and easily receiving us for the night and even giving us food, as if they hadn't even been Germans.

In one of the little German villages I happened across a familiar face. I remembered that one time in the camp, while mining rocks, a six-foot-seven SS man rushed my way and began beating me. It was a hard, heavy beating, with a billy club, and the first blow got me in the back, temporarily paralyzing me. The SS man kept bellowing and kept beating. I knew this was the end. It was apparent that he would not stop as long as I was still able to move.

In that moment another SS soldier, a short, nasty-looking fellow, emerged from out of the blue with bloodshot eyes and screamed over to my murderer, "I've got a little unfinished business with this scum!"

I couldn't imagine that I had any business at all with an SS man, but I couldn't even get a word out. While the mean-faced little fellow jerked me up off the ground and dragged me into a corncrib a few steps away, I wondered why the little SS guard didn't trust in the bigger one, who with his very first blow had revealed himself to be a master of the trade.

The nasty-looking little SS man threw me onto a bunch of cornstalks and carefully covered me with burlap bags. He wiped the blood off my face while listening tensely for noises from outside.

"Do you want a little bread?" he asked in German.

Every bit of me was smarting, but that allowed me to come to.

"I would," I stammered, not believing any of this and not understanding what sort of secret passion it could be for an SS man to feed a victim before his death.

"What's your nationality?" the mean-faced fellow asked.

"Hungarian," I replied, whereupon the SS guard put his rifle by his side and sighed.

"I'm Hungarian, too," he said in Hungarian, adding, "There will be lots of shooting around here, there will, if the situation shifts a bit."

I couldn't believe my ears.

"You're with the SS and you talk like this? How can that be?"

"I hate them. They brought me here with force, too."

"But why did you free me, of all people, when you saw that your dear colleague was bent on beating me dead?"

"You're short, too, like me. I felt sorry for you. But you're not the first. One does what he can. If only they'd all rot in hell. They aren't human beings!"

Something warm flowed down my face. Maybe it was blood, but nor is it out of the question that I cried.

The Hungarian SS guard sat there beside me all day, nursing me and caring for me. We were alone in the corncrib, and only on occasion were deportees brought down who'd been beaten dead.

Since then I hadn't seen this man who'd saved my life. Now here he stood before me, in the striped, prisoners' uniform deportees had worn.

We exchanged glances. He could tell I recognized him. He wanted to flee. I told Éliás to block his path until I trudged over.

The nasty-looking Hungarian came to a stop and, with a hard, glittering stare, waited.

"Don't you recognize me?" I asked him in Hungarian.

"No."

"Don't be afraid of me. I know everything about you, but you don't know me, and you don't even know that you saved my life. You were very good to me. I'd like to help you with something if I can."

The stern little Hungarian kept giving me a distrustful look.

"Maybe. I don't need a thing. I got papers and a prisoners' outfit, but sooner or later they'll catch me anyway. It's over for me. The tattoo is on me, the SS mark of initiation. And I want to get home."

"Do you have money?"

"I have ten marks. It doesn't matter. I'll get some along the way."

"You already have," I said, and handed him five hundred marks of Ursula's money."

"I can't accept this," he protested.

"Look, you tiny man, when you tore me from the clutches of my murderer, my life wasn't worth even ten cents. Believe me, it would bring more joy to be able to do something for you than what this rotten German money would bring you. I can get as much along the way as I want, because there are aid organizations in every town. For you it's best to hide from the authorities, because there are lots of former deportees among the bosses, and you have a face that's easy to recognize."

"Yes. I've got a pretty ugly mug, if that's what you're trying to say."

He took the money, and we bid farewell.

Éliás summed up the situation.

"Now they're the Jews. Simple as that. It wouldn't be proper if it was always the same people. But fifty marks would have been enough for him."

Again we reached a train, and now we could buy ten-mark tickets. But Éliás couldn't stop thinking of the former SS guard. Even on the train he kept pondering the matter.

"Hey, wasn't it a waste to help the guy? He was, after all, one of *them*."

"Yes, but when it was at risk of his life, he told me he hates them and would turn against them at the first opportunity, and that he saved my life not because he liked me or I was his friend but because he hated the Germans and had never been a Nazi."

Éliás nodded.

"I get it. But the situation is so chaotic that I can't see clearly. What matters most, though, is that we get home somehow."

We were able to bump along for quite a while for the ten marks, but when we got off the train to walk another sixty kilometers to the nearest station, a dismal scene greeted us at the station.

Ruins and ruins everywhere. It was as if all of Germany had perished. It seemed that for once Hitler had not been lying when he vowed to put down his arms only at ten minutes past midnight. From the look of the ruins, it might already have been 12:30 when he had. With a heavy heart I thought of Budapest. If Germany was such a dreary wasteland, what could Hungary be like? No doubt that other kind-hearted SS soldier of mine would be proven right. Everyone had died back home. Maybe it wasn't even worth going home anymore. Maybe home didn't exist anymore. Sometimes, when we got near a radio, we tried tuning into some Hungarian station, but it never worked. Hungarian radio must have died, too.

After this stretch of walk, in Dresden the train raced along with us for more than forty minutes until we were out of the ruins. For forty minutes we saw not a single intact wall. Only the twisted, burned-out iron bars of the onetime zoo indicated that at one time the Germans had there kept in captivity animals, too.

We sat, stood, and walked on trains. On arriving at one station we were greeted by the familiar crackle of rifle and machine-gun fire. A fierce firefight was underway somewhere. I thought that the war had broken out again, and we quickly hid among the ruins and waited until the weapons fell silent. American soldiers approached, and we learned from them that SS soldiers who'd dug themselves into a little patch of woods had opened fire on the Americans. The Americans shot dead every last one. The SS wasn't used to being shot back at. They didn't like that. They were used to unarmed, ragged, starving people.

In one German town the only place to sleep was the Goldener Löwe hotel and restaurant.

Most of the rooms had been shot dead, but the restaurant was perfectly intact.

An utterly emaciated German innkeeper with a nervous twitch greeted us.

He spoke fast, and it was apparent that not even he was paying much attention to what he was saying.

"There are two of us," I began as usual. "We'd like a room. Of course we don't want it for free."

"There are no rooms. Everything is finished. Go away."

"The restaurant is still here," I explained. "We could sleep splendidly even here, on the chairs or on the couch." But the innkeeper didn't even want to hear about us spending the night in the restaurant.

The next train, to Czechoslovakia, was leaving only in two days, and we couldn't exactly wander the streets in the meantime, so I tried persuading the innkeeper.

He kept protesting, his panic increasingly evident, which annoyed me.

"You listen. These here are my American documents. If you don't let us stay here for the night, I'll have this goddamn restaurant of yours shot to smithereens." Holding my American-issued travel pass under his nose, I said, "Here is the order!"

Not that I trusted much in my threat—I'd said this more out of rage than because I thought it would meet with success—but the scrawny innkeeper must have had some bad experiences with the Americans.

"Alright. Fine then. Sleep here." He added, haughtily, "I'm not in the habit of resisting the authorities."

When we asked for food, he laughed at us.

"I have only raspberry juice, and even that's fake," he said in a condescending tone. But it didn't matter to us, for we had all we needed; we'd wanted to order something only out of courtesy.

Without even replying, we took out our American canned goods and began heartily chowing down.

Two minutes later the innkeeper came over to us and whispered to us anxiously, "Gentlemen! I've lost twenty kilograms. Look. Here is my old photo. I used to be chubby, and now I'm skin and bones. Give me some food. One can, at least!"

Before I could have replied, he was summoned somewhere, and in that moment the innkeeper's wife appeared before us.

"Don't give my husband even a bite. That good-for-nothing is begging from everyone, but he doesn't give his family even a morsel! Give me a can, for the love of God."

The begging was still underway when their daughter came over.

"Don't give Mother a thing," she interrupted. "Nor Father. Only me. I'm still young. I want to eat. And I can even compensate you for the cans. Give it only to me."

The father came back and shooed away his family.

"Just give a can of meat. You two have a lot. You won't even notice. I can't take the starvation. Others would bear it better, easier, but I'm no longer young. You two were soldiers, too, we must have fought together, I recognize your SS capes. These stupid Americans don't know that." (We had gotten the SS capes from them.) "I know what the SS was, yes, I too was a Nazi. Here is my member ID. I was a follower of the Führer to the last minute. I gave lots of money to the party. Give me a little food."

Éliás, who more or less understood that the German was hungry and wanted to eat, was already preparing the huge black cans of meat and put out two more of them when I stopped him and translated the sputtering speech.

Éliás gave an understanding nod, and silently packed the food back into the suitcase we'd gotten from Ursula.

"Unfortunately we can't give a thing to Nazis," I explained to the innkeeper, who then declared that he'd only been joking, that never in his life had he been a Nazi, and in fact he wasn't even German, and even if he was, even then he'd hate the Führer and everything around him from the very bottom of his heart, so we could feel free to give him anything, and he would be as quiet as a mouse.

It seems that not even the Germans are so proud when they're hungry. Out of overcautiousness, Éliás slept atop the suitcase. The next morning our train came and we could travel on.

After ten days of travel we finally arrived at the edge of the American-occupied zone. In the village just inside the border we learned that the travel pass we'd gotten from the Americans was valid only within that zone, not in Soviet-occupied zone.

We went from one office to another and were told the same thing everywhere. The situation seemed hopeless. The only encouraging sign was that, for lack of any other zones, if we'd somehow manage to flounder across into the Soviet-occupied zone, we could then walk all the way home to Budapest.

Only a little bridge that led over some bit of water or other, separated us from the Russians. Just a little bridge. But in front of it were American soldiers, and behind it were Russians. There were no documents that could get us across. What were we to do? Return to Halberstadt, to the girls' high school? Or to Frau Rose? Were we to grow moldy in this godforsaken Germany? Airplanes that would have flown us home in minutes had long been invented, but also invented long ago were walking, and soldiers who would not let us through.

Guardedly we slunk over to the bridge. I addressed the American officer.

"Forgive me for disturbing you, but we've got to get to the other side of the bridge by all means. We're Hungarian. We have things to do in Budapest."

With a smile, the American waved a hand dismissively.

"Hopeless. We can't let anyone over to the Russian zone. That's an order."

A friendly conversation ensued, the American officer offering cigarettes and chocolate. I told him I'd lived in America for a long time, and now I'd like to live in Budapest, and not get bogged down here by the foot of the bridge.

He pondered the matter. Finally he said to his two soldiers, who stood at the ready behind his back, "Boys! If we look to the left while these two fellows here go over the bridge to the right, then we can't see them, can we?"

"Not then," said the soldiers.

"The Russians will shoo you right back, anyway, so nothing will happen."

"Nothing. Nothing will happen."

We took this as an encouraging sign. I waved over to Éliás, and on the right side of the bridge we started off toward the Russians.

Soldiers in Russian uniforms received us on the other side of the bridge.

The asked for IDs.

"I can give what documents I have," I said in Hungarian, taking out my various IDs.

But that wasn't enough for the Russian officer. In Russian he asked for even more documentation.

At this I explained, using my hands and feet, and with impeccable Hungarian, that we were deportees, and if he needed documents, we'd go home to Budapest and bring a whole lot from there, that we'd come back here and show him, if only he'd let us pass, just this once, and we'd promise never to get ourselves deported ever again.

The Russian officer looked me over, patted me down to be sure I didn't have any weapons with me, and determined that I couldn't be too dangerous to the Red Army, since he waved a hand indicating that we could go on.

Laughing and shouting, Éliás and I hugged each other on stepping over the border, which meant only that no one could now hold us up until we reached home. Even the train service was much better in the Soviet zone. In two days we reached Prague. Prague hadn't suffered a bit from the bombing, but the Czechs were still burning with white-hot hatred for the Germans. The experts we'd consulted en route had let us know in advance that we mustn't speak either German or Hungarian, because the Czechs didn't care for foreigners.

We tried finding a hotel room in Prague, but it didn't work. While sauntering along the crowded streets, in front of store displays that seemed right out of some idyllic, prewar era, on one occasion we nearly cried for joy. We saw a sign in Hungarian. "MAGYAR VÖRÖSKERESZT," it said—"Hungarian Red Cross," that is—and we entered the building. Inside, the first person we met was an old, Budapest friend of mine, Dr. Endre Déry, who at the moment was a police major who'd been sent there by the Hungarian government on a Hungarian bus to gather Hungarian deportees and return them to Budapest.

The leader of our group was a certain Mihály Lőte, an angel of a man who got us each a magnificent bed and deluged us with Hungarian cigarettes, canned goods, and all sorts of earthly delights.

We spent two days in Prague, and then rode on a Hungarian bus to a crowded train, got on, and went on toward Budapest. One ho-hum station followed another, as did waiting, standing about, and yet another train, until finally we pulled into Budapest, at the Nyugati Train Station.

I'd already come home from various reaches of the world, but never had I felt so anxious as then. The first delight was not seeing anywhere those notorious men in sickle-feather caps—gendarmes, that is—the sight of whom had always made the blood freeze in my veins.

We got off the train. Soon all would be clear. Not everyone could have died. Who among my family and friends would I find alive?

After a moving farewell with Éliás, I headed off on wobbly legs toward our apartment, from where, back then, I'd been dragged off. Along the way I stared at the streets, amazed, and noticed immediately that the SS guard had lied when he'd said that all of Budapest had perished and everyone had died, because the streets and the buildings were practically right out of a prewar past compared to the ruins of Germany.

On the way home I dropped in at Mrs. Ullman's to get news from her. It hadn't even occurred to me that she too might have died. As it turned out, I was right: she herself opened her door when I rang the bell.

"Tell me, who is still alive in my family? Don't spare my feelings—I want to know the truth."

"Everyone is. I see your father every day. Gyuri is well, too, healthy and sound. So are your little sister, your brother-in-law, the child, and everyone."

Szabó was still alive, too, longer and thinner than ever before, and it turned out that he'd risked his life to save Mrs. Ullman from the Arrow Cross.

I said good-bye, a bit relieved, though I didn't exactly believe the good news. I was afraid. I suspected that she hadn't wanted to tell me the truth.

A few minutes later I was home, and, indeed, I met my father on the stairs. He then confirmed what I didn't believe when Mrs. Ullman had told me, that—by virtue of some miracle—everyone in my family was still alive. It took me days to believe it and to understand that yet another thing was not impossible: that I too had survived.

Life is more beautiful than a dream.

Within minutes I learned that Ella Gombaszögi was alive, too, just that she'd gone off to Romania to put some weight on. As for a poor little hunchbacked friend of mine, he hadn't even been taken to Auschwitz, for he'd been killed right here in Hungary, by Márton Zöldy. I wept for this bespectacled angel, who to the age of fifty had always been in love, and always began relating his newest love like this: "On my honor, I say, she doesn't seem to be a tart."

But Zoli Stób was alive, too, with his whole family. Zoltán Egyed returned from deportation, too, but in awfully frail condition. He knew they'd only let him go home to die, yet he was full of plans all the same. He died after lengthy suffering.

My uncle in America, Márton Himmler, who had since become a US Army colonel, came, too, bringing with him greetings from my American friends. He also brought with him my favorite Hungarian fascists, among them, Ferenc Szálasi and László Endre, handing them over to the Hungarian authorities. I was especially pleased to hear that Endre was back; Endre, who, when he inspected the Jewish ghetto in the Transylvanian city of Nagyvárad, had "expressed his satisfaction." Now he, who had deified that other Himmler, trembled before Márton Himmler. It was unbelievable that it was László Endre who would be hung instead of him killing me.

Unfortunately, on the very day his sentence was carried out, I received a huge care package from America, from the film director Andrew "Bandy" Márton and his family, containing clothes and all sorts of treasures, so I was happier for the gift than for Endre's hanging. It was all like some didactic poem in which the good get their just reward, and the fascist, Szálasi, is executed.

A package arrived from Yelena, too, signaling that in Hollywood they hadn't yet forgotten about me completely. It conjured up in me the memory of a bygone life. I remembered how Yelena had inspired me and encouraged me as I wrote my first novel, an American novel at that, *Greenhorn*; how she had invited me from boring but certain Detroit to uncertain but exciting Hollywood; and how she'd then helped me become a scene writer at Paramount.

So too, I could thank Yelena for my association with Francis Edward Faragho, who had been one of America's most talented writers before becoming completely depraved. A long time earlier we'd jointly written racy stories for American magazines at forty dollars apiece. Francis was also the one who, in Hollywood, when I had neither a job nor money, had loaned me two thousand dollars with no clear repayment deadline.

He too was the one who'd gotten me a five-hundred-dollar-a-week job at Metro-Goldwyn-Mayer, and when, trembling with excitement and happiness, I went to visit him with my first weekly check, asking him to give me twenty-five dollars and to deduct the rest for my debt, he waved a hand and said, "I make three thousand dollars a week, so it's obvious I don't need your money."

"It's not that simple," I insisted. "I owe you, so I'll pay up."

"Right you are. You owe money, I'll admit, and you should pay, but not to me, who has money, but give that two thousand dollars to someone who needs it."

Ever since then I've been repaying this debt, but I will never be able to do so entirely.

I got a package from Karcsi Vidor, too, that contained everything a girl dreams of, or, at least, everything that I did.

While opening the package, I thought of the bad old times when I'd been an extra in the dream factory, and Karcsi got me my first, serious job that came with weekly pay, as an editor.

Karcsi Vidor had meanwhile become Charles Vidor, a top director at Columbia. He had taught Rita Hayworth the ins and outs of the movie business. Back then he was still on his first wife, who was a fashion designer, and in that capacity often spent extended periods in New York.

It was on such an occasion that Vidor bumped up against a gorgeous, world-famous Hollywood starlet. A storm of passion developed between the two young people, though Vidor was then still a poor assistant director alongside Alexander Korda, and every minute he hesitated about this love.

"It's not right, my going to pick you up in my little Ford, because my little car blushes on seeing your Rolls-Royce."

The world-famous starlet laughed.

"If I sit in your little Ford, that will soon become a Rolls-Royce, and then neither one of us will need to blush."

The love affair, however, ended the moment Vidor's wife returned from New York.

I asked the now world-famous director, "Say, my dear Karcsi, what will happen if your wife finds out that you cheated on her long and hard in her absence?"

Vidor's face grew dark, and he knit his thick brows even thicker.

"Who would she find out from?"

"From you. Because you're a gossip."

Vidor brooded, and then jumped up furiously.

"If she ever does find out, then I'll take her with me into the bathroom and there, in front of her, will wash up. So"—he asked, triumphantly—"what could she say to that?"

A good many years have passed since then, but never has anyone explained to me so intelligently that great truth whereby those kisses that we don't really give out of love can be washed off with water from the faucet.

I can now share this little story with a clear conscience, since his wife learned of the cheating and was not satisfied with the explanation. They divorced, and since then Charles Vidor has been married three times.

My rickety gait was history. I awoke to a new life, as if I'd been reborn. My old life with Mengele, Auschwitz, and Halberstadt now haunted me only like some foggy nightmare, and there were moments when I didn't even believe that a madman named Hitler had ever ruled on the earth.

Budapest was still licking its wounds, but we saw that the patient had gotten through the crisis and had stepped irrevocably onto the path of recovery.

Of course, it's said that a dead man's beard still grows for a day, and Hitler's craze sometimes still reared its head, but no longer was there a gold reserve to back up the reactionaries.

Every minute of the day I was happy to be alive, to have arrived once again in the land of freedom of food, and that those thin German soups were over. Now, however, money was thin, and became ever more thin, but I didn't even care about that, since life was free and beautiful. Just one thing hurt: that I hadn't managed to find out a thing about Éva.

The old building she'd lived in had vanished from the face of the earth, and those mutual acquaintances I could have asked had likewise been swept away by the whirlwind of war.

But I kept tirelessly investigating.

I immediately got a job, as it didn't matter anymore who my grandparents were. A Budapest theater hired me as a script doctor and production consultant. I wrote shows, corrected pieces, and stuck my nose in everything, because that's what I was paid for.

Sometimes I went to the rehearsals, too, figuring maybe I'd find something in need of smoothing out there too.

A day before a premier I arrived a bit late: the rehearsal was well underway and the director was enthusiastically shouting away. In the dark I fumbled my way forward, took a seat in the auditorium, and I watched.

Once my eyes had gotten a bit used to the dark, I noticed someone sitting next to me. Though I couldn't see the face, I could see that the person was wearing a red hussar dress, which is why, coupled with the fact that the show was an operetta, I thought it could only be a gal.

"What time could it be?" I quietly inquired.

"I don't know exactly," she whispered, "because I don't have a watch. Be careful to speak softly, because the director really likes to yell."

"Thank you, I'll be careful," I whispered. "Who are you?"

"I'm performing in the next scene, but I only dance and say one sentence. I'd like to be an actress."

"It's a tough career," I observed. "But it's not harder than anything else."

"Are you an actor?"

"No. But I also work here."

"What do you do?"

"I write all sorts of nonsense."

"That must be fun."

As she said that last sentence, I became giddy. Suddenly it was as if I was hearing Éva's beautiful, tinkling voice. But by then I knew I didn't have to take myself seriously in the matter of Éva, since for quite a while I'd been seeing her in every woman who came my way, and only when they got close to me did I realize that they didn't even resemble her. Often I thought I heard Éva in the voices of women I didn't know, but gradually I began to resign myself to the fact that this was all but a fantasy, and that the real, one-and-only Éva had, together with her voice, her hair, and her fairytale laughter, had forever vanished into the horrible chaos.

Now my mania grew only more pronounced when, in the dark, I even thought I recognized Éva's face, and I began fearing myself. I'd heard stories of people who had gone mad from this sort of thing.

The rehearsal was over, the lights came on in the auditorium, and I was just about to ask the hussar sitting beside me, whose part was in a variety show titled *The Soldier of Peace*, what color her hair was in real life, when it struck me that this hussar in the red dress who was sitting here beside me was in fact Éva. In person. But unfortunately I didn't believe it. Overcautiousness had led me to figure I'd suddenly gone mad, since until then it had never happened that I'd permanently seen anyone as Éva. But now, no matter how I looked at the hussar, it was Éva in every which way.

I didn't dare say a word, for fear of driving away the vision, and secretly I thought that perhaps it was really Éva, after all, in which case it might be that I am I, and she can recognize me, too. And if we recognize *each other*, why then I wasn't wrong.

The red hussar looked at me, wanting to say something, but no sound came from her throat. Her eyes—her gorgeous blue, hussar eyes—teared up, and she clutched me to her like at that proverbial straw.

"Éva," I said, or perhaps I just wanted to say, "I've never loved a hussar as much as you."

Then we spoke for a long time. She told me about her escape from a thousand deaths, and I still couldn't believe I wasn't dreaming.

It's right, after all, that the world is arranged the way it is. It dawned on me that regardless of inflation and all the talk of good money and bad money, the truth is, after all, that truly great and important things cost nothing.

Air costs nothing; a kiss, if it costs money, is then worth not a thing; health is free, too, and if I don't have it, I'd go in vain into any shop to buy health, for it can't be bought even for a fortune.

The sun also shines for free, and has since who knows when, and the sweet scent of roses is brought to me by the complimentary summer breeze.

The fascists' reign of terror had forever expired.

Beside us stood mighty Russia, and the fairytale breeze of freedom pours invincibly in the window.

Éva's eyes were blue, and life was more beautiful than I would ever have dared dream in merry Germany.

Thirty-Three

LIFE BECOMES EVER MORE BEAUTIFUL. WE'RE AFRAID AGAIN, BUT EXUBERANTLY. EVERY COW IN ADÁCS LOOKS THE SAME. EPSTEIN'S CHICKENS ARE IMMORTAL. YOU CAN HAGGLE UPWARD, TOO.

Just when I thought life could not be better and more beautiful, it turned out I was wrong. The door of every newspaper was open before me, and Gyuri Gál, the editor-in-chief at the time of the weekly satirical paper *Lúdas Matyi*, after looking for me everywhere, found me, and I joined its editorial board. True, the pay was lax, because inflation happened to be raging full force just then, but it felt good to belong somewhere.

At the same time, I became a compère at a cabaret and wrote a piece play for the Comedy Theater titled *Earthly Paradise* that was a big success, with just one staggeringly bad review. Only later, after I became a friend and colleague of the reviewer, did he admit that he hadn't ever seen the piece.

I also became a regular employee of the weekly *Illustrated Observer*, so I could barely keep up.

The big boss at both *Lúdas Matyi* and *Illustrated Observer*, a man without a rank, was Andor Gábor, whose fan I'd been since childhood, and the adoration only intensified once I met him, though then I didn't yet know that a few years later he would save my life.

The Fészek Artists' Club reopened, too, at its old location, providing a *fészek* (nest) where members old and new alike could meet and eat and drink.

And in the Downtown Theatre there opened the Királyhegyi Cabaret, where we produced not only one-act plays but also comedies and one-act shows. The company included Ella Gombaszögi, a half-dozen other friends and acquaintances, and yet others.

By then my father and I were living under one roof, at 14 Saint Stephen Park, in downtown Pest, on the second floor in a gorgeous, three-room flat. My little sister, my warm-hearted brother-in-law, Gyula, and their little girl, Julika, were to be found some twenty minutes away, likewise in Pest, on Rottenbiller Street. My little brother was the director and chief physician of a clinic in the eleventh district, on the Buda side of the Danube. He'd taken an immeasurably long journey from the days when, as a young medical student, he'd been arrested on a charge of communist agitation. The family was in a panic, knowing that if he were to be convicted, as someone with a criminal record he could never be a doctor. I ran over to Pista Lukács, who by then was a star investigative reporter at *The Evening* and associated newspapers. Andor Miklós, the papers' editor-in-chief and owner, also took part in the rescue mission. The struggle to free my little brother took three days. During that time I ceased to exist. Three days later Lukács notified us that we could go to the police, for Deputy Police Commissioner József Sombor-Schweinitzer, who had then had the rank of executioner-in-chief (i.e. chief of the political police), had promised that after a formal interrogation my brother would be released. For the time being.

We went. The police led my little brother out of cell number 200, and Sombor-Schweinitzer asked, "You have not taken part in communist gatherings and in these so-called 'excursions,' have you?"

My little brother only looked at Sombor-Schweinitzer but didn't reply. He didn't say a word. We knew he'd never lied, and not even now did he want to deny a thing, but nor did he want to confess.

I sensed that everything was lost. Silence amounts to a confession. Suddenly I interrupted.

"Mr. Sombor-Schweinitzer, I would not want you to misunderstand. I've known my brother since he was born. He is in the awkward habit of becoming completely mute at emotionally challenging times and being unable to get a word out. Even now this is the situation, but if he could speak, he would say that he is entirely innocent."

Sombor-Schweinitzer knew I was lying.

"Very well. I accept this explanation and will release him. But you won't be achieving much with this, since I'm certain he'll be back before me again. And then I won't know mercy."

That's how my little brother was freed from the hands of the Horthyists and became a doctor without being nabbed again by Sombor-Schweinitzer's goons.

It was actually my little brother who'd saved an old issue of *New Times* published after the liberation but during the period when I'd been resting up in Germany after the toils of deportation. Under the title *Our Deceased*, this issue ran my obituary, explaining that I'd been a talented writer at *New Times*, all the way until my death at Auschwitz. I was happy to see the article, in part because I was praised, and in part because few people have the opportunity to read their own obituaries.

The months passed exuberantly and diligently, and I was not robbed of my love of life even when, one day, Éva announced that she had met a very talented writer, that they'd fallen in love, and that they were getting married the next day.

I offered my heartfelt congratulations, truly so, because I knew her fiancé, who was in fact a kind, smart, amiable, and talented man.

After the editorial and other work of the day, a bunch of us would sit about in the Duna-park Café until 2 AM, and Ella Gombaszögi would usually take me home in her car.

On that day—by then it was 1950—I got home at 2:30, and I was just about to get undressed, when all of a sudden the doorbell rang. It was now 3 AM, so I felt no particular joy. I opened the little window on the door. One man in civilian clothes stood there. I was relieved. It was my understanding that two of them always come if they're planning to take you away.

"Can I help you?" I inquired.

"State Protection Authority," said this sole civilian, and at my request he produced his ID. He really was who he said he was. I let him in.

"Well, get dressed, and then let's go. The car is waiting downstairs."

"For what?"

"It's broken."

"What is?"

"The radio. The receiver and transmitter. Well, let's go. I'm in a hurry."

The matter became ever more suspicious, and I understood less and less what I had to do with his radio, be it a receiver or transmitter.

"Who are you looking for, by name?"

Opening his fist-clenched right hand, he showed me a sheet of paper baring the words, "Jenő Király, radio technician."

My father was Jenő, true, but Királyhegyi, and he knew even less about technical matters than I do.

"No radio person at all lives here," I said, "nor a Jenő Király."

"For God's sake, they gave me the wrong address, and this is the third place I've been to with no luck."

I didn't envy those other two people, either, whom he'd dropped in on with no luck. But a bit later that year, in summer 1950, at 3 AM the doorbell rang again. A uniformed police officer brought by a slip of paper according to which 1 Liberation Street, in the village of Adács, in Heves County, northern Hungary, had been designated as my mandatory residence.

As later turned out—unfortunately only months later—this ringing of the doorbell had likewise been at the wrong place; for I was forcibly relocated to the provinces instead of newspaper reporter Pál Király, who, however, was at least as innocent as I. To this day I think he is unaware that I substituted for him in Adács, where, perhaps, he'd never been in his life.

By morning the flat was full of my friends. They included the unforgettable Endre Gáspár, who wrote, spoke, and translated from every language, and with whom I used to visit the writer Jenő Heltai, who lived in the same neighborhood as I. I remembered that not so long before, when I happened to be at Gáspár's place, he'd been using an electric razor and meanwhile called over to me, "Turn on the radio."

"What language?" I asked.

"It doesn't matter to me one bit," he said, since he knew that the radio did not know any language he himself didn't understand.

Several of my friends attended my mourning, as did my brother-in-law, who helped with the packing, my little sister, who wept and consoled Dad just stood there with a wordless stare. In times of great trouble he was always calm and thoughtful.

Everyone cheered me up with good words and cash, figuring I might need it in that village, though in those days buying groceries wasn't exactly easy, for even bread was available only for coupons, as was meat, and both were in short supply.

The same evening or, rather, night, two of the friends who'd come by, Sándor Pécsi and Klári Tolnay, even went so far as to go to the police to seek mercy upon me, but Pécsi wasn't even allowed in to see the officer in charge, and Tolnay was asked why she was dealing with things that weren't her business.

And so I wasn't even surprised when, in the wee hours, the police arrived. I took my belongings and got into the back of the canvas-covered truck, which was already full of forlorn people who likewise had no business in their mandatory residences.

The truck headed off and they took us out to the railway station, where we boarded the train, which was somehow in no mood to depart. The hours passed: nothing. The car I was traveling in was full of people exiled to Adács, or, should I say, the car I would have been traveling in, but the train car, which is to say, the train, just stood there.

I began getting acquainted with the others. First I said hello to the Krausz brothers, who had started out as intestine dealers but after the liberation had voluntarily handed over their facility to the state. The younger Krausz was eighty-one; the older, who had owned the business, eighty-three. They didn't understand what had happened to them, and they complained about the lack of water.

"Older folks like us need water," explained one of the Krauszes, as if younger people didn't even know what good it was to drink water.

I felt sorry for them, and with my Auschwitz training I went over to the bayonet-wielding policeman and said, "An order has been issued! Everyone is obliged to immediately get water! The canteens need to be filled."

The policeman didn't ask where the order had come from. In those days it was inadvisable to ask lots of questions, so he began barking out at once, "Everyone get water! Fill the canteens!"

The deportees ran down the stairs and were happy to drink the water, filling up their canteens or bottles.

I got to know others, too. I went by one of the seats, where a very old man and an even older woman were waiting for their fate to turn rosier, but every time I went past them, the old woman shot me terrible grimaces.

"Your dear wife seems restless," I said to the man.

"This is not my wife, but my daughter. She's mentally ill, but very intelligent. She needs taking care of, otherwise she'll eat every medicine there is. My name is Epstein, by the way, and this here is my daughter's certification of mental illness."

"Put it away, Mr. Epstein. I believe you, besides, I'm not with the authorities, I just wanted to get acquainted with my future companions of fate. All of us here are going to Adács, which is where our forced residences will be. But as long as you brought it up, how is your dear daughter's intelligence manifested? Because well, on first impression, one would think "

Epstein lit up. "True, she can't read or write, but she is wonderful at cleaning."

I was reassured, and tried to cast a reassuring smile at the mentally ill daughter, who didn't seem older than seventy or eighty years old, at which she shot me even more frightening grimaces and nibbled at some sort of medication.

I went on getting acquainted. That's how I reached the colonel and his family. The colonel had been a captain under the Horthy regime, but the new regime took over and he became a colonel in our army. The then-defense minister had raised him as an example of what a Hungarian socialist senior officer should be like. His son was a first lieutenant in our army.

After standing about for three days, the train left, and within moments arrived in Adács.

When we arrived, we were lined up in military formation, and everyone's name was read aloud, as was the crime for which he had wound up here.

Among us was a ninety-year-old, retired state secretary, of whom it turned out that even back in the days of Franz Joseph he'd worked in the Finance Ministry in a rather low rank, and nor was he promoted under Horthy, and then after 1945 that was precisely why he'd been named as state secretary. He didn't have much to do in that position, for he was already old, and soon he'd been sent into retirement, and his pension was sent to him in Adács.

It turned out that the house at 1 Liberation Street I'd been assigned to move in to had already been occupied by more alert deportees, and so I was taken to the farm of a kulak named Balázs Győri. That is to say, he himself took me along with the Krausz brothers, who were to be my roommates, on his little one-horse carriage, and only then did we learn that our apartment had formerly been a granary, and that it was especially in our honor that he had more or less swept it out, so said Mr. Balázs, who began by giving us a veritable feast.

He gave us peppers and tomatoes, for he had no other food, and when I asked him what I owed him, he just gave a wave of his hand and said, cheerfully, "Oh, please! We are being cooked in the same pot." And yet this scoundrel of a kulak was staggeringly poor. The shirt he wore was so ragged that how he managed to put it together every morning will forever be a mystery.

Together with the Krauszes we hired a woman, Rozika, who cooked for us and cleaned the granary, if reluctantly so. Fortunately there wasn't much to cook besides potatoes, though we didn't get too much enjoyment out of those, either.

From the first days there I noticed how enthusiastically the women went about collecting horse manure in comely buckets. Only later did I learn that, here, this was the jolly joker, which could be used for anything. This is what they cooked over, since it burned pretty well when dried, and the famous adobe, which they built their houses out of, was likewise a blend of horse manure and mud.

Writing letters was permitted, and we could move freely about the village, though going beyond the village boundary was prohibited, and going to the town of Gyöngyös or similarly stunning places was allowed only in matters of life or death.

The village had one road worthy of the name, and that is what the cows got about on. I never did understand how each cow had such great sense as to infallibly find its way home, whereas every house looked the same and every cow did, too. How could it have known that it lived there, that it happened to be *that* cow? These are among the eternal mysteries of nature.

When we went to the post office with my kulak, he noticed how scared I was of all the cows as they came toward us. "Sir," he said, "Cows are gentle animals. There's no need to fear them. They don't bother anyone."

"But Mr. Balázs, I'm not scared that one of the cows will get angry with me, but that by mistake, with no anger at all, it will step on me. Any one of these cows is very heavy, after all."

Mr. Balázs laughed. But not for long, for the next day his own cow, in his own barn, pressed him to the wall in one gentle motion so hard that several of his ribs were broken. He couldn't stop spreading manure on himself, and when, four weeks later, he was back on his feet, he just dragged himself about and he wore a heavy, sheepskin jacket in July.

The only entertainment in the village was the post office, where letters could be mailed, where I received letters and telegrams, and where I could make phone calls, too. Of course this meant standing in line, since others were also interested in what was happening in the world. On one such occasion a sixtyish woman standing behind me in line asked, "Are you a deportee, sir?"

"Yes, I am."

"From Budapest, then?"

"From Budapest."

"Interesting. Sometime I'd want a look at that Budapest, too."

I was so surprised that my brother-in-law's shorts, which were a loose fit to begin with, nearly fell right off me.

"You've never been to Budapest?" I asked, amazed.

"Why? Have you been to Adács before?"

There were two chained-up dogs on the farm we lived on, Furry and Honey. The poor little things were always tied to a post and they hadn't so much as even heard of freedom. Mr. Balázs didn't dare release them, since they simply didn't want to get out of the habit of biting.

The poor things barked all night, for they were always hungry, and my kulak barely fed them; true, he didn't have anything for himself, either.

But there was trouble not only with the dogs. It turned out that it's not true that a rooster crows only at dawn. The truth was that, here, the rooster's beak didn't stop rattling on all night long. The cat meowed and the cow mooed over who knows what cryptic woe. In short, the silence of village life proved to be one fat lie. I couldn't sleep from the racket the animals made. In contrast, the Krausz brothers spent a long time choosing between their myriad Swiss sleeping pills, unable to decide which to love, and in the splendid mountain air—Adács is in the foothills of the Mátra Mountains—they would fall asleep while choosing their pills and slept till morning.

With longing I looked upon the Krauszes' ravishing pills, and though I'd never taken a sleeping pill in my life, I now stole a bunch from them. Not that it crossed my mind to take even one myself, for it was obvious that I could sleep like a lamb if allowed to do so, but the animals were restless, so they were in need of sleeping pills.

I gave the cow some ten Swiss pills. The two biting dogs also got their share, and nor did I forget about the rooster, who greedily snapped up the pills. No wonder, a new taste!

The sleeping pills were a smashing success. My most challenging patient was the cow, who at each crack of dawn paid us a visit and stuck her smart, lovely head through the hole where the granary's window should have been, but no longer did she greet us with a strident "MOOO," but only a hushed, drowsy "moo."

The rooster slept night and day, and then set forth sleepily, constantly tripping on its own two feet while blinking reproachfully toward Switzerland.

Every day on the road to the post office a blackboard caught my eye on which was written, in chalk, "The widow Mrs. Balázs Győri is an enemy of the people, an enemy of peace." Mrs. Balázs Győri was our Rozika by another name. I didn't understand why the serene, sweet-tempered old woman, who was as unshakeable as a drying oak tree, imperturbable through and through, was an enemy.

"Rozika," I said to her one time, "your name is written on the blackboard again."

"They've got the chalk, let them write what they want!"

"It's not quite that simple, Rozika. You know full well why you are on the board of shame."

"Of course I do. On account of the eggs."

I looked at the egg book, which every respectable resident of Adács had in his or her drawer. It turned out that it was July, and she'd already turned over to the state even her October ration of eggs though she didn't have a single hen. She'd been assigned to produce who knew how many eggs. But instead she'd bought them in the grocery store for one forint a piece—one hundred fillers, that is—and then turned them over, getting fifteen fillers for each one, the remaining eighty-five being her "profit." I was nonplussed. So she met her quota, lost eighty-five fillers per egg, but still didn't produce a single egg.

"I don't understand this. If you've surrendered the eggs, why are you being treated so badly?"

"Why are *you* being treated so badly?"

I kept busy dropping in on my acquaintances in the village, and so it was that I got to the Epsteins' farm. Besides, I was curious how these hapless folks were getting by in this village environment that was so foreign to them.

When I arrived, old Epstein was woefully chewing peanuts, and his little girl, who was older than even him, was cleaning. She was sweeping up with a nonexistent broom, and her dad was right, she worked intelligently indeed, since with a nimble hand she went back no less than three times to remove the last speck of nonexistent dust, and then she swept the whole of the spectral trash under the bed. Method is the soul of everything.

"How are you, Mr. Epstein?"

"We'll starve to death here, sir," he said in resignation.

While talking with him I noticed that a good many chickens were taking part in our conversation, whereupon I asked, "Whose chickens are these?"

"Mine."

"Then what's the problem? Doesn't your dear daughter like chickens?"

"We both love them. But there is no shohet here, and because of that they can't be slaughtered."

By then the kulak, Epstein's landlord, appeared, too, and he confirmed what Epstein had said.

"These folks here are going hungry, living only on peanuts and tomatoes. And here are the chickens. Only the Lord God can understand this."

"Listen here, Mr. Epstein," I said, "give me two of the chickens. I have a friend who is a shohet. He'll slaughter them, and I'll bring them back dead for you."

I figured I'd have Rozika slaughter them and settle my sin later with God. But Epstein was as sly as a fox.

"I'd like to speak with the shohet."

"It's not worth it. He's a shy and retiring shohet. He just slaughters, and doesn't say a word."

With a reprimanding wave of the hand, Epstein said, "There is no shohet in this village. I've already inquired."

Like a vanquished army I left Epstein and his intelligently cleaning daughter, but I did not lose heart. I went to the colonels and told them the sad story of Epstein and his daughter, asking his wife to help them out. Meanwhile I wrote a letter to Gyöngyös, saying there are chickens but no shohet, so a shohet should be sent, whatever the cost.

The colonel's wife gathered up some lard, flour, and similar womanly things, and we went to the woebegone, shohetless Epstein.

"Listen here, Mr. Epstein. The colonel's wife has agreed to cook you two a hot meal, and then your little girl can clean more enthusiastically."

Epstein's face turned even more gloomy.

"The cooking can't be done here. The kulak has made my plates terefah."

I questioned the kulak.

"I don't know what's come over these folks. I couldn't stand watching these poor wretches go hungry here at my place, so I cut them a couple nice big slabs of smoked bacon and without saying a word just put them on their plates. They didn't even touch it. Maybe they've gone mad. I don't get it."

I did get it. On account of the bacon, they couldn't touch even their plates. The kulak had wanted to help, as did we, but again we left in disgraceful defeat, even as the little Epstein girl alone kept sweeping enthusiastically with her nonexistent broom, unconcerned with the troubles of the world.

A few days later I happened to be on the way to the post office when I saw, coming toward me, with four million, razor-sharp knives in his breast pocket, a shohet who looked like a shohet.

"Are you the shohet who got my letter?" I asked.

"Mr. Epstein?"

"No, but I wrote it in his place. But hurry. I'll tell you exactly where their farm is."

"Sir, I'm turning right back to Gyöngyös. In this mud it's impossible to get about either on foot or by bicycle. I'm sorry. Perhaps on another occasion."

With that, he vanished on his bicycle, like an apparition. It seemed the chickens would live forever.

But not even then did I lose heart. I wrote a formal petition asking that this deported family, one half of which was mentally ill, anyway, while the head of the family was mad, be placed in some religious household where they could get ritual meals and where the little girl would have the opportunity to clean with her never-wilting broom.

Soon the permit arrived, and the Epsteins could happily travel off, leaving behind all those chickens for the kulak, who did not have to wait for a shohet.

It was a big sensation in Adács when guests of mine from Budapest arrived: Ella Gombaszögi and four other friends. I was trembling with happiness all over on hugging them. Ella was amazing, as always, because in a matter of moments she got her bearings, headed to the well to get water, and from somewhere or other conjured up coffee, whose magnificent aroma filled the area within minutes. They brought food with them, too, so I was able to serve my guests. The Krauszes also blissfully observed the unexpected miracle and drank of the coffee, which they'd long deserved for all the many splendid sleeping pills used as fodder.

The Krauszes, it might be mentioned, hadn't the faintest notion of the world that surrounded them and didn't understand one bit how they'd ended up here and what their crime had been.

On one occasion, just as I arrived home from the post office, I overheard the elder Krausz, the former company head, explaining to the younger one:

"Go ahead and take it out, it's there in the suitcase. You see! Here's the date. In 1901, the carriage we'd been transporting intestines on wasn't lit up. And we got punished, too, a five-crown fine. Obviously that's why we're here now. We should have had that carriage lit up back then."

The older Krausz, as the company boss, had traveled all over the world back in his day, but he did not know that there's a sea by Nice. All he knew was the intestine dealer there.

He traveled to Russia, too, and there, in Voronezh, a *vengerka*—a Hungarian girl of loose morals who was an indentured waitress in some local nightclub—fell in love with him. She asked the then still valiant, handsome man to redeem her from bondage as a *vengerka*, for just thirty rubles, and then they could live together happily ever after.

"And did you like that Hungarian girl?"

"I was in love with her."

"And did you redeem her?"

"No."

"Were you poor?"

"I was always rich. But I was in Voronezh on business, the intestine dealer there was Weiss, and I was there to do business with him. I didn't even think of bothering with women, either. And"—he said, with delayed nostalgia—"she was even called Judit."

That evening, when I went home for our joint meal, which consisted of nothing, I heard the older Krausz say to the younger one, "You know, I should have redeemed that gal, since I loved her. And Pál says I should have looked at the sea while in Nice."

Soon harvest time arrived. Pitchfork-wielding peasants came for us at 3 AM, and so we volunteered to help with the harvest. Such work in the fields in sultry heat is best done naked or, at most, while wearing a loincloth, but by no means a shirt, since the dry broken pieces of stalk stick so hard to any clothes that they can't be removed even with a revolver.

I got on my brother-in-law's shorts, but the older Krausz got well dressed for the harvest. He pulled on a pair of long trousers, boots, a jerkin he'd bought way back when from the Bulgarian czar, and a hat to ward off the sun, while the other Krausz got down to work likewise in plain, long pants, as well as high-top laced shoes, a jacket, and a vest.

Fortunately the field on which we worked sprawled out right here before our farm, so we didn't have to walk far. There was no pay and we got nothing to eat, so we were fired up only by zeal.

Soon it was made clear to us that our job was removing the stalks from the wheat. It turned out that they were that pesky part of the wheat that nature had invented to aggravate us. Two of us took hold of the handbarrow that we'd piled high using pitchforks, and that we carried from here all the way to there, and then we set it down and went back for yet more raw material.

I explained to the Krauszes what they were supposed to do. The older one asked, decisively, in German, "*Wo ist der Törek?*"—*törek* being the Hungarian word for "chaff," but his question meaning, "Where is Mr. Törek?" He thought we wanted to introduce him to some fellow named Törek. This, too, made it evident that he was not particularly a farmer or smallholder type. Also odd was that when one Krausz picked up the empty handbarrow the other one went searching for it far off, because they both had poor eyesight.

The peasants couldn't get enough of making fun of us. The policeman lolling about at the edge of the wheatfield laughed, too, waving me over.

"I've been watching you—you are so inept at this work, loading very few stalks onto the handbarrow so it will be easier to carry. You must really hate our communist state, mister, huh?"

"I don't hate it at all. My mother sometimes gave me a thrashing, too, but I adored her even when she slapped me. Fundamentally she was a boundlessly sweet mom. Even if your homeland is sometimes not nice to you, you can still love it."

"Hey, you put that nicely," the policeman declared, lighting up a Kossuth-brand cigarette.

"Well, I still have the strength to speak, but not to harvest," I replied, returning to my stalks of wheat.

That summer the caterpillar population in Adács reached world-record levels.

Those odious grubs were swarming everywhere, and it often happened that I was heading along the road, not a tree nearby, and three or four of these monsters fell upon my head. From where, God only knows.

The caterpillars kept making my mood worse and worse, and when some turned up even in our sickly little soup, I resolved to declare war on them and exterminate them from the village or, at least, from around our farm. After sending out some correspondence, I got a good dose of delicious, potent Swiss poison and gave it to my kulak, who diluted it with expertise and poured a monumental dose of that into the wood harvest-bucket he carried on his back, from which he could water the insects.

Hoisting the bucket-contraption over my shoulder, I gave the solution a try. I procured a solitary caterpillar (which wasn't a big challenge), and carefully sprinkled a few drops on him. The effect exceeded my wildest expectations. In a matter of moments it froze, contracted, and died. With that, I got down to serial murder. The trees were bare on account of the caterpillars, so seeing them wasn't difficult; a thousand deaths met each and every one.

I went to sleep satisfied, but the next day there were more caterpillars than ever before. When I complained about this to my kulak, he impassively quoted the title of a novel of mine published a few years earlier: "*Mindenki nem halt meg.*"—that is, "Not everyone has died."

Rather than sit back in resignation, I kept diligently watering the caterpillars, but I must admit that they won.

Increasingly bored with Adács, I wrote a letter to the newspaper *Free People*, whose editor-in-chief I knew well, but later it turned out that by the time the letter arrived, the boss had long been someone else.

My letter began with a quote from a *Free People* article according to which our party's fist had struck the right targets, and although international opinion cried out in protest, Hungary had relocated only archdukes and fascist generals, and not a single common man or intellectual was on the list.

I continued like this:

> Today in Hungary there isn't a soul who would DARE doubt in the good faith of *Free People*, but I myself do not believe that it is well-informed—I, who, as plain to the eye, am a little man; am an intellectual, as can be gathered from my letter; whose father wasn't a soldier and whose mother wasn't, either; and whose

family included not a single archduke, not to mention any Arrow Crossers. What *Free People* writes is not true, that the deportees here live amid good circumstances, for this flat we inhabit was formerly a granary, which is why mice and rats visit it so enthusiastically, for they are looking for seeds, but find only two Krauszes and one Királyhegyi.

Nor is it true that only archdukes and dukes have been relocated here, for I was a staff member of *Lúdas Matyi*, and this paper cannot be characterized as being edited by Arrow Crossers and archdukes.

I request that urgent measures be taken in this matter, and that my estimable lines be published in your paper.

P.S. Now I know that the Hungarian saying, "living like Marci in Heves" is, in fact, not really about living like a lord. In fact there's nothing to envy about Marci's life in Heves.

I sent the letter to the editor-in-chief of *Free People*, on Blaha Lujza Square in Pest. As later turned out, the staff passed it from hand to hand and, laughing, took it in to the boss, who felt I was right. He assigned one of his employees to look into the matter, and the investigation confirmed what I'd written.

Later I had the chance to read what Andor Gábor, editor-in-chief of *Lúdas Matyi*, wrote about the matter.

He wrote: "Királyhegyi is not an enemy, but a humorist."

I think that's what decided matters. Seventeen weeks later I received an official notification signed by Comrade Cziráky informing me that I could leave Adács and move back to Budapest, though I could not occupy my former flat.

I couldn't have been happier. I didn't care about the flat, only that once more I could walk on smooth pavement and meet with my friends, and didn't have to trudge along the roads of Adács neck deep in mud. I went out to the train station twice to convince myself that I was free anew, and when I boarded the Budapest train, I was still giddy with joy.

Thirty-Four

Judit, though a lab technician, is beautiful. This of course has its consequences. Not even destitution is free. Roth is the main tenant but insists on the rent. Vienna is close, but why? Our compatriots who've wound up abroad return in spring, like storks. Roulette strengthens the heart.

While working at the *Illustrated Observer* before my relocation I got to know a spine-tinglingly beautiful, eighteen-year-old gal named Judit who worked as a laboratory technician at some company, who knows why. Our initial, couple minutes of conversation developed into more serious dates, and the relocation struck amid our budding romance.

Judit was intelligent, but she was uncultivated to a high degree, and Adács broke our blossoming romance in two. At least that's what I thought, when, suddenly and unexpectedly, she arrived in Adács.

"I heard, sweetheart, sir, that you wound up here. I thought I could be of help to you, sir." (She was formal in addressing me to the day I died.)

"I'm happy to have you here, but you won't be happy I'm here. I'm here for punishment, so anyone who associates with me could face unpleasant consequences."

Without even replying, Judit got right down to work. In an astonishingly short time the granary sparkled of cleanliness. The Krauszes wept tears of joy. Beyond that, Judit knew how to cook, too, and was more enthusiastic about it than Rozika, whose specialty was rock-hard potatoes. When I'd once asked Rozika why she cooked the potatoes so hard, she said, "That's not my doing. I light up the stove with horse chips, and then sometimes it goes out. And I've got to go tend to my business."

She regarded cooking as a game of chance, while Judit kept cooking as long as it took.

When the policeman led Judit through the village for an interrogation and asked, "Why do you live with a deportee?" she answered without even batting an eyelid, "Because I love him. It wasn't me who deported him, but you people."

When it turned out that she worked in a lab and was spending her vacation in Adács, the policeman edified her, saying that what she was doing was improper indeed, but he released her, for there was no rule about what to do with those people who, though they have their own flats in Budapest, follow deportees.

Judit was adept at everything. We had lots of flies, so she made a fly swatter out of the sole of a shoe that could have killed an ox. When one day noticed a mouse climbing on the wall, she quietly picked up the swatter.

"Sorry, sweetheart," she said, and gave that mouse such a slap that it passed away at once.

She illegally extended her vacation so we could be together, whereupon she was fired from her job. She took this news, too, cheerfully, without batting an eye.

"I like village life," she observed, and often traveled to Budapest for shopping and to carry out other assignments. Her sheer presence conjured bleak Adács into a paradise.

When the notice came that the captivity was over and I could go home, Judit seemed sad even though I explained to her on the train that this marked the start of a new, happy life, that my innocence had come to light. She only wept silent tears.

When I asked her what was the matter—we were free, after all—at first she gave elusive answers, and then she admitted, "I only thought, sir, that you have lots of things going on in Budapest, but while were in Adács, I was the only thing."

"Listen here, my dear Judit, just because we're going to Budapest, no matter how many things I've got going on there, even there you will be the one and only thing."

Her face lit up; she was reassured.

In Budapest it turned out that not even city life was a rose garden. I took Judit as my wife, in part so she'd see that even in Budapest she was my thing, and in part, because I was too poor to pay with any other currency.

"The age difference between us is big, my dear Judit, so don't take this marriage seriously. If you get tired of it, just feel free to let me now, and if a young man who's right for you shows up, don't bother with a thing, we'll get divorced and your life will be on track."

"You are so silly, sweetheart!" she said, blushing.

For the time being we didn't have a flat, but I had a friend named Zoltán—Zoli, for short—whose son had, like me, left the country as a young man. Zoli tearfully lamented that the kid had signed on for a job cutting down jungles in Brazil, from which he'd die before long.

Zoli told me when the ship was arriving in Rio. That's where my older brother was a doctor, so I telegrammed him asking him to take the boy under his wing. He showed up on the ship with my Hungarian-language telegram, thus certifying to the Brazilians that they must hand over the boy to him. He then took the boy home, gave him a flat, clothes, and food, and got him a job in a pharmacy.

Zoli took us in as exchange kids. We moved into the servant's room and didn't have to pay rent.

Meanwhile I went off in search of a living, which was nowhere to be found. My articles were not accepted; no matter where I went, I was met by closed doors. Only later did I learn that I'd been preceded everywhere by that swooshing whisper of death, which meant only that I was blacklisted. All I saw was that no matter what writing of mine I took, the bosses didn't like it. To this day I do not know how I got through those hard years. I got tiny little loans with flexible due dates, and we had a place to live.

Judit's amazing nature also helped a lot. Interestingly enough, she was never hungry if I didn't have money for dinner. Or lunch. Or breakfast.

Zoli was an entertaining landlord, and though his heart was not in good shape, he adored women. For example, one gorgeous summer day his wife, Jolánka, went to the outdoor public pool. Zoli was home alone, and his first order of business was to call one of his women friends to come immediately. The woman came, and everything went as smoothly as possible, the only problem being that at the beach Zoli's wife realized she had left her bag at home that contained the things she needed for bathing.

She ran home and looked for her husband, whom she found in the bathroom, in the bathtub, with the woman.

Jolánka saw at once that there was cheating going on here, and in a dramatic voice much like Armand Duval is apt to do at the close of the second act of *La Dame aux Camélias* (The Lady of the Camellias), she shouted to the woman, "I am Mrs. Zoltán T–!"

The gal politely extended her soapy hand.

"I'm Manci," she said, and since she hadn't a clue as to Zoli's family name, she figured a new woman had arrived to visit Zoli, and she was up on her etiquette.

A big blow-up ensued, but Zoli declared that he had a bad heart, and had invited the woman over only because he was not supposed to get himself overly excited.

So we passed our time until one day my older brother wrote that he bought Zoli's boy a little photo store, taught him photography, and the kid had already moved out.

At that moment my job as an exchange kid ceased, and Zoli notified me that I should urgently look for another flat, since he needed the servant's room.

After lengthy searching we found a suitable place downtown, on Dalszínház Street, in a second-floor flat owned by Mr. and Mrs. Roth, who were the primary tenants, true—they rented the flat from the city—but who lived off subtenants, whom the flat was full of. We ourselves were housed in a walk-in closet that was dark day and night because, Mr. Roth explained, the suitcases stored in there didn't like sunlight. Our closet opened to the kitchen, the advantage being that a bit of warmth seeped in along with various fragrances, since Mrs. Roth was always cooking, for both the tenants and strangers, too, who came by for home cooking.

Being short on cash, most of the time I couldn't pay the rent, which led to spirited arguments. Roth sometimes turned off the light, and at other times didn't let us into the bathroom, saying he needed the rent we had agreed on.

Fortunately, there was an exceptional little iron stove in our closet, though we had no money for coal or wood. Here, too, Judit's genius came in handy.

She noticed that the dresser, which was leaning up against the wall, kept leaning against the wall even with its back removed. The back of the dresser was dry and old, and it burned splendidly in the little stove. Judit also noticed that the legs of our chairs were high—higher than we needed—and so it was quite alright for us to burn their lower parts, and no one would notice the difference. The closet also contained drawers that could likewise provide warmth.

Unfortunately, after a while old Mr. Roth noticed that his furniture was becoming less and less, made a big hoopla about it, and now not only demanded all the back rent but also the missing pieces of furniture, which by now had been burnt to ashes.

Fortunately, by virtue of some miracle, my older brother in Rio then sent us a package containing brand-new textiles and all sorts of other valuables. We sold it all, and with that, were able to pay up all the back rent and the cost of the furniture, too.

From then on, our landlord, the main tenant, checked every day to be sure nothing was missing of the furniture, and we temporarily switched to burning coal.

For a while I was able to pay the rent, no problem, since a dear, loyal friend of mine, Endre Gáspár, had gotten a lot more translations than he could handle himself. In secret he had me translate a few books from English to Hungarian, and only later did I learn that he paid me more than he'd gotten for them.

A few months after the so-called 1956 "counterrevolution," an incredible thing happened. Karcsi (aka Charles) Vidor, who meanwhile had become a world-famous film director, reached across the ocean and invited me to visit him. In actuality, by then he was not even in America but in Rome, at Cinecittà Studios, directing the film adaptation of Hemingway's *A Farewell to Arms*. He offered to employ me on the set as a script doctor and production consultant, but in fact he wanted nothing more than to see me again.

In no time I was issued a passport and an Italian visa. Vidor sent a plane ticket, too, and in a matter of minutes I landed in Rome, where, after so many years, I was able to meet Karcsi, in the company of his fourth wife, Doris, daughter of Warner Bros. president Harry Warner.

I arrived with a little briefcase containing half a link of Hungarian sausage and a big loaf of bread I'd bought in its old age at a grocery store.

Only in Rome did I learn that I'd happened to arrive right on Karcsi's birthday, and so I gave him the bread and the sausage, wishing him many happy returns.

The effect was unexpected. Vidor wept on seeing Hungarian bread again after so many years.

Mrs. Vidor observed, "Interesting. I bought him a Rolls Royce, but he wasn't moved. Do you understand this?"

"How many cars do you have?"

"Seven."

"There you are. You've got seven cars, but this is the only little heel of Hungarian bread you have. So of course this is what moved him to tears."

Soon work began at the studio. Karcsi called my attention to the scene in which the nurse seduces the American soldier, who was played by the then twenty-year-old Rock Hudson.

Karcsi and I spoke English even among ourselves so the others wouldn't think we were saying bad things about them. The young, virgin nurse was played by a fortyish, famous American actress.

When the scene was over, Vidor asked:

"So, how did you like it?"

"A lot. Except that I'd sooner believe that the young Rock Hudson is a virgin than I would about the woman, who seems a bit old beside him."

"Good timing, because this gentleman standing here beside you, David O. Selznick, has five million dollars invested in this film, and the lady playing the nurse is his wife."

I went pale. I would have gladly popped into thin air, like a bubble, but all at once the husband and producer spoke.

"This little man is right, and I don't even know who he is. She wants to play virgins, and yet today is her thirty-ninth birthday. This is killing me. She'll be the ruin of me, but she always has to be right."

Rome was beautiful, and Karcsi was kinder than ever. He was among those few people who can bear success.

"I just built a mansion in Beverly Hills for three hundred thousand dollars. We'll go home together, you'll have a suite there, and if you write, you write, that won't bother me, and if you're not in the mood for that, you can just look at the ocean and the sun."

"I'm going home, my dear Karcsi. I'm not interested in your suite. And I'm not interested in America. I've had enough of it. I'm a Budapester, that's where I belong, and that's where I'm happy or unhappy."

I got home and showered Judit with brand-new clothes, which Mrs. Vidor herself had chosen and bought, not trusting in my taste.

As if by magic the world changed, and again I was free to live and to write.

In 1957 my first novel to be published in years appeared, with the title *A ház közbeszól* (The House Cuts In). Lest I forget, I quickly went to get the ten thousand forints I got for it. Hungarian Radio opened its doors to me, too, and I wrote a musical. Szilárd Darvas wrote the accompanying poems.

We managed to break our way into the Puppet Theater, too, where Szilárd and I debuted a piece we cowrote, *Az emberke komédiája* (The Comedy of the Little Guy).

Life kept rounding out as Szilárd and I wrote a screenplay, too, for a film titled *Felfelé a lejtőn* (Up the Slope).

But fortune comes alone no more than misfortune does. Rather than sit back and relax, Karcsi Vidor soon directed a new film, this time in Vienna, about the life of Franz Liszt.

Again he invited me to join him, and I was happy that we could work together anew. I read the screenplay, which I found very weak, and nor was I enthusiastic about the surprisingly feminine Dirk Bogarde, in the lead role.

Once more I was a script doctor and production consultant, and now I was also the music consultant. Though I knew that injustice is the fundamental law of life, it was always heart-rending when, again and again, I met with it. Karcsi Vidor was well aware I had no ear for and no understanding of music, and yet he still appointed me music consultant.

In vain did my friend György Ferenczy—an instructor at Hungary's Franz Liszt College of Music who gave concerts in all over the world—show up in Vienna, and in vain did I explain to Karcsi that he should hire him as music consultant. Karcsi just waved a hand and said, "For me, you are the expert."

Filming lasted for eight months, during which time we were often at Schönbrunn Palace, and since, fortunately, His Majesty Franz Joseph I was no longer there, I had the opportunity to take a good look for myself at the former king and emperor's living quarters.

It turned out that he hadn't had a bathroom. He bathed only in a wretched little washbasin. It seems he didn't like to bathe, as it wasn't soldierly.

On Sundays, when we didn't work, Karcsi and I strolled about Vienna, delighting in the sights. One such day he stopped short as we walked along some little street and, spellbound, gazed upon a small painting in the window of a tiny gallery. It depicted a Hungarian hussar leaning wearily upon his horse.

"I was a hussar, too, in World War I, and I too was weary. I like this painting a lot. Too bad it's Sunday."

On getting back to the Hotel Imperial, I met Mrs. Vidor, Harry Warner's daughter, who was madly in love with her husband, was attentive to his thoughts, and who tried her best to ensure his utmost affection for her, not with much success. I told her about the hussar painting.

His wife said, excitedly, "Listen! Tomorrow you will go to that gallery and buy that painting for Charlie no matter how much it costs. If I go, as an American, they'll ask more for it right away, because these merchants are all swindlers. I'll give you a signed check, and you'll fill in the sum. But be careful not to let on which painting it is that you want. Look at the others, too, haggle over them, and then give the hussar painting a blasé look, and no matter how much the merchant wants, you just give a laugh and offer half as much. But I want to get that painting for Charlie by all means."

I nodded. The next day I went to that little shop, whose owner was a bearded old man.

"Sir, I'd like to buy this hussar painting, and before you tell me how much it costs, let me tell you that it's an American multimillionaire who needs it. Here, in my hand, is a signed check; I need only to fill in the sum. No matter how much you ask, I will pay it."

"The price of the painting is one hundred dollars. It's not worth any more."

"Alright, then. Let it be five hundred, and that's that."

"Can't be done. The painting is worth a hundred dollars and not a penny more."

"No problem. But this is an unexpected opportunity. The individual is willing to pay anything. Let it be at least four hundred."

"I can't do it, sir. I'm sorry. It's not worth more."

Since the merchant seemed poor and Mrs. Vidor was rich, I applied all my powers of persuasion to ratchet up the price, but for all I tried, it didn't work. The little old man stubbornly stuck to one hundred dollars, and I couldn't even get him to one hundred and ten.

Mrs. Vidor praised me for being so clever and haggling the price so low. I did not mention that I'd haggled upward, but with no success.

Usually several of us had breakfast together in the hotel, and I couldn't cease to be amazed at those millionaires who are full of woes. Vidor's wife in particular complained a lot, especially about how much grief she'd had the year before with her gardeners.

"I had to fire sixteen gardeners. These employees nowadays are horrible. One of them, for example, didn't prune the trees properly, and another lied that the currants were not yet ripe."

Mrs. Vidor's story lasted for forty-five minutes, during which I nearly grew mildewy with boredom while the others listened with devotion. Noticing my prolonged silence, the producer finally directed a question squarely at me:

"And how does this work in your country?"

"Well, the matter is not quite like this. If I fire ten gardeners a year, even that's a lot."

I awaited the laughter, but everyone was silent. Finally Mrs. Vidor spoke, flashing her who-knows-how-many-carats diamond ring.

"You see, even where he's from the situation's the same."

Just then a frail old man joined our table, and Vidor quickly whispered to me, in Hungarian, "Take a good look at this fellow. His name is Baxter, he's a jeweller, he's ninety years old, and he has a billion dollars."

I was thunderstruck. A billion dollars! That was a lot even for a debt. When I now took a better look at the jeweller with his gauffered face, he looked no older than a hundred.

No sooner did he sit down than he too began to complain.

"These prices are intolerable. The cost of potatoes went up again."

I turned to him.

"Is your mother still alive?"

"Of course not. I'm ninety years old. Why do you ask?"

"Nothing. It's not important. Just that I had a thought, but it only works with a mom." He didn't understand the Hungarian mother-themed bit of profanity I was alluding to. Only Karcsi was choking with laughter.

The producer then spoke, and while absentmindedly stirring his coffee, he observed, "Listen here, Paul. I've grown really fond of you these past few months, since meeting you. I'm a businessman and understand life. This is my advice: always have two hundred thousand dollars at home so if anything happens, you'll have something to draw on. I myself have paintings worth two hundred million, as well as a stamp collection worth a few million, and yet I always keep a couple hundred thousand dollars in cash at home, since nothing substitutes for money like money."

To this day I regret not having taken his advice.

When I got home, Judit received me with the news that she had fallen in love with an engineer named Pista (Stevie) and would resign from the position she'd had beside me.

I have to admit that, on the one hand, this divorce was predictable, and on the other hand, I was always glad to get divorced and always remained good friends with my ex wives. I've been married five times so far, and I can proudly say that every one of my marriages worked. All the same, Judit's resignation took me a bit by surprise. She'd held fast beside me in unprecedented poverty, she'd fought with the Roths in my place when I hadn't been able to pay the rent, and she left me when I could have offered her something of life's delights.

Fortunately, I knew the secret: life's fundamental law is injustice. In my woe I wrote a TV drama directed by the exceptional Tibor Kalmár and titled *Állati dolgok* (Animal Affairs). This saw us take lots of trips to the Budapest Zoo and work a lot with the lions, among other animals. The old zookeeper encouraged me to go right into their cages, saying they were gentle and wouldn't harm anyone. The offer didn't enthuse me, for it seemed to be a gamble one could only lose. If I didn't go into the cage, we definitely wouldn't get into a fight, but if I were to go in and a dispute would arise all the same, for these brutes were capricious, why then perhaps my whole day would be ruined.

Before and during the shooting of the scene, the lion obstinately turned its back to the camera, at which the old zookeeper standing beside her scolded her as he would a wife.

"Aren't you ashamed, you pig? I tell you to look right at the camera, and you turn around. Now look into it, or else I'll get seriously mad and give you a few good slaps right here in front of everyone! You hear?! Don't you get saucy with me, since you know you always get the short end of the stick!"

The chiding paid off. The wild animal finally had a change of heart, laughing or, rather, roaring into the camera, and the take was a success.

By then I no longer lived at the Roths', but by virtue of some miracle I'd found myself a room in an apartment on Béla Bartók Road. Aside from the original tenant, an old woman who had once been the all-powerful master of the flat, there lived another charming old lady with her two adult sons and a soldier and his wife. I was left with the tiny, servant's room.

The first day, when I'd drifted home at 1 AM from the Fészek Artists' Club, Miss Mária, mother of the two boys, was already eagerly busying herself about the kitchen.

My eyes fell absentmindedly upon the stove. *What, pray tell, is she cooking so late?* I noticed her carefully tear up an issue of the daily *People's Freedom* and toast the shreds of paper in the egg cooker. It didn't seem so unusual; I figured it was no doubt some woman's affair. *Take some paper, roast it well, and the spot will come out.* Or something similar. When I asked her what she was doing with the paper once it was nice and roasted, she replied, "I throw it out."

"Interesting. I'm in the habit of throwing old newspapers into the garbage raw, but live and learn."

"Sir, I'm crazy and have certification to prove I'm not a liar. Here, take a look at it."

Then and there I made friends with Miss Mária, and soon the other tenants also knew. That's why it didn't surprise me when one day the one-time landlady asked me, around noon, just as I was set to go out, "Excuse me for a moment. I'd like you to have a word with Miss Mária, who threatened me while we were arguing. She said she'd bash my brains in with my pestle if I go butting into the cooking. Please talk her out of it; the threat makes me uncomfortable."

I promised to do so, and that night, when I next crossed paths with Miss Mária, I tactfully broached the subject.

"I heard, Miss Mária, that you want to bash in the brains of the former landlady with her own pestle."

Miss Mária broke into a smile.

"I think it is likely, sir, with all due respect, that this will come to pass, too, if I set myself to it. You know, I can't get into any trouble, since my certification protects me. As for the pestle, with all due respect, I think if I bash in her brains it is completely irrelevant whose it was in the first place."

While admitting this, I still managed to talk Miss Mária out of the aggression and convinced her that the decisive factor in this case was not proprietary law.

"Maybe you are right, sir. I promise to postpone the matter, and to let you know if I decide all the same that I must do something against her, because, believe me, folks like this can only be quieted down a bit if you bash in their brains."

The pestle lay still, true, but the fights were a daily order of business. I resolved to seek another flat. My secret dream was to once again be a primary tenant.

I called Comrade K., who had a surprisingly high position in a government ministry. His secretary answered.

"I'm afraid I can't give him the phone, since he's not in Budapest. He's off campaigning before the election."

"Tell Comrade K. that if he is willing to receive me, I will see to it that his nominee is elected."

"Please understand that he's not in town. But when he returns, I will tell him you called, and he will call you back."

Dispirited, I hung up. But I was wrong, for a few days later Comrade K. called me in to his office. As friendly as could be, he listened attentively to the story of my relocation from Budapest and agreed to intervene.

Soon I received a new summons, this time to Major M., and it was from him that I learned that, as you might recall, I'd been relocated by mistake, since my name resembled someone else's, and he promised that he would do all he could.

In the end I got not only an apartment in the Attila József housing complex in Pest—with two rooms; central heating; hot, cold, and lukewarm water; and everything else—but also ten thousand forints with which to buy some sort of furniture.

But soon I traded my lovely little flat for another, since it was far from the Fészek Artists' Club, which was my second home. A thousand memories flared up in me every evening when I went into this favorite old haunt of mine, and I loved those with whom I shared a table, who were also my friends.

Of course this club, so redolent of age, was full of other, new faces. Missing were Jenő Heltai and Bandi Gáspár, as well as Mustache, the worst waiter on the face of the earth. I would order dinner, for example, and an hour later Mustache would come over to me and inquire, "What is this, you're not eating anything today?"

This brought to mind Mustache's incident with Géza Feleki, who, though he'd been editor-in-chief of the daily *World* and a scholar on the side, was an absent-minded, unfocused fellow with an unkempt exterior. Ferenc Molnár had said of him back then, "The spirit goes to Feleki only to throw up."

One time Feleki had ordered a coffee from Mustache—a caffè lungo, filtered, with steamed milk froth but without foam, and with plenty of milk. In a case like this, a normal waiter brings a coffee, and then whatever will be, will be. But Mustache was of a different timber. An hour and a half later he showed up at Feleki's table and put down two frankfurters with horseradish.

Feleki seethed: "Why the horseradish when you know full well that I like them with mustard?!"

The faces changed and the people changed, but in time we too will be legends.

My table includes Magda Simonyi, that grand matriarch who commiserates with everyone's woe, who knows everything, and who can sort out anything. Simonyi may have retired from her career as an actress, but she never takes a break. She is simultaneously tending to some business, talking, making calls, and writing letters, like Napoleon was not long before her. The only difference is that Simonyi has so far never lost a battle.

Taking his place beside her in no time is László Huba, the exceptional writer and journalist, who has no enemies, only impassioned friends, for he is smart, gracious, courteous, and obliging. He is the one who said, "To live is simply to help."

Tibor Kalmár is a director to behold, and he is famous for being absolutely faithful—to the female gender.

Playwright, screenwriter, and songwriter Iván Szenes is ours, too, but only in part, because his heart belongs to horse races. He's made a lot over the course of his life, but the bulk of his earnings have gone to horses. An expert, he always knows which horse will finish first, but out of caution he always wagers on the one that likewise finishes, but a bit later. His horses aren't much delayed in time, only in distance.

Tamás Garay also shows up if he is not at some film festival just then, as is director György Hintsch, whom I can thank for the exceptional success of a night of my works he directed on television.

Also in our circle, ever since the letter *M* was invented, is Károly Mécs, the remarkable actor and faithful friend, along with his wife, Éva, and indeed so is Györgyi, their daughter, who is our favorite and is likewise preparing to be an actress

Klári Szántó is always ready for a debate, and she is enthusiastic and gets right down to business when something is needed, appearing in more copies than the country's biggest daily.

Writer Gyuri Sós speaks little but writes a lot, which is why he became a boss at Hungarian Television.

And then there are the external members, those who don't religiously partake in the conversations at our table, but Gyuri Gyapjú, my best friend, would never miss an evening at the Fészek, and he inspired many of my articles.

Gyuri Gyapjú has amassed a whole boatload of trouble for himself, since he is sheer goodness, he doesn't know how to say "no," and he loves even his enemies.

A few years ago Gyuri Gyapjú and I traveled to Paris. Gyuri brought his wife along, too, and it was 3 AM when we arrived in front of our cheap little hotel.

The hotel door was locked. We kept ringing the bell and banging the door until finally out shuffled a ninetyish concierge, one of his eyes closed, the other sleeping. He looked sad.

To cheer him up, I asked, "Would you like to sleep with me, Monsieur?"

I asked this mainly to show off my knowledge of French, and also to get the old guy to laugh. He replied, "*Oui, Monsieur!*" But he said this not because he had an eye for me but because he was Parisian, and even at 3 AM, half asleep, his sense of humor was intact.

The next day I had to go somewhere on Rue Kléber, so I went over to a policeman and said, in French, "*Parlez-vous français, Monsier?*" at which the policeman tried tooth and nail to explain that, of course, he does, for he was born here.

"*Donc vous êtes français*" (So you are French), I added, "*Alors dites-moi où est Rue Kléber.*" (Then tell me where Rue Kléber is.)

The policeman kept ardently explaining at length, but I didn't understand a word.

To signal that I had not the slightest as to what he'd just said, I repeated my question: "*Je vous remercie. Mais où est la Rue Kléber.*" (Thank you. But where is Rue Kléber?)

Again he issued a drawn-out reply, again I thanked him, and again I asked him, at which he left his post behind, walked one block with me, stopped, and, with his billy club, pointed at the pavement.

"*C'est Rue Kléber.*" (This is Rue Kléber.)

In Paris, even if you're just walking along the road, it's as if you're in the theater. It's colorful, interesting, exciting. I'd traveled the world, and had loved Chinese restaurants everywhere. By virtue of some miracle, fantastic Chinese dishes somehow bear close relation to Hungarian dishes, though at first sight they are entirely different.

And so in Paris, too, we stepped into a pretty little Chinese place. The proprietor was a stunningly beautiful young Chinese gal, most of the patrons Hungarian. I didn't much wonder about this, since I knew there wasn't a single spot on earth where one wouldn't cross paths with Hungarians.

Gyuri Gyapjú and I ordered some Chinese dish with an impossible-to-pronounce name. We waited, but it didn't come. Gyapjú was increasingly anxious, but he said nothing, for he knew neither Chinese nor French.

Finally even I thought we'd waited long enough.

"May God smite this wretched Chinese dive where you just wait and wait, and these Chinese pigs don't bring a thing!"

Of course I wasn't so discreet, for I wove even the proprietor's mother into my zestful Hungarian cursing, likening her to a whore, right when the proprietor herself was swooshing past our table. We nearly fainted when this oriental wonder stopped before us and said, in ornate Hungarian, "Take it easy.... Not a whore, not her mother. Everything will be here shortly."

And come it did, though we could barely eat in our wonderment. Soon it turned out that the restaurant had previously had a Hungarian owner and that Hungarians had eaten here all the time. The beautiful Chinese gal had bought it from her, but most of the Hungarian patrons had kept coming and taught the new owner the lovelier Hungarian expressions. Soon things got to the point where she could swear in Hungarian better than her teachers. A triumph of Hungarian culture!

From then on we often dropped in at this exceptional Chinese restaurant, though at such times I always recalled my unforgettable dinner at the Japanese embassy in Budapest. Of course, it is improper to mistake the Chinese for the Japanese.

It was back in the Horthy era that a friend of mine said to me, "Tomorrow night we're invited to dinner at the Japanese ambassador's."

"How would *I* be invited when I don't even know the ambassador?"

"I was invited, but I said I'm going along with my friend. The ambassador is a likable, decent fellow who speaks impeccable English, since he knows that no one speaks Japanese."

The ambassador lived in a beautiful villa on Gellért Hill. Plush carpeting, opulence everywhere.

A white-gloved Hungarian lackey served us. The first course was raw fish head, ground. I went pale. It didn't even occur to me to taste it, since the very smell made me faint. My friend ate politely, choking back revulsion.

Second course: raw fish in vinegar and some other, revolting fluid. I stared before me, and my not at all favorable opinion of Japanese cuisine began to develop in me.

And in no time the third course arrived: raw fish, à la God only knows.

My friend ate with a clenched-fist face, and by then I'd lost my appetite for weeks. They served three more such courses for gourmets, and meanwhile my friend kept gesticulating in my direction, hands and feet, coupled with whispering in Hungarian, to let me know that in Japan it is the greatest offense not to eat of food you are served. I thought to myself, *May the ambassador be offended, but as long as I don't have to see dead fish and live Japanese for months yet, I am not going to taste this abomination. Besides, I don't like fish.*

My friend emerged from the hospital six weeks after his dinner of raw fish, but his body was still full of rashes even then.

A few months later he invited the Japanese ambassador for dinner at his gorgeous flat in downtown Pest. On offer was everything that entices Hungarian eyes and mouths: ham, salami, stuffed cabbage. And what took me aback: the Japanese man wolfed down the scrumptious Hungarian fare with enthusiasm. I didn't get it.

"How can it be," I asked with that discretion which the Creator had bestowed me with, "that you fed us all that horrible fish calling it dinner, from which my friend nearly died, when you love Hungarian cuisine so much?"

The ambassador smiled.

"Well, I thought you gentlemen would surely be inspired by Japanese specialties."

My first introduction to Japan was much more pleasant. It had happened in Hollywood, a long time back, that an enormous, forty-ish American man, Mike Levy, had come by to see me at my office in Paramount Studios, on the boss's recommendation.

"Is it true that you're Hungarian?" he asked.

"It's true, but through no fault of my own."

"Well, that's wonderful. I have a four-year-old girl. I'd like you to teach her Japanese."

It turned out that the American was a well-to-do millionaire with a yacht and a daughter. They wanted to sail to Japan, and he wanted the girl to be able to speak with the natives.

"I already have an occupation here, at the studio," I explained, as it seemed completely hopeless to persuade him that Japanese and Hungarian were not one and the same.

The American was hard as nails, and rich too, so he didn't give in so easily. The money he offered would be ten times an average monthly salary today.

"OK, I accept," I said, and figured I'd buy an English-Japanese language textbook and dictionary, and for that much money I too would learn Japanese; at worst, my accent would not be perfect.

But it turned out that in all of America there wasn't a single English-Japanese dictionary, not even to speak of a Japanese language book. I made up my mind. I taught the girl, named Goldie—Hungarian. *Let her have a major world language at her fingertips.*

Little Goldie was charming, lovely, and smart. She learned brilliantly, and soon we were talking only Hungarian to each other. Her father was delighted to see how fast his daughter had gotten down the Japanese language.

Every hour I spent with her was a pure, unmitigated joy, which is not even to speak of the loads of money the father showered me with.

Catastrophe came crashing down on me unexpectedly.

"A Japanese friend of mine from Tokyo is visiting this afternoon. I'll introduce you to him, and then the three of you can talk in Japanese."

I went pale. *What will become of this?* I fretted. *What crime have I committed by teaching the girl Hungarian? No matter, within minutes it will all turn out.*

In terror I awaited the Japanese gentleman, and when the door opened I didn't dare so much as stir. Goldie, who already knew that we were going to talk Japanese, ran up to the Japanese man, and greeted him as I'd taught her.

The blood froze in my veins when, all at once, I heard the stranger's reply.

"*Isten áldjon meg, édes kislányom*" (God bless you, my dear little girl), he said in Hungarian.

It turned out that the Japanese gentleman who'd just come from Tokyo was called Péter Molnár, marking him as Hungarian a mile away, and spoke Japanese as fluently as I.

In no time I explained the situation to him, turning the conversation from Japanese to Hungarian so he'd understand me more. He did.

Fate works in such wondrous ways! I thought. *Lo and behold, abroad everyone who matters is Hungarian, and when these millionaires go on their yacht to Tokyo and the dad is struck to find that the Japanese do not understand their daughter well, he will be certain that it's they who don't speak the language, for he'd heard with his own ears how cute little Goldie was chatting away in Japanese.*

Not long ago my dear girlfriend and I traveled once again to Vienna, since an old friend of mine, Sándor Fülöp, had phoned to say he wants to see me one more time before his death. Of course, when it comes down to it, everyone is before his or her death so long as they're alive, and so we went and, fortunately, found Sándor in the best of health.

This Sándor was a legend in his own time. He'd been a millionaire more often than he'd gone bankrupt, though he'd also tried his hand at poverty now and again, but that never worked.

For a long time he lived in Romania. It was from him that I learned that trouble can be turned around, too. One day in the run-up to World

War II a young Iron Guardist dropped by his shop, where Sándor had unsuspectingly been selling grains and other things. (The Iron Guard was to Romania what the Arrow Cross was to Hungary, if not worse.)

"Give me a thousand *lei*, because if you don't, I'll attack you in the Iron Guard newspaper."

"I won't give you a penny," said Sándor, and stood up straight, all six-foot-seven of him.

"Then give me eight hundred."

"I won't."

"Five hundred."

"Not a penny. But listen here. You're an Iron Guardist. Go to the Iron Guard's boss and ask him for a barley export permit, and I'll give two thousand lei."

The Iron Guardist happily ran there and back, triumphantly bringing with him the permit, which back then was impossible to acquire.

Sándor handed him the two thousand lei.

That's as far as Sándor got in recounting his story when I, who'd been listening in bad spirits, asked, "Why did you give that murderer two thousand when even he himself asked for just a thousand?"

Sándor smiled.

"It was worth it. I made fifty thousand dollars on it."

The only thing he didn't say was that he didn't earn this for himself; for after the liberation, with him now in Vienna, whenever a Hungarian dropped by to see him who'd been a forced laborer, who was a refugee, or who was poor, he gave them enough to get by on in the form of food and drink, as well as pocket money, and those who played cards even got money for cards.

Sándor gave me a warm welcome in Vienna, too.

"Needless to say, I'll cover your hotel and half your meals."

"And the other half?"

"Naturally, me," he said humbly. "A room is waiting for you in the Sacher."

Nusi, his wife, was the niece of the great poet Endre Ady's legendary love, Léda. She and Sándor had a happy marriage, though Sándor adored women. Many years earlier, when they were still a young couple, when one day Sándor had gotten home from a business meeting, his wife was surprised to notice that her husband's handkerchief was full of lipstick, though Sándor himself never used cosmetics. She stared numbly at the telltale handkerchief.

"What is this?" she asked with blood-curdling repose.

"Don't worry about it," he said evasively. "I'm unwilling to talk to you about the matter. You don't understand business affairs, anyway."

In Vienna my girlfriend and I were bowled over by the astronomical prices. The Stadtkrug, one of the city's most exclusive restaurants, advertised its beef soup in an illuminated display in its front window, for ninety schillings. There, too, we were guests; not paying guests, of course, since the proprietor was a friend of ours, but even so, I found everything too expensive.

Meeting up with my friend Szóbel was a true pleasure and fun. He'd invited us to his nightclub, where not only the dancing girls undressed completely while performing, but so too did the woman singer, who, it seemed, could not sing otherwise.

While talking with Szóbel the subject veered onto our student days, and I asked him, "Where did you go to school?"

"I graduated from business school."

"What business?"

"The girl business."

"Interesting. Your life must be exciting among so many beautiful, naked women."

"I'm self-critical. I'm no longer young. I never was an Adonis. Still, I know the women love me not only for my money."

"Why, then?"

"For my gifts."

Back to my friend Sándor, who was charming, kind, and generous. Some weeks earlier he'd been in Monte Carlo, and he told me a story about that.

"You know, there the Casino de Monte-Carlo is the country, the industry, and everything. Never in my life have I risked even a cent on cards or roulette, it didn't interest me, but there it's impossible not to pay attention to it all. One day I noticed a remarkable old woman at the gaming tables. She was as ugly as the Devil's grandmother, laden with wrinkles, and was accompanied by two handsome young men wherever she went. Of course she regularly went to the Casino, and without batting an eyelid she'd lose half a million dollars or win a million, and all the jewelry sagging from her would have been enough to pay off the debts of a smaller country. I heard a lot about this daring gamer, and so I began to look into who this odious and staggeringly wealthy ancient artifact of a woman could be.

"Just as there are Hungarians all over the world, here too there was an old Hungarian who, as a Casino employee, knew everything about everyone. When I inquired about the old woman, he said that back in the Nazi era she had served Hitler and, above all, herself, as an exceptional murderer and SS general. When the troubles came, claiming to be a hermaphrodite he had himself operated on to become a woman and changed his name, too."

One day in Vienna I was having a coffee at the Café Europa when an amiable, fortyish man approached me.

"Mr. Királyhegyi, right?"

"No doubt, but who might you be?"

"Dr. Zoltán Schlesinger, a Hungarian doctor from New York. I left Hungary thirty years ago to get away from Horthy. Ever since I've lived in New York. I think we'll be good friends."

Starting then, Dr. Schlesinger has traveled back home to Hungary every year, and each time he grows fonder of the country and Budapest in particular.

Every year, with feverish excitement he counts how much money he has in America and how much he could live on in Budapest if he returned for good. But every year he returns to New York yet again, only to then come back and count anew.

In the Vienna hotel Schlesinger was staying at when I met him there was an unsightly Hungarian whose ugliness wasn't even mitigated by his broken nose. He was excruciatingly elegant, his neck full of gold chains, his hands with diamond rings; and those who knew him said that he'd formerly been a gangster.

When I asked him if the rumors were true, he laughed.

"Nonsense. It's true that I've got a roulette club in New York even these days, and it's true that I don't have a permit for it. But if roulette is okay in Las Vegas, why is it prohibited in New York? Only laws contrary to common sense can be violated."

"Well, not even a roulette table is something to be sneezed at. A customer goes in rich, and by the time he comes out, he's been plundered, right?"

"Sure, some folks lose, that's true. But at my place you can win, too. But it's also true that in the long run only the house can win. The problem with the players is that they're greedy. When they win, they can't stop. And then, when they're completely burned out, they stop, since they have no choice. They all want to get rich quick."

"You've got to have a heart for this sort of club, no?"

"No. I listened to my heart only once, and even then I paid for it big time."

"Why? Did you cheat to benefit a player?"

"No. But that's nearly what happened. About a year ago this agreeable young fellow showed up in the cardroom and began playing. In no time he lost fifteen hundred bucks. The next day he came in again, and lost two thousand. Of course in the meantime he'd been winning, too, but he wouldn't rest until he lost. After a two-day break, it seemed he wanted a change. He switched to playing roulette. He lost again, three thousand this time."

"The next day a young woman comes into my office," he continued. "She was so gorgeous I didn't even dare believe it. She seemed sad."

"'What can I help you with?' I asked.

"'Sir, our lives are in your hands. My husband, George, has so far lost six thousand five hundred dollars in your club in a few days. We're newlyweds and that was all the money we had. That's what we wanted to use to open a little shop with; we'd already settled on all the details—where we'd order the goods from, and the bank loan seemed a sure thing, too—when he drifted into this club and lost all we had. He never played before. He never even had cards in his hands. For the love of God, give back that money. It doesn't mean a thing to you, but it's about the lives and happiness of two people.'

"'But ma'am,' I replied, 'Imagine what would become of me if I made a habit of returning losses. All the gamblers in the world would come here, where they can win without risk. Don't even dream of it.'

"'I know it was crazy of me to come here, but I had no other option. If you don't help us, we're finished. Have a heart. I know I'm wrong; I know that a loser can't get back his money, but for the love of God, make an exception just this once. No one will find out about it. Have mercy on me!'

"The gorgeous young woman knelt down before me and, I have to admit, I felt sorry for her.

"'Listen here, ma'am. I'll give you the money back on one condition. If you get lost, and your husband never sets foot in this club again as long as he lives.'

"The woman again fell to tears, kissing my hands and completely beside herself with joy.

"'I swear we'll never come even near the club ever again!'

"'Alright,' I said, and gave the crying woman the money back, though even before myself I was ashamed at my weakness.

"Three days later the husband again dropped in at the club.

"I watched him. He won two thousand dollars. I had him called into my office.

"'Put that two thousand dollars down here on the table immediately. You know full well that your wife was here to see me three days ago, and she begged until I gave back the money you lost here. But on condition that you never set foot in here ever again. And now here you are once more. Well, I won't stand for this!'

"'I don't know what you're talking about,' the man said, looking surprised.

"'Of course you do. I'm talking about your wife, who promised that you two would get lost and you'd never play at my club ever again.'

"'Sir, you've gone mad. I've never been married in my life.'"

Thirty-Five

WRITING A PLAY IS EASY, HAVING A FLOP IS HARD. LANGUAGE SKILLS: POWER. MY TROUPE AND I TRAVEL THE COUNTRY. I CAME FROM AMERICA, BUT WHEN?

A few years ago the Hungarian Theater produced my play *Lopni se szabad* (Not Even Stealing is Permitted). At first the piece was meant to be a comedy, at least that's how I'd intended it, but in the hands of its brilliant director it degenerated into a drama. As I watched the rehearsals, I sensed a flop fast approaching, but as for what did end up happening, not even I had counted on that. The piece was such a flop that even the theater was rebuilt afterward. Indeed, even the square on which the theater sat was renamed, to ensure that nothing could remind viewers of the piece.

Now, I did think the main theater publication went a bit far in its review in noting, more or less, that not since the Mongol invasion of the thirteenth century had our homeland suffered such a blow.

Fate works in mysterious ways. Two years later the director at the theater in the small city of Szolnok, József Bor, somewhere happened upon the original piece and produced it just as I'd written it. Thanks to great directing and outstanding actors, its success was such that I'd never seen the likes of before. The applause didn't stop, the curtain fell, and then came more applause; it was everything a playwright dreams of, which is not even to mention that the audience laughed through even the intermissions.

Later I joined Bor and his theater company in the Tisza, which, it turned out, was not Hungary's second largest river, as I initially thought, but a hotel and bar. There, over dinner, the wonderful director voiced this sentence, which I have been unable to forget since: "Today the audience was a bit cool. You should have seen it yesterday!"

Two years ago two staff members of the national musical and cultural events agency looked me up proposing that we organize, and tour the country with, an evening of entertainment comprising excerpts of my works.

I agreed, because the agency employees were awfully kind to place their trust in me, though at the bottom of my heart I would have gone with Gyuri Gyapjú's advice not to take this on, both because I was too old by now for long trips to the provinces, and because audiences even on the outskirts of the capital didn't appreciate my quintessentially Budapest humor.

Since then we've held 250 performances across Hungary, and audiences in smaller towns are just as delightful as those in Budapest and larger towns and cities. The name of the show, which I wrote and present: *Amerikából jöttem* (I Came from America). I've traveled across America, Europe, Africa, and Australia, but, aside from Budapest, never in my life had I voluntarily paid a visit to Hungary. In the course of the national tour I've never ceased to be amazed at the fine roads we have connecting our country's far-flung places, and at how gracious and exuberant the audiences are.

We've held numerous performances in villages large and small, and most of the time I engage the audiences in conversation. In one little village the director of the local cultural center, where we performed, was an amiable, pretty young woman. She had two children. The younger one, a four-year-old girl, was named Aranka, and the older one was seven, and called Róbert. They are both sweet, and their mother told a charming story about them.

"I'm careful to be sure the kids feel I love each of them the same. Yesterday, for example, I gave Aranka two bars of chocolate. 'One is for you, and I want you to put away the other one for Robi when he comes home from school.' At this Aranka attentively broke her own piece in two, put one of them into the pocket of her little apron, and ate only the other one immediately. Finding this odd, I asked her why she'd done so, to which she replied, in a didactic tone, 'You don't understand this, Mommy. If I eat the whole chocolate and then give Robi his share, then he'll see only that I don't have any chocolate. That's why I put away half of mine, so when Robi gets his, he'll see that I have chocolate, too, and won't feel that he needs to give me his half. Do you understand now, Mommy?'"

What will become of this little girl later on? Say, in a week?

On another occasion we were in a village of three thousand people, with sparkling, beautiful houses and a surprising number of cars everywhere. That's not to mention its brand-new, fetching cultural center, with both a TV and a library.

On the stage they're already arranging the set as I stand on the steps by the performers' entrance. Below me two local men are smoking pipes. They're chatting.

"Hey," says one to the other, "there's going to be some theater show here tonight."

"What the hell."

"That's right. I read the poster. Some guy Királyhegyi came down from Budapest with his company."

"Who is that Királyhegyi?"

"Hell knows."

"Is there gonna be a ball?"

"No."

"Well, then let's go to the pub."

This is the sort of Hungarian village we met Mr. János in, too. A fifty-eight-year-old, strapping, handsome, brawny man. He was the head of the local state agricultural cooperative. He had an adventurous, exciting life. He escaped the army, became a partisan, fought against the Germans, and blew up trains. The Nazis caught him three times and sentenced him death, but each time he managed to escape and keep fighting.

He'd never been sick in his life, and he got through the war without even a scratch.

Now he'd gotten married. A twenty-year-old girl. It was a big wedding, with the whole village there, celebrating the new couple. Everyone loved Mr. János whether he was getting married or not.

We were talking with him in the library of the village cultural center. The young director, who has a job on the side as a high school teacher, takes the risk to ask, "Say, Mr. János, you just got married, you're fifty-eight years old, and your wife is a twenty-year-old girl. That's a big age difference. Aren't you worried about this marriage?"

Mr. János breaks into a smile.

"Well … I've been in more dangerous situations."

Usually our tour doesn't take us too far from Budapest, and we get home the same night, but that particular evening we were no less than 180 kilometers from Budapest. In the car aside from Józsi, the driver, and myself were other members of the company, including the director, György Máday; Magda Scheer; and Bea Révy.

We were racing home when all at once one of the front tires dropped right off, and our crippled car fell flat on the pavement. Nothing else happened to us, just that we stood there in the cold night, on December 7. We flagged down a bus coming toward us with four good tires. Three stalwart young men emerged from the bus and lifted our car, but not even that helped, since it turned out that we were missing some part. Alas, such a car has a surprising number of parts.

As the director, Máday stayed there by the car along with the driver. The three of us girls got on the bus.

Magda took over command.

"We'll stop at the next train station, right?"

"No, ma'am," said the bus driver. "That's not the way the bus is going."

Magda conjured up her loveliest smile, which didn't exactly have its desired effect in the dimly lit bus.

"She'll go wherever you want her to. Just stop there long enough for us to get off, and then you can be on your regular way."

Bea, who must have been tired, slept standing up on the jam-packed bus.

"That's true," came the driver's gracious reply. "Well, if the passengers don't mind, I could take you as far as the train station."

We got off. Bea sleepwalked. Sprawled out inside the little station was a gorgeous, enormous iron stove of the sort that can give off heat that's just out of this world—if it's burning. But it wasn't lit, and there wasn't a sign of coal or wood anywhere. And so it was cold both outside and inside. We were rapturously cold, only Bea was sleeping unrelentingly, even while talking.

The station master bore a striking resemblance to Francis II Rákóczi, that Hungarian nobleman and prince of Transylvania with the handlebar mustache who led a peasant uprising in the early eighteenth century. Only that he seemed much younger, and he had enough hair on his head to dam the Danube, and even then there would have been hair left over.

Cheerfully we shivered. It was 2 AM, and Francis II Rákóczi notified us that the next train would leave only at 3:40.

We were free to freeze in the meantime—with the exception of Bea, that is, who, on getting the news, lay down, asleep, on the bench, and so she didn't hear Francis II Rákóczi now also informing us that at this hour, the whole village was asleep, not only her, and neither a hotel nor a bar was open.

But Magda was not the type to give up so easily.

"But maybe some lower class train leaves from here earlier?"

"Yes. But that's just a freight train. It doesn't carry passengers, just coal."

"If it has a locomotive, then maybe we can get on that?"

"Maybe. But it leaves in five minutes. You've got to run if you want to make it."

We ran nearly a mile in numbing cold, though Bea fortunately kept sleeping even while running, eyes closed, as we held her hands to keep her from having bad dreams. The cold was, by now, knee-deep.

We made it to the locomotive. It was still standing there when, after a brief argument, for a hundred-forint banknote we were allowed to grip our way up its steep and slippery ladder. Bea was sleeping even while gripping. "Trouble? What trouble?" said Magda, when she slipped back down. "Hardships must be overcome." Her skirt ripped.

Finally the train left, carrying a whole lot of freight, at a speed of ten miles a week.

The stoker, as per his name, stoked, from which the furnace with its gaping mouth then belched out heat. This made Bea sleep once more. Again while standing.

The heat became unbearable. That's when I felt, for the first time in my life, what it is to have the skin blush right off your face.

After racing along for twenty kilometers, the train stopped in the middle of the road; that is to say, the track. The engineer explained the situation.

"We're going only this far. But you can get on another freight train that will get you all the way to Kiskunhalas. There you can then catch the express train that doesn't even stop until Budapest, just here and there."

Onto another locomotive! There, getting aboard was harder: the ladder was slippery, because it had snowed or otherwise precipitated while we'd been on the earlier train, and some of the rungs had fallen off over time. But by then we had practice at climbing ladders, so we each fell back no more than four or five times, and by now only an expert would have recognized the girls' skirts for what they were. Bea was meanwhile sleeping while awake, as we climbed with monkeylike skill; which is to say, there are clumsy monkeys, too.

Fortunately, the furnace in our new lodging was even warmer, whereas we'd believed that the earlier heat had already been as hot as could be. That's not to mention that every minute the engineer emitted whistles that would have popped the eardrums of even the most tried and tested beat musicians. But let's forget that, I'm not a musical sort.

Half roasted and entirely frozen, sooty, grimy, and in rags we finally arrived after who knows how long in the small town of Kiskunhalas, on the plains still well to the south of Budapest, where we had nothing to do.

Fortunately we missed the express train by only five minutes.

The slow train, which stopped at every single station along the way, left from there, too, at only 3:40 AM, and by 8 in the morning we were already home.

Only later did we learn that Máday and the driver managed to fix our car in an hour. They went straight to the train station to fetch us, but by then we were far away, since we had urgent business.

Lesson: what's urgent can wait.

Máday, our director, is like the rest of them, after all. He's always saying how harmful smoking is, how smokers should kick the habit. Newspapers here and there, too, are talking ever more about why quitting is imperative, since smoking is harmful.

No one talks about the crux of the matter, though, which is how hard it is to GET INTO THE HABIT of smoking.

I remember how much I suffered when I started. No one in my family smoked—neither my father nor my mother nor my siblings—so I had no one to learn from.

Father was a merciless antismoker notwithstanding the fact that at home, a great many cigars and cigarettes lay idle in a golden box, solely for guests. Let strangers suffer!

I wasn't quite twelve years old when I took particular notice of one such smoking guest. He was smoking exuberantly; it was clear how much he enjoyed the smoke. It seems that, back then, Hungarian cigarettes were still good. I also noticed that the guest inhaled the smoke deeply, down to his ankles, but nothing came out. To this day I don't know how he did it.

Father, noticing my illicit interest, gave me a stern rebuke.

"Don't you even think of lighting up, or else I'll break your ..."

He didn't even get to saying what he'd break, because I was already running down to the second floor, Apartment 5, where my friend Karcsi Schatz lived.

"Big news! I'm taking up smoking!"

In a matter of moments Karcsi saw that this was our big chance. After deft financial maneuvers, which he was a genius at, we went out and bought a carton of 100 Magyar brand cigarettes, which back then were the cheapest and strongest cigarettes on the market. Like eagles we raced upstairs to the roof terrace, and the festive moment arrived. We lit the first cigarette.

Then the second, because the first was horrible. Then the third, which was even more horrible than the first two. *What on earth do blockheaded adults like about this?* I thought. Standing there beside Karcsi, I made as if all that foul smoke was a divine pleasure, though my belly was churning with revulsion and I would have liked to die. I felt no pleasure at all. But who is to say, anymore, how many cigarettes we smoked on that awful terrace, for back then we believed that the process was the key, and that we mustn't stop, that we must wait until it turned good. Sooner or later something pleasurable would surely happen. The smoke rose and rose, but tasted increasingly bitter. We suffered like cattle in a slaughterhouse, and got so sick from this pleasurable pastime called smoking that we nearly died of it.

For a while this put a brake on our desire, but a few weeks later Karcsi himself came by, out of breath.

"Listen here! I figured out what we were doing wrong! The smoke's got to be inhaled. Nice and deep. Into the lungs. That's the real thing. We were just blowing it like crackpots. That was the problem."

I nodded, since I always had trusted in Karcsi's voluminous brains, and then upstairs on the terrace—where the uncultured and blockheads went sunbathing instead of smoking, like good Hungarians should—we began the whole torture from the start, this time inhaling. Of course not even that was easy. We coughed and gagged, and though I would been in the mood to abandon smoking altogether in the ensuing minutes, iron diligence was to beget a miracle. We got sick again, a bit better than the first time, but we didn't lose heart. The dizziness couldn't last forever, we figured, since all those smokers can't be crazy.

Only months later, after fathomless suffering, did we arrive at the point where, even if the blow wasn't good, it wasn't so deadly.

Much water was yet to flow down the Danube until we could finally join the populous camp of real smokers, who die of the craze only later.

Then everything went like clockwork. There were times when we got sick from the foul smoke only so-so, and by now we also knew that there was such a thing as recess, which was my favorite subject in school, too; which is to say, we knew that we could take a break now and again and didn't have to practice smoking all the time.

So too we heard rumors that some folks smoke just ten or twenty cigarettes a day, since even that much is enough to make you sick.

Quitting: that's nothing. You throw away the cigarettes, and that's that. No need to light up ever again. Getting into the habit, that's the hard part.

Smoking gets bad publicity. Everyone is lashing out at smoke, with worse and worse rumors circulating about it in the newspapers and on radio.

Not long ago I read somewhere that American scientists had regularly pumped cigarette smoke into the lungs of twenty little mice. In seven weeks twelve of the mice had lung cancer. The obvious conclusion is that mice should give up smoking if they simply can't take it even that much.

Last December, Hungarian Television aired a two-hour show sponsored by the national lottery in which I starred, too, reciting my own routine, and being solely responsible for the laughter. I spoke about good luck and bad luck.

The next day I was stopped on the street by a scruffy old man with a long, snow-white beard.

"I saw you yesterday on TV!"

"I can't help it."

"Don't you remember me?" he inquired while lovingly twiddling his beard.

"I don't know who you are."

"Don't be silly! There's no way you can't remember me, when we went to third grade together."

"That's impossible. I'm certain that there were no bearded kids."

Strangers often accost me on the street, congratulating or scolding me by turns. The other day I'd just left for my favorite café, the Quint, when all at once a spine-chillingly ugly old woman gave me a bear hug and planted a peck on each of my cheeks.

"Don't mind me, but I read so many nice things about you that I felt I owe you this much."

I cast the woman a sullen look.

"Believe me, I wouldn't have sued you."

But I had an even more awkward encounter. I'd just gotten off the underground at Vörösmarty Square, in Pest, or, rather, I'd only wanted to, because the train arrived at its last stop with a big thud, plopping me right back on the seat, when a pretty young woman helped me up.

"Excuse me, I don't even know you, but I must thank you for having ensured me an unforgettable experience last night when you sang in *La Traviata.*"

"Well, a man just sort of sings this and that," I stammered out, bemused, and slunk off. I can't even imagine whom she mistook me for when it's common knowledge that I don't even go near the opera, since I can't stand a racket.

With this, I ask forgiveness of this anonymous music-lover for not having disclosed my identity, but I was reminded of my own personal Traviata, which is to say, one of my life's greatest mistakes.

When, a good long time ago, I let my father know that I wanted to go to America, he couldn't stop trying to talk me out of it, and when he saw that I was adamant, this is what he said: "OK, just go ahead. I'm sure you will be greeted by virgins in white dresses, the whole city will be lit up in your honor, and there will be fireworks, as at every large affair. Go ahead!"

I went. And when I arrived in New York, the whole immense city was bathed in light, fireworks flashed resplendently across the sky, people in rapture swarmed the streets, and the whole city was drunk with joy. It occurred to me that perhaps I'd gone mad, which was why I was now seeing my father's scornful prophecy come true. Only later did I realize that I'd arrived on the Fourth of July, Independence Day, and that the city adorns itself every year for the occasion, fireworks crackling and the red, white, and blue fluttering even if I am not arriving in America on that day.

To be continued, but for now,
the end

Glossary

1956 Revolution. The Hungarian Revolution of 1956 was a revolt against the government of the Hungarian People's Republic and its Soviet-imposed policies, lasting from October 23 until November 10. More than 2,500 Hungarians and 700 Soviet troops died, and 200,000 Hungarians fled the country as refugees. In this book Királyhegyi gives but passing mention to this major event in his country's modern history, which may seem surprising, given the detail he devotes to other cataclysmic events he lived through. But the book was first published in Hungary in 1980, during the communist era, when any substantial, drawn-out discussion of the event that might have been interpreted as critical of its suppression would have been edited out. Hungary's post-1956 regime tolerated only the term "counterrevolution" (*ellenforradalom*) in referring to the event, hence Kiralyhegyi's use of it, in one brief mention.

Ady, Endre (1877–1919). Regarded by many as the greatest Hungarian poet of the twentieth century, Endre Ady devoted his lyrical verse to key questions of human existence, including love and love of nation. His style and content marked a break with the influence of such poets as the mid-nineteenth-century romantic figure Sándor Petőfi.

Appell During roll call (German: *Appell*) in concentration camps, prisoners would have to stand still, wearing thin clothing, for hours on end in any weather. The block **kapo** would count the number of prisoners before reporting to the SS officer. If the number appeared incorrect, it would take hours until the SS officer finally made the numbers tally. Anyone unable to stand was taken away to his or her death.

Arrow Cross. The Arrow Cross Party (Hungarian: *Nyilaskeresztes Párt-Hungarista Mozgalom*, literally "Arrow Cross Party–Hungarist Movement") was a fascist, national socialist party led by **Ferenc Szálasi**, which ruled Hungary from October 1944 to March 1945. During its time in power, more than ten thousand Jews, Romani, and others were murdered by forces associated with the party, and 80,000 people were deported from Hungary to concentration camps in Austria. This came in the wake of the mass deportation of Hungarian Jews to camps abroad that had ensued with the German occupation of Hungary earlier that year. After the war, Szálasi and other Arrow Cross leaders were tried and many executed as war criminals by Hungarian courts.

Aster Revolution. The Aster Revolution or Chrysanthemum Revolution (Hungarian: *Őszirózsás forradalom*) was a revolution in Hungary led by Count Mihály Károlyi after World War I that ended 400 years of Habsburg rule over Hungary. Facing political crisis in March 1919 over Hungary's ceding of territories to neighboring countries, Károlyi turned over power to a coalition that quickly established what was to be the short-lived Hungarian Soviet Republic.

Aussenkommando. A term for subcamps in the context of Nazi Germany, referring to those outlying detention centers that came under the command of a main concentration camp run by the SS. Survival conditions in the subcamps were, in many cases, poorer for the prisoners than those in the main camps.

Curtiz, Michael (1888–1962). Born Manó Kaminer, also known as Mihály Kertész, Curtiz was a Hungarian-born American film director, recognized as one of the most prolific directors in history. He directed classic films from the silent era and numerous others during Hollywood's Golden Age.

Endre, László (1895–1946) was a Hungarian right-wing politician and a Nazi collaborator during World War II.

Fészek Artists' Club. Downtown Budapest's Fészek Club (*fészek* meaning nest in Hungarian) has been a second home for writers, painters, singers, actors, musicians, architects, and sculptors for more than a century. In addition to housing a restaurant on its ground floor, it has a theatre, gallery-style rooms, an arts library, and other spaces for performance artists and guest speakers to share their work and their ideas. In its early heyday, it was a private, members-only space, with prominent people from other backgrounds like bankers, politicians, and academics also allowed to join.

Franz Joseph I (1830–1916) was Emperor of Austria and King of Hungary, as well as King of Bohemia from December 1848 until his death in November 1916.

Herczeg, Ferenc (1863–1954) was a Hungarian playwright and author who promoted conservative nationalist opinion in his country. He was nominated for the Nobel Prize in Literature three times.

Himmler, Márton. Királyhegyi's uncle in America, Himmler was a US military officer of Hungarian descent who, during and after World War II, participated in the hunt for top Hungarian government officials suspected of war crimes.

Horthy, Miklós (June 1868–1957) was a Hungarian admiral and statesman who served as regent of the Kingdom of Hungary between World Wars I and II and throughout most of World War II, from March 1920 to October 1944.

Hungarist Movement. See "Arrow Cross."

József, Attila (1905–1937) was one of Hungary's greatest twentieth century poets and is the best-known modern Hungarian poet internationally. Though he was hailed during the communist era of the 1950s as Hungary's great "proletarian poet," his life and works are today being re-evaluated.

kapo. A prisoner functionary in a Nazi concentration camp who was assigned by the SS guards to supervise forced labor or carry out administrative tasks. Designed to turn victim against victim, the prisoner functionary system minimized costs by allowing camps to function with fewer SS personnel.

Korda, Sir Alexander (Sándor) (1893–1956) was a Hungarian-born British film producer and director. In the late 1920s he worked in Hollywood, and from 1930 he became a leading figure in the British film industry, the founder of London Films, and the owner of British Lion Films, a film distribution company. Korda was the first filmmaker in the UK to be officially knighted.

körözött. The Hungarian name for a popular, paprika-spiced cheese spread made with sheep's milk cheese, goat cheese, or cottage cheese and butter or margarine and typically eaten on an open sandwich, toast, or crackers, or as a filling in cold dishes such as stuffed tomatoes, peppers, or hard boiled eggs. In Austria the comparable food is known as *Liptauer.*

kulak. A term for purportedly affluent peasants in the later Russian Empire, Soviet Russia, and the early Soviet Union that became prevalent across much of Eastern Europe. Under Stalin's campaign to collectivize the peasantry, peasants who owned a bit more livestock or land than their neighbors were labeled "kulaks" and scapegoated and persecuted by the communist state.

Protective letters, Swiss. Late in World War II the Swiss government, represented in Budapest by Vice-Consul Carl Lutz, issued protective letters, or passes, to thousands of Hungarian Jews. Once the fascists took over Budapest in 1944, they began deporting Jews to concentration camps. Under a deal he negotiated with the Hungarian government and the Nazis, Lutz gained permission to issue protective letters to 8,000 Hungarian Jews for emigration to Palestine, but he is credited with saving some 62,000 lives in all.

Protestant faith, conversion to. Királyhegyi refers more than once in this book to his Protestant faith, though he otherwise readily identifies himself as of Jewish background. Presumably this is because he had converted to Christianity, as had many Hungarian Jews in the first decades of the twentieth century, whether to assimilate or to survive. Ultimately, doing so did not help him avoid deportation to a work camp and, subsequently, to concentration camps.

Rákóczi, Ferenc (Francis) II (1676–1735) was a Hungarian nobleman and leader of the 1703–11 Hungarian uprising against the Habsburgs as the ruling prince of the Estates Confederated for Liberty of the Kingdom of Hungary. He was also Prince of Transylvania. Hungarians today regard him as a national hero.

Radnóti, Miklós (1909–1944) was a major Hungarian poet who died in the Holocaust. Born into an assimilated Jewish family, Radnóti, whose life was shaped profoundly by his mother's and twin brother's death at his birth, identified strongly as a Hungarian. His poetry mingles avant-garde and expressionist themes with a new classical style, and he is also known for his love poetry. Radnóti converted to Catholicism in 1943, among numerous Jewish writers who had done so due to pervasive anti-Semitism.

Rejtő, Jenő (1905–1943), whose pseudonyms included P. Howard and Gibson Lavery, was a Hungarian journalist, pulp fiction writer, and playwright who died as a forced laborer during World War II. Despite the "pulp" nature of his writings, he is not only widely read in Hungary, but is also much appreciated by literary critics. It is a prevalent opinion that he lifted the genre to the level of serious art.

Saujude. A derogatory reference in Nazi Germany to Jews that derives from *Judensau* (German for "Jews' sow").

Shohet. A person officially licensed by rabbinic authority as slaughterer of animals and poultry for use as food in accordance with Jewish laws.

Szálasi, Ferenc (1897–1946) was the leader of Hungary's fascist **Arrow Cross Party–Hungarist Movement** and the "Leader of the Nation" (*Nemzetvezető*), being both head of state and prime minister of the Kingdom of Hungary's "Government of National Unity" for the final six months of in World War II, after Germany occupied Hungary and removed Regent **Miklós Horthy** by force. During Szálasi's brief rule, his men murdered 10,000–15,000 Jews and others. After the war, he was tried in Hungary and executed.

terefah. A member of a kosher species of mammal or bird, disqualified from being considered kosher, due to pre-existing mortal injuries or physical defects.

Vidor, Charles (1900–1959) was an American film director of Hungarian descent, with whom Pál Királyhegyi, as the latter recounts in this book, stowed away on a ship to New York City. The second Karcsi (Charlie) to figure prominently in Királyhegyi's story, Vidor, who was born to a Jewish family in Budapest, he first came to prominence during the final years of the silent film era. His many film successes included *The Bridge* (1929) and *A Farewell to Arms* (1957). Though Királyhegyi does not note this in *My First Two Hundred Years,* Vidor died in Vienna, of a heart attack, aged fifty-eight, while filming *Song Without End*—which Királyhegyi had been in Vienna consulting him on. It is possible that Királyhegyi had left Vienna prior to Vidor's death.

Publisher's Acknowledgments

As someone with no prior publishing experience, I relied on the kindness and advice of many as I worked over the last two years toward bringing Pál Királyhegyi's *My First Two Hundred Years* to readers of English.

In the very beginning, Rita Tímár pointed me in the right direction to secure the English -language book rights in Hungary, and also gave me useful contracting advice.

I feel gratitude toward the HoFra Theatrical and Literary Agency, and especially Hajnalka Ihárosi, for giving me a chance to take on this project, despite my having no writing, translating, or publishing track record at all.

Perhaps no one did more in Hungary to keep Királyhegyi's legacy robust than József Köves at K.u.K. Book Publishing. After republishing this book in Hungarian in 2015, he also compiled and published two volumes of Királyhegyi's other writings. His encouragement and his help in interpreting certain sentences of the book were very helpful.

I also want to thank my friends Miklós Kuti and János Gellér for helping analyze an important paragraph of the text.

I was most fortunate to work with the book's translator, Paul Olchváry, owner of New Europe Books. I personally know no one, other than Paul, who grew up outside of Hungary, and has such an astonishing command of, or a more nuanced understanding of "our beautiful and useful" (and notoriously difficult) Hungarian language, as well as Hungarian history and culture. In addition to being an experienced and excellent translator, he was a pleasure to work with. These remarkable qualities of his ensured that Királyhegyi's subtle humor, characteristic wordplay, and cheerful tone made it from the Hungarian pages to the English ones. I have no doubt that I couldn't have had a better partner to get this job done so well. I am looking forward to future projects together with Paul to publish in English other favorites from our outsized Hungarian literature. Paul, an accomplished book publisher, also selflessly gave me plenty of advice about various details of the book publishing trade.

Editor Matt Henderson Ellis's many thoughtful recommendations were accepted almost without exception.

The Hungarian National Museum's prompt permission to use the photo of the author much enhanced the appearance of the back cover.

I wish to express my gratitude to the competent Createspace team for their expertise and patience.

My brother George gave me this book thirty-five years ago. He has better sense of humor than anyone I know, and his wisdom, counsel and encouragement I also appreciate very much.

My mother Erika, who is one of the many readers touched by Királyhegyi's humanity and humor, helped this project in innumerable ways, especially taking care of issues in Hungary that needed personal presence there, since I live on this side of the ocean.

Lastly, and most importantly I thank my wife Sara for supporting this project by accepting the inevitable toll it took on my limited free time, and graciously resigning herself to the fact that this project —which, after all, centered on the remarkable life of an immigrant—came with the territory of marrying an immigrant.

COMING IN 2018

Greenhorn

a novel by Pál Királyhegyi

(Paul King)

"Greenhorn is charming…[with] a very quiet but sure humor."
—*New York Times 1932*

"Mr. King enjoyed America for all its accurately placed punches on the chin. And readers will enjoy his account of his sojourn here, written in a merry tone throughout but leaving out none of the less pleasant angles of his experience."
—*The Saturday Review of Literature, 1932*

Published in 1932, written in English under the pen name Paul King, this largely autobiographical novel covers the author's life from his adolescence in Budapest through New York, until he leaves from Detroit on a Hollywood-bound train. *Greenhorn* describes this particular period of the author's life on about twice as many pages and in much more lovely and vivid detail and with more subtle "Paul King humor" than the book you are holding in your hands, while also providing fascinating insight into the triumphs and travails of one immigrant in America in the Roaring Twenties. If you liked *My First Two Hundred Years,* you will certainly enjoy *Greenhorn* as well.

"One of the most pleasant things I have ever read," wrote Harry Salpeter, noted book critic of the time. No disaster "can really touch that core of sweetness and strength which makes him take it on the chin without a whine."

These 1932 words are astonishing for us, who know today that these qualities of Királyhegyi would be put to the ultimate test in the years ahead, during the Holocaust, as he was to recount in *My First Two Hundred Years.*

About the Translator

Paul Olchváry has translated many books of Hungarian prose literature to English, including György Dragomán's novel *The White King*, Vilmos Kondor's novel *Budapest Noir*, Ádám Bodor's *The Sinistra Zone*, Ferenc Barnás's novel *The Ninth*, and Károly Pap's *Azarel.* He has received translation grants from the National Endowment for the Arts and PEN American Center in the United States, and the Milán Füst Prize by the Milán Füst Foundation of the Hungarian Academy of Sciences. He is the founder of New Europe Books. A native of Amherst, New York, Olchváry was born to Hungarian parents and lived in Hungary for many years as an adult. He lives currently in Williamstown, Massachusetts.

About the Author

Pál Királyhegyi (pron. Pahl *Keer*-rye-hedyee; 1900–1981, AKA Paul King) was a Hungarian writer, journalist, humorist, TV personality, and screenwriter—and perhaps the most quotable Hungarian of the twentieth century. He was the author of several novels and books of nonfiction. As told in *My First Two Hundred Years*, which relates much of his life story, in 1920 he and a fellow Hungarian stowed away on a ship bound for New York City. There, after years of hardship, hard work, and adventures aplenty, they moved to Hollywood and began working in the film industry. His friend went on to become a major director under the Americanized name Charles Vidor, while Királyhegyi wrote an autobiographical novel, in English, about an immigrant's life, titled *Greenhorn* (new edition forthcoming from Boulder Books)—published under the pseudonym Paul King. In 1931, homesick, he moved back to Hungary, where he worked as a journalist and theatre critic. Though of Jewish heritage, it may have been during this time--in the 1930s, with anti-Semitism and Hungary passing "Jewish laws"—that Királyhegyi converted to Christianity. Urban legend has it that he first that he first converted to Roman Catholicism and then within weeks to Protestanism (probably the Hungarian Reformed, or Calvinist, denomination) "in case they (the Nazis) ask what his previous religion was". In 1938 his country's turn even further to the right led him to move to England, where he worked for the *Daily Telegraph* and in the film industry and remained until 1941. Homesick once more, he returned again to Hungary, only to eventually be sent to an internal labor camp, and before long, in 1944, to Auschwitz and other concentration camps abroad, where he nearly perished. Perhaps his most famous line, one emblemizing the humor for which he is loved by all Hungarians who read his works: "My trip home was urgent, lest I miss the Auschwitz Express." In 1945 he managed to return to Budapest, where he wrote pieces for cabaret theatres. As a writer and an intellectual who had lived abroad, he found it increasingly difficult to find work after Hungary became a one-party, communist state in 1948, and in 1951—apparently by mistake, he writes in *My First Two Hundred Years*—he was sent to the countryside for a time in internal exile. In 1956, around the time of the Hungarian Revolution, he reportedly went to America, only to soon return again to Hungary. This is glaringly absent in *My First Two Hundred Years,* which was published in 1980, when any candid discussion of the revolution would have been censored.